AN ENDLESS LINE OF

Revivals and Their Leaders from

EARLE E.

Splendor

the Great Awakening to the Present

CAIRNS

Tyndale House Publishers, Inc. Wheaton, Illinois

Cover illustration: *Revival Meeting,* attributed to
Alexander Rider, c. 1815. Courtesy of the Billy
Graham Center Museum.

First printing, June 1986

Library of Congress Catalog Card Number 85-52060
ISBN 0-8423-0770-2
Copyright © 1986 by Earle E. Cairns
All rights reserved
Printed in the United States of America

TO BEN, MANDY, AND MELISSA

An endless line of splendor,

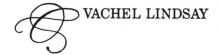

VACHEL LINDSAY

These troops with heaven for home,...

CONTENTS

ILLUSTRATIONS

FOREWORD

This is not a book on evangelism, although in modern times the word *evangelism* has come to be synonymous with *revivalism* in many parts of the world, especially in the American South. However, in a strict sense, revivalism has to do with interior spiritual renewal within the true church. Evangelism is the proclamation of the gospel to unbelievers—the outreach of a renewed church to the world. Evangelism, while invariably and inevitably the outgrowth of revival, is not Dr. Cairns' main concern in *An Endless Line of Splendor*. His concern is not primarily with the horizontal extension of the church (evangelism), but with the vertical revitalization of believers, God's chosen people. It is this revitalization process and its ebb and flow down through history which is so accurately and relevantly recorded in this work.

I read the manuscript of *An Endless Line of Splendor*, savoring the chance to be reading the work of a capable historian of the church. I took notes. It was a fresh learning experience for me. I was inspired. I saw my own ministry in much better perspective. I imagined what a wonderful thing it would be if all evangelists and revivalists in the world were able to read this work.

I have no doubt but that all believers who read *An Endless Line of Splendor* and who are receptive to its message will be renewed. As a textbook for seminaries and colleges, this book is incomparable. I cannot think of another survey of revivalism that compares with its breadth of analysis and comprehension.

My recommendation is quite beyond my capacity to express. To the perusing reader who had reached this point, I would urge: Read on. The book in your hands may well be God's instrument to effect a spiritual renewal in your own life. That, I have no doubt, is Dr. Cairns' highest goal for *An Endless Line of Splendor*.

JOHN WESLEY WHITE
Billy Graham Evangelistic Association

PREFACE

Revival means different things to different people. To many, revival means evangelism or some phenomenon associated with mass meetings, like those of Billy Graham. It conjures up images of nonbelievers making their first commitment to Christ. But revival primarily applies to *believers* and results in a deeper Christian walk, witness, and work, both at home and abroad. Evangelism is both a product of revival and a stimulus to revival.

Books on revival demonstrate weaknesses in understanding the nature of revival. Because many writers have not adequately studied firsthand or primary sources, their works are shallow and reflect common misconceptions about revival. Biases frequently lead to distortion. William Warren Sweet, in his brief history of American revival, spoke of revival in connection with the frontier and mistakenly stated that the day of revival is past. Writers who reject the supernatural also deny the workings of God in revival and brand the experiences as merely emotional.

I first became interested in revival forty-five years ago when, as a candidate for the M.A. and Ph.D. degrees, I carefully studied primary and secondary sources concerning by-products of missions in Africa. Such diverse phenomena as translation of the Bible, early road-building, exploration, education, and political change were the result of missionary efforts based on revival. All of these were in addition to the missionaries' primary work of soul-saving and church-building. Two years of intensive study of primary sources in the Billy Graham Center Library and Archives at Wheaton College reinforced this view and led me to attempt to describe and analyze the revivals that caused these results. It was revival, after all, that stimulated the missionary impulse.

The approach in this book is primarily biographical, pointing out how God works through men and women. Revival leaders such as Lorenzo Dow or Lyman Beecher were very colorful, interesting characters. Reading about their lives and work, one notices that foibles as well as virtues can be a part of the personality of a great person.

This book is descriptive and inductive. I have endeavored to gain accurate accounts either from primary sources or from two or more secondary documents for each fact. Thus the work draws on numerous sources in attempting to give a broad history of revival. I hope this has led to helpful generalizations about revival and a careful interpretation of revival.

The organization is simple. The major part of the book is devoted to an overview of the facts, or history, of Protestant revival. The fruits—results—of revival are then considered. The faith or theology of the leaders of revival is summarized. Attention is given to the hymnology of revival and its reflection of the theology of revivalism. Finally, the forces—the methods, manifestations, and means—of revival are discussed in order to make revival relevant to the present Christian scene.

I hope that this account of revival will help to dispel myths about revival that appear in many works. Many who hold to the frontier interpretation of religious history advanced by William Warren Sweet and others relegate revival to the scrap heap of history. They consider only environmental determination for religion and forget the sovereign action of God in history. Since World War II, the facts of revival have been hard on this theory.

Most writers either ignore or downplay the role of revival in the South in the United States. In fact, the camp meeting, a technique of revival, emerged in Kentucky. A major awakening occurred during the Civil War in the Confederate army. Evangelist Sam

Jones was to the South what Dwight L. Moody was to the North in the same era.

Many writers on revival perpetuate the myth that revivals were mainly emotional orgies. It is true that the camp meetings in the United States and the revivals in Wales were accompanied by peculiar physical manifestations. In the Great Awakening, evangelist James Davenport went to extremes in whipping his audiences into emotional frenzy, though he later recanted his excesses. The twentieth-century Pentecostal awakening was also emotional. Yet revival is much more than emotion. Jonathan Edwards read his sermons in a calm, solemn manner. Charles Finney's dignified, logical approach won many lawyers in every city where he held meetings. Dwight L. Moody's commonsense approach prevailed in his meetings.

Evangelists from Finney to Graham have been pictured as "hot gospellers," intent only on winning converts. Yet all of them were active in promoting the renewal of believers. Finney usually addressed Christians to revive them in the first week of his meetings. The revived Christians could then become soul-winners in successive meetings. The same has been true of many other evangelists. I have preferred to call these men *revivalistic evangelists* in order to represent them as they were, since they were concerned not only with making new converts but with renewing the faith of persons who were already Christians.

Many think revival was and is a Protestant phenomenon. While this is true in the main, revival has sporadically occurred in the Roman Catholic Church. Such individuals and groups as the Waldenses in the twelfth century, Francis of Assisi and his followers in the thirteenth century, Wycliffe and Hus in the fourteenth century, Savonarola in the fifteenth century, and Luther in the sixteenth century were used to draw people back to God. Jay P. Dolan gives evidence for revival in *Catholic Revivalism: The American Experience, 1830-1900* (University of Notre Dame Press, 1978).

I am deeply indebted to Robert Shuster, the archivist, and to

Ferne Weimer, the librarian, and their staffs at the Billy Graham Center Library and Archives for their helpfulness and courtesy in making the sources available. My Sunday school class of mature men and women in College Church of Wheaton, to whom I first presented this material, have given me many helpful ideas, made me rethink profitably some of my interpretations, and helped to clarify many points. My wife has ably edited and typed the manuscript. I am indebted to Jim Orme who generously let me use his word processor.

I hope this book will dispel some of the common myths and errors that mark many accounts of revivalism. It should help Christians to be more intelligent concerning their spiritual heritage of revival and incite them to personal and group revival in the present.

EARLE E. CAIRNS

INTRODUCTION

The church is in need of perennial revival because of recurrent spiritual decline. The second generation of Israelites is pictured in Judges 2:7, 10–13 as a people who forsook the Lord because they themselves had not experienced God's miracles on their behalf in Egypt and the wilderness. Jeremiah frequently uses the word *forsaken* to describe the Hebrews' straying from God. John accused the Ephesian church of losing its "first love" (Rev. 2:4). Spiritual decline, crisis, and renewal form a common pattern in the Bible and church history.

One should also remember that the world, the flesh, and Satan (Eph. 2:2, 3) seek to lead the Christian away from God. Christ had to face the Devil in the temptation in the wilderness (Matt. 4:1–11). Christians have the same enemy. The world's manner of life tends to pull believers down spiritually (1 John 2:15). The flesh, defined by John as the lust of the flesh and eyes and pride of life (1 John 2:16, 17), although not evil in itself, panders to worldliness. Christians constantly need spiritual revitalization.

Moreover, in a society pledged to toleration of sects outside of a state church (as in the British Isles, Scandinavia, or Germany) or to separation of church and state (as in the United States), people are not all born into the church by baptism and confirmation. Evangelism, flowing from revival, becomes a means of bringing people into voluntary association with the church. The 1857 lay prayer ecumenical revival, for example, brought approximately a million people into the churches of the United States of America and the same number into the churches in the British Isles.

REVIVAL FROM THE GREAT
REVIVAL /

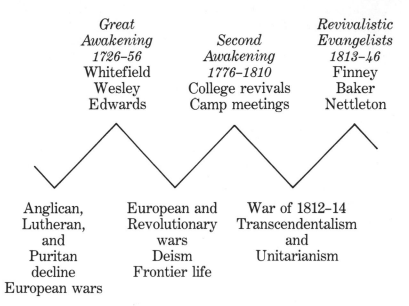

| Great Awakening 1726–56 Whitefield Wesley Edwards | Second Awakening 1776–1810 College revivals Camp meetings | Revivalistic Evangelists 1813–46 Finney Baker Nettleton |

| Anglican, Lutheran, and Puritan decline European wars | European and Revolutionary wars Deism Frontier life | War of 1812–14 Transcendentalism and Unitarianism |

DECLINE, SPIRITUAL

Revival and *renewal*, terms frequently used in the present, have often been used interchangeably with *evangelism* or *missions*. *Revival* has often been the term used to describe special services in the local church, particularly in the South. Revival is not the mass evangelism of Moody or Graham, although revival of the church usually preceded or accompanied their meetings. Evangelism and missions are the fruits of revival, but are not synonymous with revival.

The derivation of the terms *revival* (and *renewal*, now commonly used as a synonym for *revival)* will help in arriving at a working definition. *Revival* comes from the Latin *revivere*, meaning "to live again." *Renewal* is derived from *re*, meaning "back" and *novus*, meaning "new." Thus the essential idea is a new surge of spiritual life, life that is already present but flickering feebly.

AWAKENING TO THE PRESENT

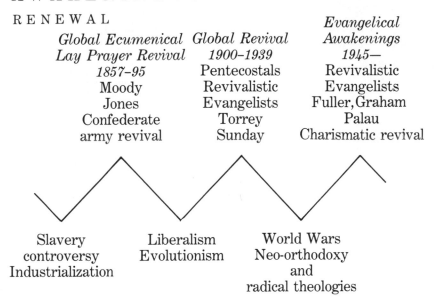

RENEWAL

Global Ecumenical
Lay Prayer Revival
1857–95
Moody
Jones
Confederate
army revival

Global Revival
1900–1939
Pentecostals
Revivalistic
Evangelists
Torrey
Sunday

Evangelical
Awakenings
1945—
Revivalistic
Evangelists
Fuller, Graham
Palau
Charismatic revival

Slavery
controversy
Industrialization

Liberalism
Evolutionism

World Wars
Neo-orthodoxy
and
radical theologies

COLDNESS, AND CRISIS

Revival is for believers only; it is the Christian who needs revival. Evan Roberts often prayed in the Welsh revival, "Bend the church and save the people."

Various definitions of revival have been given. Some define it as "times of refreshing from the presence of the Lord" (Acts 3:19). Robert Baird, an early nineteenth-century historian of American church history, spoke of revival as an "extraordinary season of religious interest." J. Edwin Orr, an authority on revival, adopts a similar definition in some of his books. Charles Finney spoke of it as "renewal of the first love of Christians." When he lectured on "What Revival Is" to his New York church in 1834, he spoke of it as believers being awakened and sinners converted. C. E. Autrey believes it is "reanimation of God's people."

Certain common elements occur in the various definitions of

revival. All suggest a decline of the church from a prior, higher spiritual experience. The decline eventuates in a crisis, primarily spiritual and moral. Individuals (one, a few, or many) are led to pray fervently for revival and to study their Bibles. Then the faithful preaching of the Word—by leaders commissioned by God—coupled with the supernatural work of the Holy Spirit results in the restoration of Christians to their first love and to a better Christian walk, witness, and work (Ps. 85:6).

I define revival or renewal as the work of the Holy Spirit in restoring the people of God to a more vital spiritual life, witness, and work by prayer and the Word after repentance in crisis for their spiritual decline. The permanent elements in revival are the Word, prayer, the Holy Spirit, and a sovereign God who uses man as his instrument.

Revival may take place in an individual, a family, or a congregation, such as Jonathan Edwards's Massachusetts congregation in 1734 and 1735. Cities may be revived, as Rochester, New York, was under Charles Finney in 1830 and 1831. Saskatchewan, a province of Canada, experienced revival in 1971. Global revival was experienced from 1857 to 1895 and from 1900 to 1945.

Renewal of the vertical spiritual relationship of Christians with God has resulted in a more meaningful horizontal relationship of Christians with man, a relationship expressed in witness, social reform, and true ecumenicity of spirit. It is God who turns the hearts of his people to himself (1 Kings 18:37; Ps. 80:3, 7, 19) when the conditions of humility, prayer, seeking God's face, and turning from sinful ways (2 Chron. 7:14) are the heartfelt expression of God's people.

The history of the Hebrews offers many instances of revival in this sense. The decline of the Israelites into idolatry while Moses was on Mount Sinai receiving the Ten Commandments was followed by the restoration of the people and the building of the tabernacle (Exod. 32–36).

Spiritual failure marked the taking of the ark of the covenant by the Philistines for seven months (1 Sam. 4:11, 18, 19–22; 6:1) and its sojourn for twenty years in Kiriath-jearim. This was followed by a spiritual crisis and an awakening when the ark was brought back to its rightful place with the aid of the Lord in the nation's difficulties (1 Sam. 4:1–11; 7:1, 3, 6, 10, 12).

Spiritual decline came again to the northern kingdom in the days of Ahab and Jezebel (1 Kings 16:30–33) with consequent idolatry. Revival came to the people after Elijah humiliated Baal and his priests (1 Kings 18:21–39). Elijah challenged the people not to halt between serving God or Baal, but to serve God only.

Spiritual death in the days of Rehoboam and Abijah was followed by renewal under the godly King Asa (2 Chron. 15:2–4, 12, 15). This revival continued on into the reign of Jehoshaphat, who was blessed by God in leadership (2 Chron. 17:9, 10, 12).

Apostasy occurred again in the time of Ahaz, who relied upon other gods (2 Chron. 28:2–4, 16, 24, 25). God used Hezekiah to bring revival (2 Chron. 29:1–4, 18, 29, 30; 30:12, 18, 19; 31:4, 10, 20, 21). This revival prepared Judah and Hezekiah to stand against Sennacherib of Assyria, whom God humbled before them (2 Chron. 32:21; Isa. 37:33–38). Hezekiah's experience suggests that revival can prepare people to face a crisis as well as to witness and work.

Josiah was the godly son of the evil Manasseh, who led Israel astray. Josiah sought God with his people by repairing the temple and by having the Law read to the people. Little wonder that the Passover was so memorable (2 Chron. 34:3–33; 35:18).

After the seventy years in Babylon, the nation again failed God as they entered into mixed marriages with the people around them and participated in their sins. Ezra led them to repentance and renewal (Ezra 9–10).

When Nehemiah had the Word of God read and explained to the people, repentance for sin and forsaking of sin followed. Then there was a turning to God with consequent blessing by God (Neh. 8–10; 13).

In each Old Testament example, spiritual falling away resulted in a crisis which led to conviction of sin, a leader finding and proclaiming the Word of God, true repentance, and godly conduct. Isaiah had such an experience (Isa. 6). Realization of the holiness of a sovereign God led the prophet, good man though he was, to a sense of sin. God then cleansed and commissioned the prophet when he expressed a willingness to do God's will.

Waves of revival occurred in the medieval church. The Waldenses studied and preached the Bible under the leadership of Peter Waldo in the twelfth century. They were persecuted by the church, but their views are still held by the Waldensian Church in northern Italy.

Francis and Dominic founded two separate orders of friars in the thirteenth century. These orders were in their early days marked by spiritual vigor and moral earnestness, which led the friars to preach with power.

The lay Brethren of the Common Life in the Netherlands, Wycliffe and the Lollards in England, and Hus and his followers in Bohemia all proclaimed the Word of God as the authority for faith and morals and declared the power of God to justify repentant sinners. Lollards, the lay preachers who followed Wycliffe, spread a pure gospel through England as Hus's followers did in Bohemia in the fourteenth century. The friar Savonarola, who was brought up to love the Bible, became a flaming denouncer of sin and a preacher of biblical righteousness in fifteenth-century Florence.

While the sixteenth-century Reformation was not a revival in the classic sense, it laid the foundations for Protestant revivals after 1726. Luther called man to a rediscovery of the New Testament pattern for life by making the Bible the sole authority for faith and life. He preached justification by faith rather than by works. He preached the spiritual priesthood of all believers. Protestantism emerged as the Roman Catholic Church rejected the Reformers and forced them and their earnest followers out of the church. The formulation of Protestant teaching made the later waves of Protestant, Anglo-Saxon, transatlantic revival possible. The revival leaders all preached the basic doctrines of the Reformation.

Puritanism (ca. 1560 to 1660) in England was not, strictly speaking, revival, but a struggle to cleanse the church from elements of "popery" (empty ritual and formality). However, it did create the spiritual vigor and moral earnestness of Oliver Cromwell in England and John Cotton in New England. Puritans, except for the Separatists, were willing to remain within the Church of England, but wished to put the control of the church in the hands of the local congregations. Most Puritans stood for a strong Calvinistic theology and for political freedom.

The ideas of Jansenism, the Roman Catholic equivalent of Puritanism, were set forth by Cornelius Jansen (1585–1638), a professor at Louvain University. Jansen desired to revive Augustine's theology in his posthumous *Augustinus* (1640). Blaise Pascal (1623–62), the famous scientist and author, cooperated with Jansen's followers at Port Royal nunnery. A Jansenist church was later founded in Germany, Austria, and Switzerland.

Pietism was a movement among Lutherans in the late 1600s and 1700s. Lutheran orthodoxy had become overly doctrinal and not concerned enough with Bible reading, holy living, and fervent preaching. The Pietists—led by Philipp Jakob Spener, August Francke, and others—helped to restore biblical preaching, Bible study, and good works among the Lutherans in Germany.

Puritanism in the Church of England, Pietism in the German Lutheran churches, and Jansenism in the Roman Catholic Church all reacted against the dead orthodoxy of these churches and sought a more vital faith.

Waves of Protestant, Anglo-Saxon, and transatlantic revival have been a characteristic of British, American, German, and Scandinavian church history in the modern period. (See diagram on pages 20–21.) The Great Awakening, led by pastors for the most part, in the British Isles and the thirteen colonies between 1726 and 1756 should be linked with the Pietist and Moravian movements in Germany.

The Second Awakening, from 1776 to 1810, produced the Methodist church, especially in the South under Devereux Jarratt and Francis Asbury. College revivals, such as those in Hampden-Sydney and Yale, and camp meetings in Kentucky were products of the Second Awakening. Voluntary societies and a "Benevolence Empire" began in England through the Clapham Sect.

Contrary to the usual practice of dating the Second Awakening from 1795 to 1846, this writer believes that the period from 1813 to 1846 constitutes a separate period of revival. The era was marked by the *Erweckung* in Germany and the *Réveil* in Switzerland, France, and Holland through Robert Haldane. In the United States the work of Beecher, Finney, and Baker was important in revival. Until the time of Finney, revival was looked upon as the work of a sovereign God and was led by pastors, some of whom were itinerants. Finney conducted protracted meetings in which he used "New Measures." He felt that revival could be brought about by the use of human means under the power of the Spirit of God. He and his successors practiced a dynamic revivalism in contrast with the more passive Calvinistic revivalism of the first two eras (1726 to 1810). Americans, following the lead of the voluntary societies in England, created missionary and reform agencies. These agencies were financed by the "Benevolence Empire," created through generous giving by such wealthy men as the Tappans, Wanamaker, and Ryman.

The period from 1857 to 1895 was one of global lay interdenominational prayer revival which awakened professing Christians and brought about the salvation of millions. Great Christian organizations, such as Keswick, the Salvation Army, and the China Inland Mission emerged in this era. Moody in the North and Sam Jones in the South carried on professional, urban, mass, and organized revivalistic evangelism outside of church buildings.

Another period of global revival came between 1900 and 1945. The Pentecostal awakening, the Welsh revival, the Korean revival, and the East African revival were sovereign works of God through his Spirit. Revivalistic evangelists such as R. A. Torrey and Billy Sunday promoted mass revival and evangelism.

In the period following World War II, revival has occurred in the United States, Canada, and Ethiopia but has been regional rather than global. Radio and television have been used by such revivalistic evangelists as Charles Fuller and Billy Graham.

The motion of waves of the sea may picture the relation of one era of revival to another. Each wave is distinct, yet there is mingling as one wave recedes and the other comes in. Isaac Backus, who was saved in the Great Awakening, was an active revivalist during the Second Awakening. Asahel Nettleton and Robert Haldane were won to Christ during the Second Awakening but were active in promoting revival in the period from 1813 to 1846, respectively in the United States and in Switzerland, France, and Holland.

One can only hope that the cry of the psalmist (85:6) and Habakkuk (3:2) may be the cry of the church now and that the wave of revival since World War II may be extended and broadened to global proportions.

PART ONE *The Facts of Revival*

1. THE GREAT AWAKENING IN GERMANY AND AMERICA

THE most important factor in bringing about the Great Awakening was the decline of genuine religious experience in Germany, the thirteen colonies, and Britain. Although the Lutherans, Congregationalists, and Anglicans in these countries held to the doctrines of the Reformation, they were not insistent upon a warm Christian experience. The Half-way Covenant in 1662 in Puritan New England brought many unconverted persons into the church. (Prior to the Half-way Covenant, only persons who had had conversion experiences could be church members.) Third-generation children and their parents who "owned the covenant" were given membership in the church. As members of the church, they gave no verbal evidence of a conversion experience. Thus many unconverted persons became members of the church. The people were orthodox in belief but not Christian at heart. This situation also existed in Britain and Germany.

The Great Awakening occurred in three areas: Germany, the thirteen colonies, and the British Isles. The Pietist movement emerged in the last quarter of the seventeenth century under

Spener and Francke. The Moravian denomination was born in the Pietist movement under the leadership of Count Zinzendorf from 1727 to 1742.

The American Awakening occurred from 1726 to 1741 in the middle colonies among the Reformed and Presbyterian groups, in the New England Congregational churches, and in the South among the Baptists. In England, Wales, and Scotland, the Awakening was predominantly Calvinistic. In England, the awakened Christians formed a Methodist group which later broke into Moravians, Calvinistic Methodists under Lady Huntingdon, and Arminian Methodists under the Wesleys.

These groups formed *ecclesiolae in ecclesia* (little churches within the church) in the established churches in Germany, England, and America. Eventually they broke off and went their own way as new denominations. Schism or division accompanied revival as the state churches' loveless majority forced the revived minority to withdraw.

PIETISM AND THE MORAVIANS IN GERMANY

Pietism was a people's movement which emphasized an internal and individual return of the soul to the authority of the Bible, to prayer, and to piety. It stressed commitment rather than creed in a practical, sometimes mystical, manner. It was a reaction to the cold orthodoxy of the Lutheranism of the seventeenth century. Pietists went back to the Bible, the New Birth, and the priesthood of believers in a religion of experience. While holding to orthodox Lutheran teaching, they chose to emphasize the emotional aspects of their faith, aspects which had been neglected because of the theological controversies and religious wars of the first half of the seventeenth century.

Philipp Jakob Spener (1635–1705) studied at universities in Switzerland, Germany, and France and served as a Lutheran pastor in Frankfurt from 1661 to 1686. He organized meetings called *collegia pietatis* for his converts. These meetings, which

PROTESTANT TRANSATLANTIC REVIVAL

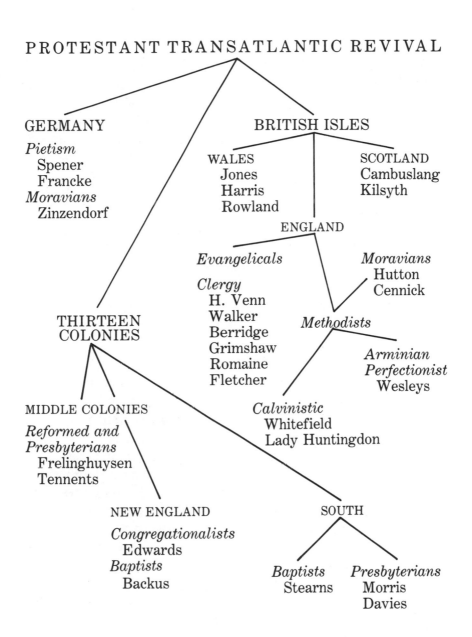

GERMANY

Pietism
  Spener
  Francke
Moravians
  Zinzendorf

BRITISH ISLES

WALES
  Jones
  Harris
  Rowland

SCOTLAND
  Cambuslang
  Kilsyth

ENGLAND

Evangelicals

Clergy
  H. Venn
  Walker
  Berridge
  Grimshaw
  Romaine
  Fletcher

Moravians
  Hutton
  Cennick

Methodists

Arminian
Perfectionist
  Wesleys

Calvinistic
  Whitefield
  Lady Huntingdon

THIRTEEN COLONIES

MIDDLE COLONIES

Reformed and Presbyterians
  Frelinghuysen
  Tennents

NEW ENGLAND

Congregationalists
  Edwards
Baptists
  Backus

SOUTH

Baptists
  Stearns

Presbyterians
  Morris
  Davies

1 7 2 6 – 1 7 5 6

resembled modern cottage prayer meetings, cultivated personal piety among the converts as they engaged in practical Bible study and prayer.

He published *Pia Desideria* ("Pious Desires") in 1675. This work called for practical biblical training along with internships in the training of ministers. Such training would produce more spiritual leadership.

Spener was called to a church in Dresden as a court preacher in 1686. When his condemnation of drunkenness, the ruler's weakness, forced him out of Dresden in 1691, he accepted an important pastoral position in Berlin which he held until his death in 1705. He is considered the founder of Pietism.

Pietism became a strong spiritual influence, infusing new life into Lutheranism. It promoted an experiential personal religion rather than the institutional religion Lutheranism had largely become. The universities in Halle and Württemburg became centers for education and missionary effort.

August Hermann Francke (1663–1727) was a kindred spirit to Spener. In 1692 Spener was able to obtain an appointment for Francke as professor in the University of Halle, opened in 1691. Francke served there from 1692 to 1727 and helped to make Halle a pietistic center of higher education and revivalism. Francke had earlier organized a *Collegium Biblicum*. This group met weekly after the Sunday evening services to study the Hebrew and Greek texts of the Bible and to find the literal meaning of the text and its practical and devotional applications.

Francke also organized a free elementary school for poor children in 1695 and a *paidogogium* (high school) in 1698. He also founded an orphanage in 1696. His friend Baron von Canstein created a society to publish and circulate the Scriptures.

The first two Protestant missionaries were Pietists, Bartholomew Ziegenbalg (1682–1719) and Heinrich Plütschau (1677–1747). They were sent in 1706 by the godly King Frederick IV of Denmark to begin missionary work in southern India. Ziegenbalg translated the entire New Testament and the Old Testament from

THE GREAT AWAKENING IN BRITAIN AND GERMANY

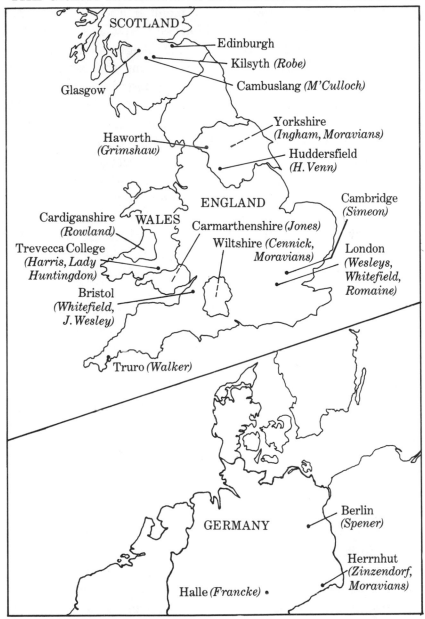

SCOTLAND

Edinburgh

Kilsyth *(Robe)*

Cambuslang *(M'Culloch)*

Glasgow

Yorkshire
(Ingham, Moravians)

Haworth
(Grimshaw)

Huddersfield
(H. Venn)

ENGLAND

Cambridge
(Simeon)

Cardiganshire
(Rowland)

WALES

Carmarthenshire *(Jones)*

Trevecca College
*(Harris, Lady
Huntingdon)*

Wiltshire *(Cennick,
Moravians)*

London
*(Wesleys,
Whitefield,
Romaine)*

Bristol
*(Whitefield,
J. Wesley)*

Truro *(Walker)*

Berlin
(Spener)

GERMANY

Herrnhut
*(Zinzendorf,
Moravians)*

Halle *(Francke)* •

1 7 2 6 – 1 7 5 6

Genesis to Ruth into Tamil before his death. By 1719, 428 persons were baptized and 280 received into membership in the church.

Johann A. Bengel (1687–1752) published a New Testament text with critical apparatus in 1734 to further August Francke's emphasis on biblical study. Bengel's work was the beginning of modern scientific work in the field of textual criticism.

The Moravian denomination emerged out of Lutheran, United Brethren and Pietist groups in the second quarter of the eighteenth century under the leadership of Count Nicholas L. von Zinzendorf (1700–1760). After his father's death, he and his mother lived with his godly grandmother. He was a delicate boy who was threatened with tuberculosis for twenty-five years. He "firmly resolved to live for him [Christ] alone" at the age of six.

Zinzendorf studied at Francke's high school from 1710 to 1716. He was an above-average student, learning the classics and Greek New Testament as well as Latin and French. He formed the boys into prayer and testimony groups.

He went to the University of Wittenberg in 1716. Although he majored in law, his first love was theology. In 1718 he founded the Order of the Grain of Mustard Seed. Members wore a ring inscribed "No one liveth to himself" and a silk sash with a cross and mustard seed.

Zinzendorf traveled in Germany, the Netherlands, and France in 1719 and 1720. In the Dusseldorf art gallery he saw Felti's *Ecce Homo*, a picture of the thorn-crowned Christ with the question underneath it: "What have you done for me since I have done this for you?" He was deeply moved to further commit himself to Christ.

He did legal work at Dresden from 1722 to 1727. He married and moved to Berthelsdorf, an estate, in 1722. His wife took charge of the finances because Zinzendorf was not good at managing money. John A. Rothe served as the Lutheran pastor on the estate. This estate became a refuge for persecuted United Brethren from Bohemia in 1722 under the leadership of Christian

THE GREAT AWAKENING IN THE THIRTEEN COLONIES

MASSACHUSETTS
Northampton *(Edwards)*

NEW HAMPSHIRE
Hanover
(Dartmouth College)

CONNECTICUT
New Haven
(Yale College)

Boston

New Brunswick
(G. Tennent)

RHODE ISLAND
Providence
*(College of
Rhode Island)*

PENNSYLVANIA
Neshaminy
*(Tennent's Log
College)*

NEW YORK

NEW JERSEY
Raritan River Valley
(Frelinghuysen)

Canonsburg
*(McMillan's
Log College)*

Freehold
(J. and W. Tennent)

Hanover County
(Davies)

Princeton
(College of New Jersey)

VIRGINIA

Philadelphia
(University of Pennsylvania)

Sandy Creek *(Stearns)* •

Fagg's Manor
(Blair's Log College)

NORTH CAROLINA

GEORGIA
Savannah *(Bethesda Orphanage)*

1726 – 1756

David. A Brethren village called Herrnhut ("Lord's Watch") had been built on the estate by 1724.

Although both Zinzendorf and Rothe wanted the refugees to adopt Lutheranism, they consented to the drawing up of laws to govern their religious and civic life in Herrnhut on May 12, 1727. Twelve elders were elected, and Zinzendorf organized the people into "bands" of about seven or eight each. This marked the legal organization of the Moravians. Their spiritual birth occurred in a Communion service on August 13, 1727, led by Rothe and Zinzendorf. The presence of the Holy Spirit was felt in a marked way. Rothe, loyal to the Lutheran church, left in 1737 when it became clear that they were emerging as a new denomination. Zinzendorf became a bishop of the Moravian group.

By 1731 Pietism had reached Sweden through the Moravians. Henrik Grundelstjerna, who had visited Herrnhut in Saxony in 1727, asked Zinzendorf to send a mission to Sweden. A Moravian delegation went to Sweden in 1731. Zinzendorf himself visited Sweden later.

All-day prayer began on August 12, 1729, with twenty-four men and twenty-four women praying each hour of the day. This prayer ministry, coupled with Zinzendorf's zeal to spread the gospel, led to missionary work in which the Moravians are credited with one missionary for every sixty members.

He met Daniel Ulrich, a West Indian slave, and two Eskimos from Greenland on a trip to Denmark in 1728. These meetings led to missionary work in the Caribbean and Greenland. The Moravians' first missionary work began in 1732 with Leonard Dober and David Nitschmann in St. Thomas in the Caribbean. Work began in Greenland in 1733 under Christian David and two brothers, Matthew and David Stack. Lapland became a mission field with the residence of Johann Nitschmann and two others there in 1734. They began work in the American colonies in 1735.

A notable Moravian convert, the Russian Baroness Barbara Juliana Krüdener (1764–1824), even influenced European diplomatic relations. An unfaithful wife, she was brought under conviction by seeing a male friend drop dead. She was afterward led to Christ by a Moravian shoemaker in Riga. During the Napoleonic Wars she greatly influenced Alexander I of Russia to think that he was Christ's emissary to bring peace to Europe. He proposed the Holy Alliance (organized in 1815) by which the rulers of Great Britain, Russia, Prussia, and Austria agreed to follow Christian principles in international relations.

Zinzendorf was ecumenical to the point of being friendly with leading Roman Catholics in France. He traveled to the thirteen colonies in 1741 and 1742 in an effort to unite the German Protestants of Pennsylvania in a church union. He was unsuccessful because they were suspicious of him. He traveled much because he was exiled from Saxony by the state for several years.

Peter Böhler, one of his faithful lieutenants, and John Wesley organized a society in London in 1738. This became a Moravian church in 1742, after the Wesleys, Whitefield, Lady Huntingdon, and others withdrew in 1740.

Great credit must go to the Moravians for their ecumenical spirit and missionary zeal which led them into extensive missionary work sixty years before William Carey.

THE GREAT AWAKENING
IN THE THIRTEEN COLONIES

The Great Awakening in the thirteen colonies is usually associated with Jonathan Edwards in Northampton, Massachusetts, in 1734 and 1735. But revival came to the colonies several years earlier among Dutch Reformed and Presbyterians in the middle colonies. It was predominantly Calvinistic in theology and stressed the sovereign act of God in bringing revival.

Revival was needed to counteract the spiritual decline which characterized the colonies. Puritan pastor Cotton Mather of Massachusetts complained that Christian life and duties were neglected. His father, Increase Mather, had bewailed the spiritual state of New England in his book *The Glory Departing from New England* (1702). Jonathan Dickinson in New Jersey and Samuel Blair in Pennsylvania complained that experiential religion was declining because the Half-way Covenant brought many unconverted persons into the church.

The frontier in the thirteen colonies isolated people from religious influence and pastoral care. Frontier life brutalized people as they had to struggle hard to survive in the wilderness and to counter the Indian threat. People turned grain into a liquid cash asset, whiskey. Consumption of whiskey brought violence and loose living; drunkenness abounded. In many areas there were no churches present to tame the people. Revival was needed.

Revival in the Reformed Churches in the Middle Colonies. Revival began about 1726 in the Dutch Reformed churches of the Raritan River Valley in New Jersey. The leader of the revival was Theodore J. Frelinghuysen (1691–1747). Frelinghuysen was born in Westphalia, Germany, and educated by his father, a Reformed pastor, until he went to a university in the Netherlands in 1711. He remained at the university until 1717, when he was ordained and became a chaplain in East Friesland. He was somewhat influenced by Pietism.

The Dutch Reformed classis (presbytery) at Amsterdam sent him to America, and he arrived in New York early in 1720. He preached in New York for Henricus Boel. Frelinghuysen desired "inner transformation" rather than outward fulfillment of religious ceremonies. Boel was upset by his evangelical proclamation of conversion, his teaching on the need of a holy life, and his omission of the Lord's Prayer in the service. Frelinghuysen accused Boel's copastor, Dubois, of extravagance because he had a large mirror in his house.

He served four Dutch Reformed churches with names such as Six Mile Run and North Branch. His parish in the Raritan River valley, just west of New Brunswick, New Jersey, covered an area more than fifteen miles long and ten miles wide. He wanted to limit church membership to the converted who would participate in worship. Many were won to Christ in a revival that peaked in 1726 and spread to other churches in New Jersey.

Nearly seventy members, who were perhaps more interested in money and beer than Christian living, filed a *Complaint Against Frelinghuysen,* which was published in 1725. The complaint contained sixty-nine signatures and accused him of unorthodox views. His opponents were unable to prove their accusations, however. Frelinghuysen, not a tactful man, wanted to nominate elders and deacons. Dubois and Boel supported the rebels and referred the case to the classis of Amsterdam, where the case dragged on for eight years.

In 1747 the Dutch Reformed Church in New Jersey split into prorevival and antirevival groups. New York City pastors opposed revivalistic country pastors. The prorevival group founded Queen's College (now Rutgers University). Gilbert Tennent, a Presbyterian pastor in New Brunswick, was influenced by Frelinghuysen and revival came to his church.

Frelinghuysen carefully catechized the young and admitted only converted persons to Communion and church membership. He began meetings for prayer, Bible study, and mutual spiritual help for his converts. He also used lay "helpers" to lead prayer meetings and church services. He began to itinerate, a new approach to outreach, to bring revival to other churches. He exchanged pulpits with Gilbert Tennent and began to practice extemporaneous preaching.

Gilbert Tennent (1703–64) was one of William Tennent's four preacher sons. Tennent trained his own sons and about fifteen others in a school that was derisively called the "log college." William Tennent, Sr. (1673-1746) was born in Ulster (northern Ireland), graduated from the University of Edinburgh, and was ordained in 1706 in the Episcopal Church in Ireland. He went to Philadelphia in 1718, and the Presbyterian synod there accepted him as a minister. He supplied two churches in Long Island until 1726, when he became pastor of churches at Neshaminy, twenty miles north and east of Philadelphia. He remained there until his death.

Tennent opened his "log college," a building by his manse, in 1726 and maintained it until 1746. His "log colleges" became the forerunners of modern seminaries. James Logan donated fifty acres of land for Tennent's college in 1728. George Whitefield visited him when he was instructing the students in a twenty-by-twenty-foot building on the donated land. Tennent's four sons, Gilbert, Charles, John, and William, and another fifteen men, including Samuel Blair and James Finley, were his pupils.

Samuel Blair (1712–51), born in Ireland, became pastor of Fagg's Manor, forty miles southwest of Philadelphia. He also set up a school with a classical and theological curriculum like that of Tennent. James Finley and Samuel Davies, the organizer of Presbyterianism in Virginia, were Blair's pupils. John McMillan set up another school at Canonsburg in western Pennsylvania in which James McGready was trained. These schools served as Presbyterian "seminaries" until the founding of the College of New Jersey (now Princeton University) in 1746.

The revivalistic preachers founded the College of New Jersey when David Brainerd was expelled from Yale. Jonathan Dickinson, the first president, opened the college in his home in Elizabethtown, New Jersey, in 1746. The college was later moved to Newark and finally located in Princeton in 1756.

William Tennent's sons John and William experienced revival in their church at Freehold, New Jersey, in 1732. But Gilbert Tennent was much more influential in Presbyterian revival. He came to America with his father, received his ministerial training in his father's "log college," and later assisted his father there. He was granted an M.A. by Yale in 1725 on the basis of his training. He was ordained and installed in a Presbyterian church in New Brunswick, New Jersey, in 1726. His church experienced a great revival. When George Whitefield visited New England and the middle colonies in 1739, Gilbert itinerated with him in New England and New York. Tennent continued to itinerate in 1740 and 1741 after Whitefield had left. He preached the New Birth with fiery zeal and moral earnestness. In the three months from December 1740 to February 1741, approximately six hundred in Boston were convicted of their sins.

Gilbert Tennent was called to the Second Presbyterian Church of Philadelphia in 1743 and served there until his death. He went to England and Scotland with Samuel Davies from 1753 to 1755 to raise money for the College of New Jersey. They were able to raise about £3,200, thanks to Lady Huntingdon, the Earl of Dartmouth, and George Whitefield.

Tennent's fiery sermon on "The Danger of an Unconverted Ministry," preached at Nottingham, Pennsylvania, on March 8, 1740, and based on Mark 6:34, aroused opposition. Tennent discussed the character of the old "Pharisee teachers," then urged pity for them, and concluded with suggestions for expressing that pity. The pastors reacted angrily, and in 1741 the Presbyterian Church split into Old Lights (antirevivalists) and New Lights (prorevivalists). When they finally reunited in 1758, the prorevivalist forces were much stronger.

James Davenport (1716–57) helped to discredit revival because of his excesses. He graduated from Yale in 1732 and was converted under the preaching of George Whitefield and Gilbert Tennent. He was ordained as a Presbyterian and given a church in Southold, Long Island, in 1738. He became an itinerant revivalistic pastor and persuaded a group to burn theological books and finery in New London, Connecticut, on March 6, 1743. He even added his worn-out pants to the fire and paraded around in his underclothing. He had a strange singing tone when he preached. He was tried, and the court pronounced him deranged and sent him home to Southold. He retracted his extremism in a letter in the *Boston Gazette* on July 18, 1744. From 1738 to 1757 he served churches in New York and New Jersey. Because of Davenport's fanaticism and Tennent's sermon on unconverted ministers, Whitefield received much opposition when he later came to the Northeast.

Revival in New England Congregationalism. Revival in New England came to Northampton, Massachusetts, as early as 1670. Solomon Stoddard (1643–1729), Jonathan Edwards's grandfather, was pastor from 1670 until his death. He was an earnest soul-winner who had five "harvests," as he called them, in his church in 1679, 1683, 1696, 1712, and 1718. Many young people were won in the last three periods of awakening.

Stoddard practiced open Communion or "Stoddardeanism," hoping that Communion would be a regenerating influence for sinners. He preached the law and damnation to bring conviction of sin but then proclaimed Christ's love and forgiveness for sin through his death on the cross. These were extemporaneous sermons without notes. He believed that preaching could be much improved. While he thought revival was still the sovereign act of God, he also felt that more attention should be given to the methods of revival. He wrote several books in the period from 1708 to 1724 on the why and how of pastoral revivalism. Revival, he thought, would awaken Christians to witness to the lost.

His grandson, Jonathan Edwards (1703–58), was to be more famous in the annals of revival. He was born at East Windsor, Connecticut, into the home of Timothy Edwards, pastor of a Congregational church. An only son with ten sisters, Jonathan was such a precocious student that he learned Latin at six and read Locke's difficult *Essay Concerning Human Understanding* at fourteen. Locke's essay greatly influenced his thinking. He went to Yale in 1716 at the age of thirteen and graduated as valedictorian at the age of seventeen. He studied theology at Yale from 1720 to 1722 and received his M.A. in 1723. His reading of 1 Timothy 1:17 at Yale in 1721 resulted in a deep spiritual experience. He served the Scottish Presbyterian Church in New York in 1722 and 1723. He returned to Yale as a tutor from 1724 to 1726.

His grandfather asked for his assistance in 1727. He was ordained that year and was Stoddard's assistant until 1729, when Stoddard died. Edwards then diligently pastored the church until

1750. He felt that a day was lost if he didn't study thirteen hours for his sermons, which he usually read from manuscripts.

In the fall of 1734 he held prayer meetings and began a series of sermons on justification by faith alone. A young woman was convicted and converted in December. Revival came and continued until more than three hundred were added to his church by May 1735, when the revival died down. The converted were about equally divided between men and women. Edwards was busy with personal conferences with the convicted in order to help them to accept Christ.

Edwards described the revival in the first of four books on revival between 1737 and 1746. The book, really a letter to Benjamin Colman, a Boston pastor, was called *A Faithful Narrative of the Surprising Work of God*. First published in London in 1737, it was widely read in the British Isles and in the colonies, especially in Boston. Edwards claimed that Northampton was "never so full of the love of God, nor full of joy." People loved the Bible and sought to help others.

The revival spread up and down the Connecticut River valley until over one hundred communities had experienced renewal of Christians and salvation of sinners by 1737. Zealous pastors preached to convince the people of God's hatred of sin and of his boundless mercy toward the repentant. Edwards's sermon ("Sinners in the Hands of an Angry God") at Enfield on July 8, 1741, well illustrated the Puritan concept of God's wrath upon sinners, and people cried out for the divine mercy that Edwards assured them was available.

When Charles Chauncy, liberal pastor of the First Church of Boston and leader of the Old Light (antirevival) Congregationalists, opposed the revival in a 1743 publication, it fell to Edwards to answer him. Edwards endeavored to formulate a theology of revival, making a synthesis of Calvinistic theology and the experiences of people who genuinely experienced spiritual transformation. The best formulation was in his *Freedom of the Will* (1754), which he wrote in about five months. He argued that the will was

free to act in the ordinary matters of life but that it was
bound—helpless—morally. It could respond to revivalistic preaching only when inclined by the Holy Spirit. Renewal could not be
worked up but was an act of the sovereign God.

Edwards's congregation later became dissatisfied with him
because he wanted all members of the church to be converted. A
dispute also arose over his salary. His public denunciation of
young people who had read a book on midwifery finally led the
congregation to dismiss him by a vote of 230 to 23. He preached
his farewell sermon on July 2, 1750, with grace and charity.

He went to a frontier church in Stockbridge, Massachusetts, in
1751 to minister to the settlers and Indians. He spoke to the Indians through an interpreter and protected them from exploita-
tive settlers. He wrote *Freedom of the Will* during the time he
was in Stockbridge. He also edited and published the *Journal of
David Brainerd* in 1749. (Brainerd had been engaged to
Edwards's daughter Jerusha, who had nursed him in his illness
from tuberculosis. Both died of the disease in 1747.)

Edwards, widely known as a scholar, was asked to be president
of the College of New Jersey on the death of his son-in-law, Aaron
Burr (father of the statesman Aaron Burr) in 1757. He assumed office on February 16, 1758, but died from a smallpox vaccination in
March of the same year.

His four books on religious experience (including the *Treatise on
Religious Affections* and *Thoughts on the Revival)* analyzed
revival and documented many facts of the Awakening. *Freedom of
the Will* provided, in a sense, a reconciliation of Calvinism and
revivalism. His *Journal of David Brainerd* inspired people like
Henry Martyn to missionary work. Edwards was one of
America's greatest intellects. His mark on theology in New England lasted long after his death. His belief that conversion in-
volves both the mind and the emotions has not, regrettably,
always been held by late generations of revivalists.

Another great New England revival occurred from 1740 to 1743
and must be linked with George Whitefield (1714–70). (The story

GEORGE WHITEFIELD (1714-1770), English preacher who reached thousands in America and Britain. Gifted in voice and gesture, Whitefield was the outstanding preacher in the Great Awakening. *(Courtesy of the Billy Graham Center Museum)*

of Whitefield's early life and his work in Britain is told on pages 68–73.) He crossed the Atlantic thirteen times before his death in Newburyport, Massachusetts. He often stayed at Benjamin Franklin's home and was his friend, although Franklin never gave up his deism. In a ten-week period in New England, Whitefield preached approximately 130 sermons and traveled eight hundred miles. He first spoke at Newport, Rhode Island, in September 1740. When the crowd in Boston was too large to be housed in the church, he spoke in the open air to five thousand on Boston Commons. Attendance rose as high as fifteen thousand in these meetings. A careful estimate by Franklin determined that Whitefield's voice could be heard by twenty-five thousand people as much as half a mile away. Hundreds of people went to their pastors for spiritual counsel as a result of Whitefield's preaching. When Whitefield left, he asked Gilbert Tennent to itinerate. Tennent itinerated for four months with much success. Whitefield visited Edwards in Massachusetts, preached in his church, and enjoyed good fellowship with him and the large Edwards family. He went to New York after his New England tour.

The revival produced 150 new churches in New England, New York, New Jersey, Pennsylvania, and Maryland. Whitefield's later visits, while fruitful, were not as successful as the 1739–41 tour. Other visits to the thirteen colonies were made (1744–48, 1751–52, 1754–55, 1763–65, and 1769–70). He was in the thirteen colonies seven times, including his first visit to Georgia in 1738. He died in Newburyport and was buried under the pulpit of the Presbyterian church.

A monument to Whitefield's visits to the colonies was the Bethesda orphanage at Savannah, Georgia. He was interested in charitable works and, like other leaders of revival, he was also interested in education. The tabernacle erected for his meetings in Philadelphia housed a charity school which later became the University of Pennsylvania. He helped Samuel Davies and Gilbert Tennent raise money for the College of New Jersey (later Princeton). He also aided Samson Occom, the Indian preacher, in raising a large sum for what became Dartmouth College in New Hampshire.

Whitefield was also interested in public affairs. The commissary, Sherburn, enlisted his efforts on behalf of the expedition to capture Fort Louisburg in Acadia from the French in 1745. Whitefield was also a friend of the leader, Colonel George William Pepperell (1696–1759). Whitefield preached the final sermon to the expedition before it left and even suggested the motto, *Nil desperandum Christo duce* (Fear nothing while Christ is leader). The expedition was successful.

Whitefield's many intercolonial journeys helped to promote an ecumenical and national spirit in the thirteen colonies. People focused on religion as the first real common interest among the colonists. He was the unifier and catalyst of revival in both America and Great Britain. He gave mobility to revivalism. He linked evangelistic passion for souls with social zeal that produced his orphanage. He also advocated kind treatment of slaves by masters in his preaching, though when James Habersham, supervisor of his orphanage, advocated a plantation to help finance his orphanage, he bought one to be worked by slaves.

Baptists in New England grew in number through the Great Awakening. Many converted Congregationalists became New Lights or Separates, wanting only regenerates as church members and opposing compulsory religious taxes to support the state church. Some of the New Lights or Separates later adopted Baptist principles and membership. Isaac Backus was one such individual.

Isaac Backus (1724–1806) was born in Norwich, Connecticut. On August 24, 1741, he was converted by the preaching of Eleazar Wheelock. He joined the First Congregational Church in Norwich the following year. He withdrew his membership in 1745 to become a New Light Congregationalist. In an experience in the woods in September 27, 1746, he felt a call to preach, and he itinerated in Connecticut, Rhode Island, and Massachusetts. Sixteen persons formed a New Light Church in Titicut parish in

Middleborough, Connecticut, on February 16, 1748, and in March asked Backus to be the pastor. He was ordained in April. By 1749 he was convinced that immersion was the correct mode of baptism. He and six members of his church were immersed on August 22, 1751. Backus became the pastor of this new Baptist church and was ordained as a Baptist minister on June 23, 1756. He served as pastor of the Middleborough church for fifty years. From 1756 to 1766 he traveled nearly fifteen thousand miles and preached more than twenty-four hundred times as a pastoral revivalist.

The College of Rhode Island (later Brown University) was chartered in February 1764. The following year Backus was named as trustee; he served in that capacity until 1799.

Backus also led the fight in Massachusetts for religious toleration and the end of the established state church. His own mother had been jailed for thirteen days in 1722 for not paying the state church tax. As agent of the Warren Baptist Association, he drafted a petition of redress in 1769 and wrote a letter to the General Assembly. He also wrote a letter to Samuel Adams in January of that year, stating the case for separation of church and state. He went to the first Continental Congress in the fall of 1774 to ask for civil rights for dissenters. The First Amendment, prohibiting establishment of a state church, came in 1789, partly as a result of Backus's work.

His historical interest, stimulated by this struggle, led him to study Baptist church history. He wrote the three-volume *A History of New England with Particular Reference to the Baptists (1777-1796)*.

Backus longed for revival and, along with twenty-two New England ministers, he set up a National Concert of Prayer for revival in 1794 that lasted until 1800.

Backus was so modest and diffident that he shut his eyes when he preached or spoke in his sharp, clear, distinct voice. He was six feet tall but became corpulent in middle life; this may have led to the stroke that killed him.

There were 312 Baptist churches with 26,638 members in New England by 1804. In all of the colonies there were 1,200 Baptist churches with about 100,000 members. Many of these became members as a result of revival. Shubal Stearns, the apostle of the Baptists in North Carolina, was a product of the Great Awakening.

The Great Awakening in the Southern Colonies. The Great Awakening in the South occurred mainly among dissenting Presbyterians and Baptists. Samuel Morris, a planter or, more likely, a bricklayer in Hanover County, Virginia, read a variety of books to friends about 1740. The readings included Whitefield's sermons, Luther's *Commentary on Galatians*, and a number of other books. So many people attended his readings that "reading houses" were built.

Many were converted in the ensuing revival which had no denominational connections. Learning of this, the New Light Presbytery of New Brunswick sent William Robinson to them in July 1743. Robinson, who had studied in the "log college," led them to become Presbyterians.

Samuel Davies (1723–61), of Welsh descent, studied at Samuel Blair's school in Fagg's Manor from 1738 to 1746. He was ordained in 1747 and visited the converts in Virginia. He returned to them in 1748 and led them until he became president of the College of New Jersey in 1759. He was licensed to preach by the governor and in 1748 received permission to open seven preaching centers. He organized Hanover Presbytery, the first presbytery in the South, on September 3, 1755. He educated the slaves in his congregations and set up missions to the Indians.

He was on leave from his churches for eleven months from 1753 to 1755, traveling to England, Scotland, and Ireland with Gilbert Tennent to raise money for the College of New Jersey. Although he experienced seasickness and worried about his ill wife, he and Tennent raised £3,200 for the college. His oratorical preaching won him acclaim. He became president of the college in 1759.

Davies was the able poet of the Great Awakening, composing some one hundred poems. He told his friend Thomas Gibbons that he tried to preach as if he would never preach again and "as a dying man to dying men."

Shubal Stearns (1706–71) helped to spread the Baptist cause in Virginia and North and South Carolina. He was born in Boston but moved to Connecticut, where the Great Awakening influenced him spiritually. He joined the New Light Congregationalists in 1745, but was immersed and ordained as a Baptist on March 20, 1751. He became a pastor in Tolland, Connecticut. People noted Stearns's small stature, penetrating eyes, and "holy whine" (a rising and falling of his voice) in preaching.

He moved to Opekon Creek, Virginia, in 1754 along with Daniel Marshall who was married to his sister Martha. When the regular Baptists opposed them, he and fifteen others moved to Sandy Creek, North Carolina. The group of sixteen organized a Baptist church and built a thirty-by-twenty-six-foot church in September 1755 on land given by Seamore York. The original sixteen soon became six hundred, and by 1772 there were forty-two churches and 125 ministers. Stearns organized the Sandy Creek Association in 1758. These Baptists united with the Regular Baptists in 1788.

Daniel Marshall (1706–84) ably seconded him in this work. Marshall was born in Windsor, Connecticut. He was converted at the age of twenty and preached to the Mohawk Indians for about eighteen months. Stearns ordained him as a Baptist pastor in 1758.

These Presbyterian and Baptist preachers laid the foundation for the work of their respective denominations in the South. Devereux Jarratt, an Episcopalian minister, led revivals in Virginia which resulted in a strong Methodist movement, but his work more properly falls into the early stages of the Second Awakening.

2. THE GREAT
AWAKENING IN BRITAIN

EVERY stratum of society in the British Isles of the eighteenth century needed revival. Gambling was in vogue in the upper and middle classes. Charles James Fox, who became a prominent politician, owed £100,000 in gambling debts and once lost £11,000 in a twenty-four hour period.

Brutal and cruel sports amused the ordinary people. Cock-fighting and bearbaiting, with consequent cruelty to animals, were common. The gallows at Tyburn were the center of "hanging shows" when ten to fifteen might be hung at once while the crowd watched. In the eighteenth century people might be hung for any of 160 offenses. These included picking a pocket of one shilling or shoplifting five shillings' worth of goods.

Drunkenness helped to make the people brutal and cruel. In 1724 the tax on gin was lowered and drunkenness became an epidemic. In 1684 the British consumed 527,000 gallons of spirits; in 1750 they consumed 11 million gallons, mostly potent gin. In one part of London in 1750, about one-fourth of the houses were selling gin. Signs over gin shops advertised: "Drunk for 1d, Dead-drunk for 2d; Free Straw." When the bishop of Chester rebuked a cleric for drunkenness, the man replied that he was never drunk on duty. The bishop then asked when a clergyman was not on duty.

Corruption and immorality were rampant among politicians of all levels. Three sons of George III, including the Prince of Wales, openly kept mistresses. Seats could be bought in Parliament; the advertised price in *The Times* of London rose from £1,000 to £5,000 early in the eighteenth century. Robert Walpole, England's first "prime minister," lived an immoral and drunken life. On one occasion he made the cynical remark that every man in the House of Commons "had his price."

A wave of materialism seemed to affect the clergy. Those in the upper echelons were paid disproportionately to the parish clergy. The archbishop of Canterbury received £7,000 annually, the archbishop of York, £4,000, the bishop of Durham, £6,000, and the bishop of London, £4,000. In contrast, half of the parish clergy received less than the legal minimum of £80 per year. Of 10,000 parishes shortly after the year 1700, 6,000 paid less than £50 and 1,200 paid less than £20 per year.

It is hardly surprising that clergy neglected their flocks. Spiritual duties were not given priority. Many bishops failed to ordain and visit their clergy or confirm children. Bishops were appointed by the government, and this led to corruption. One minister bet Lady Yarmouth £5,000 that he would not get a bishopric. She pulled the proper strings, he got his bishopric, and she got her £5,000.

Lady Huntingdon and the Earl of Dartmouth visited George III to request that Frederich Cornwallis, the archbishop of Canterbury, stop "routs and feasts" at his Lambeth palace. The king wrote a letter of severe rebuke to him and ordered him to end those practices.

The intellectual climate among the clergy and upper class was rationalistic and deistic. The poet Alexander Pope, in his *Essay on Man*, reflected the intellectual trends of the day and advised men to know themselves rather than God, for "the proper study of mankind is man." Deism was a religion of reason which ruled out miracles, prayer, and the deity of Christ. Its doctrines were: God exists; man should live ethically; and man will be rewarded or punished in the hereafter. Preachers told people to respect the upper class and be good. "Enthusiasm" in religion was frowned upon. Early in the reign of George III, Blackstone, the famous lawyer, said that it would be hard to tell from the sermons in English churches whether the preacher was Moslem, Confucianist, or Christian. Leslie Stephens characterized sermons as "dull, duller, and dullest." Britain was ripe for revival when it occurred in the 1730s.

Local revivals in the British Isles brought renewal to professing Christians and salvation to sinners before the Great Awakening. An early awakening took place in 1625 in Antrim in Ulster (northern Ireland). Robert Glendenning, a Welsh preacher, preached the law, the terror of the wrath of God, and grace for those convicted. Prayer meetings were held monthly in Hugh Campbell's house. Many came under conviction, were converted, and were added to the church.

Revival also came to the parishes of Stewarton and Irvine in Scotland in 1625. David Dickson (1583–?) earned his B.A. from the University of Glasgow. From his ordination in 1618 until 1642 he was the minister at Irvine and Stewarton. He lectured in the church on market days. Hundreds came to him under deep conviction for spiritual counsel. People called this preoccupation with salvation the "Stewarton sickness." The "sickness" ran from 1625 to about 1630 and brought renewal to the church and salvation to hundreds.

Another remarkable revival occurred at the kirk (church) of Shotts, Scotland, under the ministry of John Livingstone (1603–72). Livingstone was born in the manse at Kilsyth and earned his B.A. in 1625 from the University of Glasgow. He was licensed in 1625 and became curate at a church and chaplain to the Countess of Wigton. In 1625 he was the instrument of local revival. For five years after that he engaged in evangelism. He spent some time in Ireland but was suspended by the bishop of Down for nonconformity. From 1638 to 1648 he served at Stranraer and from 1648 to 1660 at Ancrum. At the restoration of Charles II, he fled to Holland, where he prepared a Hebrew-Latin Bible.

Livingstone had a leading role in the revival that fell upon the kirk of Shotts in 1630. Shotts lies a few miles west of Edinburgh. A carriage belonging to some ladies of high standing broke down at the kirk of Shotts. The minister, John Hance, took the ladies in and helped them with repairs. In gratitude they offered him a new manse and asked him to hold a Communion service at his church.

He held the Communion service on June 20, 1630, and invited John Livingstone to speak the following day. Livingstone's sermon in the churchyard on Ezekiel 36:25–26 resulted in five hundred coming under conviction, confessing their sins, and being converted. The revival spread to other areas as Livingstone spent another period as an itinerant evangelist.

A revival among Scottish soldiers in 1642 was instrumental in the beginning of the Presbyterian church in Ireland. Charles I sent General Robert Munro and seven Scottish regiments with Presbyterian chaplains in 1642 to keep order after the 1641 uprising. Revival broke out among the soldiers; regimental churches with sessions of elders were set up. The first presbytery was organized in 1642 with elders from four regimental churches. A synod of thirty-two ministers became the Presbyterian Church of Ireland some years after other Scottish ministers had come to help spread the revival. Many ministers from this church later came to America. Francis Makemie (1658–1708), the most notable, was sent to America by the Presbytery of Laggan when Colonel Stevens of Maryland asked for a minister. Makemie organized the first presbytery in Philadelphia in 1706. (For information of Makemie's work, see page 307.)

Early manifestations of revival came in the Church of England with the organization of religious societies of young men. The

German-born, Oxford-educated Anton Horneck (1641–97) organized such an Anglican society at Savoy Chapel as early as 1671. His "awakening" sermons brought many young men into the church. These religious societies were to foster spiritual life by Bible lectures, prayer, and religious counsel. Around 1700 there were thirty such groups in London. Samuel Wesley, father of John and Charles, organized one at Epworth. Both Whitefield and Wesley used this system in their work. Howel Harris had used the same system in Wales even earlier. These weekly meetings were for the culture of a deeper spiritual life, Bible study and prayer, and works of charity.

THE GREAT AWAKENING IN WALES

Revival in Wales preceded that in England. Griffith Jones (1683–1761), a shepherd boy, was called by a dream to be a preacher. He was educated in the Elizabethan Grammar School as an older boy. George Bull ordained him in 1709 after theological training. After serving as curate at Langharne for a short time, he became pastor of Llandowror in Carmarthenshire in 1716 and served there until his death. His passionate and powerful preaching brought revival in 1716. Daniel Rowland, another minister, was converted in his meetings.

Jones pioneered in itinerant field preaching. He organized the churches that sprung up into circuits. He also clothed and fed the poor. But it was his charity schools that made him most famous.

The biblical ignorance he discovered in catechetical classes led him to train and pay teachers to travel on the circuits. They would travel from church to church and spend several months at each church, teaching the people to read. He began his first Circulating Welsh Charity School in 1730. By 1737 he had 37 schools with 2,400 pupils. By 1777 the pupils who had gone through his schools numbered 500,000. He persuaded the Society for Propagation of the Gospel to supply him with 30,000 Welsh Bibles. When he died, 158,000 pupils were being taught to read the Bible in Welsh in nearly 4,000 schools. This godly revivalistic pastor not only brought many Welsh to Christ, but he taught them to read the Bible to guide them in faith and life.

Daniel Rowland (1713-90) was curate to his brother in Llangeitho, Cardiganshire. Although he had been ordained in 1733, he was an unconverted, sports-loving preacher. He was converted in 1735 when he heard Griffith Jones's sermon at Llandwei Brefi. Before his conversion he had been unable to help those convicted by his sermons. After his conversion he balanced the law with the love of Christ in his preaching. When he was removed from his church in Ystrad Ffin in 1763, his people built a chapel for him in Llangeitho. He itinerated widely and had two thousand communicants in his own church by 1742. He later helped to organize the Welsh Calvinistic Methodist Church by moderating its first meeting in January 1743.

Howel Harris (1714-73), the third of the trio of Welsh revivalists, was born in Trevecca near Talgarth in southern Wales. His brother Joseph, a blacksmith, had become chief assayer at the Tower of London by 1748. His brother Thomas, a tailor in London, became a wealthy country gentleman. Joseph helped him in 1728 to attend a grammar school at Llwyn-Llyd where he learned Greek and Latin.

Harris became a teacher at Llan-gors near his home in 1732. He went downhill spiritually in the eighteen months he was there, with his interests mainly in cards, drink, and girls. Joseph got him another school at Llangastry.

The vicar, Pryce David, rode to hounds and drank but did his work in the pulpit on Sunday. On Palm Sunday in 1735 he spoke of the need to receive Communion. He said that if one was not fit to come to the Lord's Table, he was not fit to live or die. Harris was convicted, read religious books, and tried to earn salvation by good works and asceticism. He read in *The Practice of Piety* that if a person believed during Communion, his sins would be forgiven. He believed and was saved in May 1735, but he did not have a clear view of free grace by faith until he met George Whitefield in 1739. Whitefield, on first seeing him, said, "My heart was knit closely to him."

Harris went for a time to St. Mary's College, Oxford, but soon left. Griffith Jones advised him to seek ordination, but he was refused ordination on two occasions because of his views on itinerating. He carried on all his revivalistic work as a layman in the established church.

He opened schools in Trevecca and Talgarth in 1736, but he lost the Talgarth school in 1737 because he was more interested in preaching and neglected his teaching. He taught school by day and preached as an Anglican exhorter in the evening in the open air. His itineration often involved six sermons a day. He itinerated twenty-five hundred miles on foot and spoke 125 times in a two-year period. He organized his first society in late 1736, and by 1739 there were many societies. He was the organizing genius in 1743 when the Welsh-English Calvinistic Association of Churches was set up with George Whitefield as its moderator. Harris filled in for Whitefield at Moorfields Tabernacle in London while Whitefield was in North America and made twenty-five visits, with each visit a month in length, to London to preach. He preached at the opening of Wesley's "Foundery" on November 11, 1739.

His best period of revivalism was from 1735 to 1750, with many Christians being renewed and people saved. This was followed by intolerance and bouts of passion in 1750. Harris retired to Trevecca and, with the example of Zinzendorf's Herrnhut, founded a religious community, the "Family." They lived under semi-monastic rules. There were 120 in the "Family" by 1755.

Harris was captain of a company of Breconshire militia from 1759 to 1762 during the war with France. He continued to preach during this period and founded a chapel at Yarmouth where he was stationed.

Lady Huntingdon rented an old Tudor building from him at Trevecca to house the college which she founded in 1768. Harris talked to the students regularly. His good common sense enabled him to make many practical innovations in hedging and ditching which improved Welsh agriculture.

William Williams (1717–91) of Pantycelyn was won to Christ by one of Harris's open-air sermons at Talgarth in 1738. He became an itinerant revivalist, especially in Pembrokeshire. He was the Charles Wesley of Welsh hymnody and is best known for his hymn, "Guide Me, O Thou Great Jehovah" ("Redeemer" in the original).

These men stirred nearly all of Wales in the second half of the eighteenth century. Schools and colleges were founded by them to meet the need of Wales.

THE GREAT AWAKENING IN SCOTLAND

The Scottish churches suffered spiritually because of the Patronage Act (1712), which gave the landowners on whose land the church was located the right to select the minister. If he were not spiritually vital, the owner might force the people to engage unworthy ministers. Theological dissension and consequent secession in the eighteenth century further weakened the church, but revival came to Cambuslang and Kilsyth from February to August 1742.

Cambuslang was about five miles southeast of Glasgow. The pastor from 1731 was William M'Culloch (1700—1771). He graduated from Glasgow University in 1712, taught mathematics for a time, and became tutor and chaplain to a Mr. Hamilton. He was ordained in 1731 and appointed to Cambuslang, a town of two hundred families engaged in weaving, agriculture, and mining.

Hurricane, famine, and a cold 1739–40 winter gave his parishoners concern about the hereafter. M'Culloch preached several sermons on the New Birth in 1740 and 1741. In January 1742, ninety heads of families asked for a Thursday service. M'Culloch organized prayer societies that February. When he preached on John 3:35 on February 14, 1742, Catherine Jackson came to the manse crying, "What must I do?" On February 16 many met at the manse for prayer. When M'Culloch spoke on Jeremiah 23:6 on February 18, fifty came to his house for spiritual counsel and fifteen became Christians. By the end of April of that year over two hundred had been converted.

The crowds became so great at the daily services that M'Culloch had to have the aid of other ministers. George Whitefield, who was in Scotland for the second of his fourteen visits there, helped with the Cambuslang "Wark" for the week of July 11–17, 1742. On July 11 he spoke to a crowd he estimated to be twenty thousand. People wept over their sins, and some fell prostrate. Over seventeen hundred took Communion in this open-air sacramental service. Whitefield returned again on August 15 to speak at an open-air service to about thirty thousand people, with three thousand taking Communion. Nearly nine years later, in a report dated April 30, 1751, M'Culloch could count four hundred in his own parish who were going on spiritually as a result of this six-month revival in 1742.

James Robe (1688–1753) was educated at Glasgow University. He was ordained in 1713 and served as pastor at Kilsyth from 1713 to 1752. In 1740 he began to speak for a year on the subject of regeneration, just as William M'Culloch and Jonathan Edwards had done. On May 19, 1742, four or five were convicted. Robe was present at the Cambuslang revival and told his congregation about it in mid-May. About thirty people were counseled by him and the elders. Nearly three hundred were soundly converted in the period from May to August, 1742. Whitefield spoke on June 15 to about ten thousand in the open air, and fifteen hundred participated in the Communion service that followed.

Revival spread all over the Scottish Lowlands from these two centers. Prayer, serious preaching of the New Birth, and private counseling of the convicted formed the pattern of these revivals.

This revival rescued Scotland from the coldness of rationalism and restored it to orthodoxy. Missions began, first with Claudius

Buchanan of Cambuslang, and later with Alexander Duff, going to India. Gerardus Kuyper heard of the revivals by letter, and a revival broke out in his church in Amsterdam in 1748.

THE GREAT AWAKENING IN ENGLAND

Though the name Methodist was often used to designate all who were revivalistic in the eighteenth century, one must distinguish the Calvinistic, predominantly upper-class, Evangelicals* who remained in the established church from the lower- and middle-class followers of Whitefield and Wesley who worshiped in chapels. Estimates of Evangelicals indicate that they comprised about 5 percent of the population. The Methodists provided the foot soldiers and the Evangelicals the leaders in the late eighteenth- and early nineteenth-century social reforms. George M. Trevelyan, historian, wrote of the Evangelicals as a "Bridge Between Establishment and Dissent." Parish clergymen, clergymen teaching in universities, and laymen of the Clapham Sect made up that leadership.

William Law (1686–1761) greatly influenced Evangelicals, including Henry Martyn, Henry Venn, James Hervey, and Thomas Scott, and also the Methodist leaders such as Whitefield and the Wesleys. Born at King's Cliffe, Northants, Law graduated from Emmanuel College, Cambridge, and was ordained in 1711. He lost his college fellowship and church for refusing to take the oath of loyalty to George I. He served as tutor and private chaplain to the father of the great historian, Edward Gibbon, at Putney from 1727 to 1740. He returned to King's Cliffe in 1740 and wrote his *Treatise on Christian Perfection* (1726) and *A Serious Call to a Devout and Holy Life* (1728). The members of the "Holy Club" at

---

*When the word *evangelical*—used either as a noun or as an adjective—is used to refer to Christians who emphasize personal piety, evangelism, and fidelity to the Bible as the infallible rule of faith, the word is lowercased. However, many times in this book the word refers to an identifiable party within the Church of England, a group whose work reached its apex in the Clapham Sect. When this Church of England party is being referred to, as above, *Evangelical* is capitalized.

Oxford carefully studied his writings, especially the latter books. They were strongly influenced by these works as well as those of earlier Puritan writers.

The Evangelicals.

WESTERN ENGLAND. Western England, especially Cornwall, was blessed with early Evangelical leadership long before the time of the Wesleys or Whitefield. James Hervey (1714-58), a member of the Holy Club in Oxford, graduated from Lincoln College, Oxford, in 1737. When he went to Cornwall for his health, he spoke at St. Genney's for the pastor, George Thomson, an even earlier Evangelical. Whitefield's advice to read Romans and Galatians resulted in his conversion in 1742. With better health, Hervey served as curate of Biddeford near Exeter from 1740 to 1743. He spoke twice on Sunday, gave two Bible readings during the week, and faithfully catechized the children. Dismissed for his evangelical Calvinism, he went to Weston Flavell in Northamptonshire in 1743. There he served as curate and then successor (1752-58) to his father.

Samuel Walker (1714-61), another Evangelical cleric, was greatly admired by his fellow ministers. He graduated from Exeter College and was ordained in 1737. During the period from 1738 to 1746 he tutored a noble's son for two years and held a curacy for six. He went to Truro, Cornwall, in 1746 to indulge his love of card playing and dancing in the pleasure centers. He was converted about 1748 through the ministry of George Conon (1710-?), an Evangelical layman and head of the noted Truro Grammar School for many years. Conon, a Scot and graduate of Aberdeen University, also helped Thomas Haweis to become a Christian.

Walker began preaching salvation by faith in daily services and private counseling. He organized religious societies for his converts in 1754. The Parsons' Club, which he formed for ministers in 1755, helped many fellow clerics. He, however, disagreed with the Methodists' itinerancy and emphasis on feelings.

YORKSHIRE. Yorkshire was another center of Evangelical revival in the north of England, with leaders such as Henry Venn and William Grimshaw. Henry Venn (1724–97) graduated from Jesus College, Cambridge, where he excelled at cricket. After earning his M.A. in 1749, he was ordained and served at Clapham from 1754 to 1759. He was made vicar of Huddersfield in 1759. There he preached 6,250 sermons to the rough and ignorant weavers of Yorkshire. He retired to Yelling, near Cambridge, in 1771.

Venn had to resort to open-air preaching because so many wanted to hear him. Twenty-two of his "lads" became ministers. Their training was facilitated through financial assistance from the Elland Society, an organization set up in 1767 to help poor boys train for the ministry. Venn greatly influenced Charles Simeon and Joseph Jowett. From 1792 to 1813 his godly son, John Venn (1759–1813), was the rector of Clapham Common Anglican Church, which the proponents of social reform attended.

An even more colorful speaker was the powerfully built William Grimshaw (1708–63), who graduated from Christ's College, Cambridge, in 1730. He had been awarded a scholarship because he was poor. After ordination he served at St. Mary's Chapel at Todmorden from 1731 to 1742. From 1742 until his death he was pastor at Haworth, Yorkshire, where the congregation was pleased with his ability to jump over a five-bar gate and with his humorous homespun preaching in market language.

He came under conviction at Todmorden in 1734 when he was unable to console John and Susan Schofield about the death of their baby girl. He began secret prayer in 1735. Three years later he was praying four times a day in an effort to please God by his works. He read Owens's book on justification and began to study the Bible. He finally found peace in 1742.

Grimshaw's parish experienced revival from 1742 to 1748. Many were converted in the crowds of a thousand or more. On one occasion he left the church with the congregation singing Psalm 119.

Taking a riding crop, he went to Black Bull Tavern and forcibly brought the men to church.

He itinerated widely over eight thousand square miles in four counties. He walked to all of his services, some of which began as early as 4:00 A.M. His extemporaneous open-air preaching, congregational hymn-singing, house-to-house visitation, and weekly class meetings helped him to win and disciple many. His policy was to "preach down man and preach up Christ." His irenic spirit led to cooperation with Whitefield who preached in Haworth. John Wesley was also a close friend.

THE MIDLANDS. John Berridge (1716–93), a very witty, colorful eccentric, earned his B.A. at Clare College, Cambridge. After his conversion in 1749 he served as curate at Stapleford near Cambridge from 1749 to 1755 and rector at Everton from 1755 to 1785. His church experienced revival under his preaching of justification by faith only. He began itinerant preaching and cooperated with the Wesleys and Whitefield. He was very influential at Cambridge University.

When the French skeptic Voltaire was asked to select a character as beautiful as Christ, he pointed to John W. Fletcher (1729–85). Fletcher was a Swiss, educated in Geneva, who went to England as a tutor in 1752. He was converted through the Methodists and ordained in the Church of England in 1757. His only church was the parish of Madeley in Shropshire, to which he was appointed in 1760. When Lady Huntingdon opened Trevecca College in Wales in 1768 to train preachers, he became principal. He resigned in 1771 because of his strong Arminian views, expressed in his book, *Checks to Antinomianism*. He was saintly in life, a zealous revival preacher, and loved by all.

LONDON. William Romaine (1714-95) became the leading preacher in London. The son of a grain dealer who became mayor of Hartlepool near Durham, he earned his M.A. at Christ Church, Oxford, in 1737 and was ordained in 1738. Crowned heads of Europe subscribed to his translation of the Hebrew concordance and lexicon of Marius de Calasio. For a time he served as professor of astronomy at Gresham College.

He held curacies near and in London from 1738. In 1749 he became a lecturer at St. Dunstan's-in-the-West in Fleet Street, London. In spite of some internal difficulties in the church, he held that post for forty-six years, and St. Dunstan's-in-the-West became a center for London Evangelicals. Romaine was given another lectureship at St. George's in 1750. Under Whitefield's influence he became an ardent revival preacher and Calvinist. He also was one of Lady Huntingdon's chaplains for several years. From 1765 to 1795 he was the preacher in St. Anne's and about 1766 in St. Andrews-by-the-Wardrobe. He spoke Sunday morning and evening in these churches. He had large congregations for his sermons and lectures.

Another notable London preacher was Martin Madan, a lawyer. Asked to hear Wesley so that he could mimic him before his drinking friends, he listened but was converted instead. He became preacher and chaplain at Lock Hospital in 1750.

Those Anglican clergy who loved the Church of England joined with Whitefield and the Wesleys in itinerant preaching of salvation by faith only. They met opposition from the Anglican clergy who thought salvation was by good works and who disdained intense religious feelings ("enthusiasm"). The Evangelicals persuaded wealthy, influential Anglican laymen to form voluntary societies about 1795 and to promote social reforms such as the abolition of the slave trade and slavery between 1772 and 1833.

Other leading clerics of the Evangelicals, college clergy like Simeon and Milner, will be discussed in the chapter on the era from 1776 to 1810 when they did most of their great work. These early Evangelicals laid the foundations for the Evangelicals who became numerous in the Church of England.

The Methodists. While the Evangelicals became a potent force within the parishes, the Methodists also worshiped and received the sacraments in the parish churches. They also worshiped in their chapels, but did not separate from the established church until the period from 1784 to 1794. The Wesleys wanted them to remain in the Church of England. It was only after John Wesley's death that the separation came with the Plan of Pacification in 1795. Until then they were like the Pietists in the Lutheran Church and the prorevival American colonials within the Presbyterian and Congregational churches in the North and within the Anglican Church in the South.

THE MORAVIANS. Any discussion of the Methodist movement should properly begin with a look at the Methodists' connections with the Moravians. (The Moravians are discussed more fully on pages 36–39.) The United Brethren *(Unitas Fratrum)* from Bohemia settled on Zinzendorf's Berthelsdorf estate in Saxony and built Herrnhut as a new home. They existed within the Lutheran Church until 1727, when they began to form a separate Moravian denomination with Zinzendorf's consent. By 1742 the separation was complete.

A team of ten Moravians en route to join August Spangenberg in Georgia stopped in England in 1735. Later twenty-six sailed on the *Simmonds* with the Wesleys. John was impressed with the courageous bearing of the women and children in a terrible storm.

James Hutton (1715–95), a London bookseller, had met the Moravians on a visit to the *Simmonds* before they sailed. He formed a small group for prayer and Bible study which the Wesley's later attended. The Moravian leader Peter Böhler preached justification by faith to them. This group was superseded by the Fetter Lane Society, for which John Wesley and Böhler drew up rules on May 1, 1738. This became the first informal Moravian church in July 1740, when John Wesley, Lady Huntingdon, and about eighteen others withdrew. (Wesley opposed their doctrine of "stillness" which repudiated ordinances of the church in stressing justification by faith.) James Hutton went with the Moravians, as did Benjamin Ingham, who was converted in 1737 and had been with the Wesleys at Oxford and in Georgia. The separation was made formal by 1742.

Benjamin Ingham (1712–72), who visited Herrnhut with Wesley in 1738, became the Moravian apostle to Yorkshire and Lancashire. He won approximately twelve hundred, who were organized into Moravian societies by 1742.

John Cennick (1718–55), who had headed Whitefield's school at Kingswood near Bristol, and who wrote many hymns, went to Wiltshire as a revivalist. He also preached in Dublin and the Moravians soon organized societies there.

WHITEFIELD, LADY HUNTINGDON, AND THE ENGLISH CALVINISTIC METHODISTS. The second wave of Methodist revival in England began with the work of George Whitefield (1714–70) in Bristol. He also linked revival in England with that in the thirteen colonies in his seven visits there (See pages 46–49 for an account of his work in the colonies.)

He had a graceful body, a radiant face, and a strong, clear voice. His enemies called him "Dr. Squintum" because of a squint in one eye as a result of measles.

His father owned the Bull Inn, a three-story building with a large hall. George was the last of his seven children. When his father died in 1716, his mother remarried. From 1726 to 1729 she sent George to St. Mary de Crypt grammar school in Gloucester where he displayed a good memory and mastery of dramatic elocution.

In 1730 and 1731 he served in the inn. A student who had been at Oxford told George's mother that her son could earn his tuition at Oxford as a servant to other boys. Subsequently he entered Pembroke College in November 1732, only to be surrounded by an immoral and drunken atmosphere. Whitefield, however, became religious.

Charles Wesley came to know of him in 1733 when George told him of a woman in distress. Charles asked Whitefield to join the Holy Club which he, Robert Kirkham, and William Morgan had set up about 1728.

John Wesley assumed leadership of the club when he returned to Oxford in 1729. Members studied the Greek New Testament and the church fathers, had long and early devotions each day, and fasted on Wednesday and Friday. But in seeking to do good works, they were practical as well as ascetic. They visited prisons in Oxford and set up a school for prisoners' children.

Charles Wesley loaned Whitefield the book *The Life of God in the Soul of Man* by Henry Scougal (1650–78). The son of the bishop of Aberdeen, Scougal had become a professor of divinity at the age of twenty-five. His book, published in London in 1677, had wide influence. Susannah Wesley, mother of Charles and John, liked it. It defined religion as "the union of the soul with God, and Christ formed in us." Whitefield, under the influence of Scougal and the Holy Club, became very ascetic. He ate only coarse bread and drank only sage tea for six weeks during Lent in 1735. His studies and health began to suffer. His tutor arranged for a doctor to see him, and the doctor confined him to bed for six weeks. By March 1735, he had turned from a religion of works to Jesus Christ who "revealed himself to me and gave me the New Birth."

Whitefield recuperated from his severe asceticism in the home of Gabriel Harris, son of the mayor of Gloucester. Harris gave him Matthew Henry's *Commentary on the Bible.* He studied it and the Greek New Testament on his knees. Later that year his witness brought a religious society into being.

Benson, bishop of Gloucester, hearing of Whitefield's abilities from Lady Selwyn seven months after his return to Gloucester, gave him £5 to go back to Oxford and promised to ordain him. Benson ordained him as a deacon late in June 1736. Whitefield's first sermon, delivered a week after ordination at St. Mary de Crypt Church, was on Ecclesiastes 4:9-12. Three hundred attended, and fifteen were convicted.

George was granted his B.A. Thomas Broughton, also a member of the Holy Club, asked Whitefield to supply for him in the chapel of the Tower of London. Here he had great success. He preached his first extemporaneous sermon on December 29, 1737, and gave his first extemporaneous prayer on December 24, 1738.

He decided to become a missionary to Georgia after a short

curacy. Before leaving he preached in Bath, London, and Bristol. Lady Huntingdon had him speak in her salon, and Lady Frankland became a Christian. He also raised £1,000 for charity schools and £300 for the poor of Georgia.

He sailed for Georgia as Governor Oglethorpe's secretary in 1738. He left with five aides, one of whom, James Habersham, later headed up his orphanage in Savannah. (John Wesley, returning from Georgia on the *Whitaker*, told him not to go as the lot he cast had been against George going to Georgia.) He served as chaplain to one hundred soldiers during the seven-week trip to Gibraltar and won many to Christ. On arrival in Georgia, he served as secretary to Oglethorpe and set up schools. When he saw the plight of orphans in the colony, he remembered Charles Wesley had suggested opening an orphanage.

He returned to England on November 30, 1738, and preached each Sunday in the four churches in London open to him. He was present at the meeting with Wesley and others on January 1, 1739, when they experienced an unusual sense of the Holy Spirit moving them. Bishop Benson also ordained Whitefield as priest in 1739.

From Howel Harris he learned of open-air preaching and preached on a hillside to the unchurched, neglected miners of Kingswood on February 17, 1739. Crowds increased from two hundred to five thousand, ten thousand, and even twenty thousand. Whitefield also founded Kingswood School for the miners' children. He asked Wesley to come Bristol while he went to North America and persuaded him to take up field preaching. Wesley said he had before thought souls could only be saved in the church.

Whitefield spent four weeks in London preaching to crowds as large as thirty thousand at Kennington Common. He organized the many converts into bands on April 17, 1739.

On his way to America he wrote, "The whole world is now my parish!" He landed at Lewiston, Delaware, on October 30, 1739. On this trip he met William Tennent at Neshaminy and became a friend of Benjamin Franklin. He also spoke at Yale to the students. He was most successful in his preaching tour in the Northeast.

He laid the first brick for his Bethesda orphanage near Savannah on March 25, 1740. He planned a school for freed Negroes in Pennsylvania, and William Seward, a wealthy widowed stockbroker and Whitefield's friend and traveling companion, gave £2,000 for the five thousand acres. Seward later died of injuries at the hands of a mob, and Whitefield sold the property to the Moravians, who named it Nazareth.

Whitefield found many churches closed to him on his return to England because a man named Cooper had published Whitefield's *Journal* without permission. Wesley had tried to stop publication because of Whitefield's criticism of Anglican clergy in the *Journal*. An additional problem arose because Wesley's sermon on "Free Grace" had been published in the fall of 1739 as a twenty-four-page booklet with Wesley's approval. (Wesley's sermon expressed clearly his Arminian theology. Whitefield was a Calvinist, and this difference caused problems between the two men.) Wesley had dismissed Cennick as the head of the Kingswood School and put the title to the school and the New Room meeting place in Bristol in his own name. Thirty thousand in Whitefield's societies were also turned over to Wesley. Whitefield's letter to Wesley, replying to his free grace pamphlet, was published without Whitefield's knowledge and distributed in Wesley's Foundery. As a result, in 1741, the Methodists broke into two groups, the Calvinistic group following Whitefield, and the Arminian group following Wesley. In all of this Whitefield was very irenic and conciliatory although Wesley was at times tactless and domineering. Later the two friends were reconciled.

Whitefield first visited Scotland in 1741 and on his second visit in 1742 he participated in the revivals at Cambuslang and Kilsyth.

At about this time Whitefield was chided by a friend for giving £5 to a widow. Later a thief took Whitefield's coat and left his old ragged coat in exchange. Whitefield found £100 in the lining of that tattered coat! He remarked to the friend that God had given a 2000 percent return on his £5.

He married Elizabeth James, a widow, on November 14, 1741. Although she loved Howel Harris, and he loved her, they gave each other up so that she could marry Whitefield and establish a home in London.

Whitefield returned to America in 1744 and, at the suggestion of James Habersham, bought a plantation which he called Providence in South Carolina. The plantation was to be worked by slaves, and the profits were to be used to help support the Bethesda orphanage. When he received a legacy, he paid off the debt on Bethesda.

Lady Huntingdon later made Whitefield one of her chaplains and he often spoke to the upper-class friends in the salon in her Park Street, London, house. Noblemen and bishops came to these meetings. The Earls of Buchan and Bath became Christians, and the second Earl of Dartmouth (1731–1801) accepted Christ in 1756. He became influential in the royal household. He contributed a large sum to found Dartmouth College, named after him, in Hanover, New Hampshire.

Not all heard Whitefield with pleasure. The Duchess of Buckingham wrote to Lady Huntingdon that Whitefield's doctrine was "most repulsive" and that it was "monstrous" to be told that your heart was "as sinful as the common wretches that crawl the earth."

He preached in Scotland during more than a dozen trips and won many converts from the large crowds of listeners. He was frequently in Wales, the home of his wife. At least twice he traveled to Ireland, and he preached all over England. During his life he made seven trips to the thirteen colonies.

By 1764 he had become somewhat corpulent and asthmatic. The latter ailment resulted in his death.

He was a sincere, humble, and self-abasing man and England's ablest preacher. David Garrick, the actor, said he longed to say "Oh" with the same emphasis with which Whitefield spoke it.

Whitefield preached approximately eighteen thousand times in his life, often to congregations as large as twenty thousand to forty thousand. He was the first of the revivalists in England to organize bands and societies, to use lay preachers, to preach and pray extemporaneously, to preach in the open air, and to preach to children.

He helped to foster the cause of education by opening a school in Kingswood, and by permitting the tabernacle built for his preaching in Philadelphia to be used as a charity school. That school later became the University of Pennsylvania. He helped Tennent and Davies to raise money for the College of New Jersey and helped Samson Occom to raise a large sum for what became Dartmouth College.

He was interested in bettering the social conditions of the poor. He supported Bethesda orphanage for more than thirty years at much personal cost and worry. He preached better treatment of slaves by their masters.

He helped to unify the thirteen colonies as he gave them a common interest in religion in his preaching tours from Maine to Georgia. He unified the work of revival preachers on both sides of the Atlantic. He helped to organize the Welsh Calvinistic Methodist Church in 1743 and became its first moderator. He was most certainly the prophet of the Methodist awakening.

Selina Hastings, Lady Huntingdon (1707–91) was closely associated with Whitefield from the beginning of the Great Awakening. Lady Huntingdon was married to the ninth Earl of Huntingdon, Theophilus Hastings. She was a friend of the great composer, Handel. She read the Bible much, prayed, and performed charitable deeds, but it was through Lady Margaret Hastings, her sister-in-law, that she was converted. Fearing death, she simply said, "My God, I give myself to thee."

Her husband died in 1746. After his death, she turned her attention to spreading the gospel. She had been one of the Fetter Lane group but broke with it in 1740, along with the Wesleys. She had asked Whitefield to preach in her home before 1744 and made him her chaplain in 1748. She met Griffith Jones and Daniel Rowland on a visit to Wales in that same year. A tabernacle was opened for George Whitefield in 1753 with her help. She later helped to build Spa Fields and Tottenham Chapels.

Lady Huntingdon was also interested in the cause of education. When Samson Occom was in England, she invited him to her home and helped him to raise money for Dartmouth College. Earlier she had given money to the College of New Jersey through Davies and Tennent.

In 1768 she got a Tudor building in Trevecca from Howel Harris. This building was to house Trevecca College where ministers could be trained for her "connexion." Whitefield preached the dedicatory sermon on Exodus 20:24 on August 24, 1768. John Fletcher was principal until 1771 when he resigned because his Arminianism was not compatible with Lady Huntingdon's Calvinism. Lady Glenorchy of Scotland gave £1,000 and John Thornton two gifts of £500 each to the college. Lady Huntingdon provided board, room, tuition, and clothes for the students at her own expense during the three-year course. The ministerial students regularly went out preaching on Sunday. The college was moved in 1792 to Cheshunt about fourteen miles from London and renamed Cheshunt College. In 1911 it was moved to Cambridge. It became the source of ministers for the new congregations that came from the Great Awakening.

Lady Huntingdon's chapels were for a long time like the Methodist chapels in relation to the Church of England. She had to register them as dissenting chapels in 1781 under the Toleration Act. Her connexion had evolved into the English Calvinistic Methodist Church. She had six men ordained as ministers in 1783. She made Lady Anne Erskine the trustee of her connexion by her will, and in 1790 the first association was formed. Like Wesley and Whitefield, she would have preferred to keep her followers in the Church of England. Her followers later joined with the Congregational Church.

Whitefield willed the Bethesda orphanage to Lady Huntingdon

and she supervised it from England after his death. Several missionaries were sent to Georgia from Trevecca.

Lady Huntingdon's contributions to the Christian cause were numerous. She gave £100,000 in her lifetime to Christian causes. She helped to build sixty-seven chapels, of which six were her private property. She bought the right to name ministers to many parishes and appointed Evangelical men in them. Others, like Whitefield, she made her private chaplains. She founded Trevecca College to train ministers. And her salon was a center for preaching the gospel to the wealthy and titled.

JOHN AND CHARLES WESLEY. If Whitefield was the passionate preacher of the English Great Awakening, John Wesley was its energetic organizer and Charles Wesley its joyful songster. But the two brothers learned from Whitefield's open-air preaching and his class and society organization.

John Wesley (1703–91) was the fifteenth child of Samuel and Susannah Wesley. Samuel was a graduate of Exeter College, Oxford, ordained in 1689, and rector of Epworth parish in the fen country. He was a poor businessman with a large family and a stubborn, unforgiving, domineering disposition. He even spent time in a debtor's prison. He was, however, a literary man and an earnest pastor to his rough and ignorant people.

Susannah, the mother, was similar to Monica, the godly mother of Augustine, or Aletta, the mother of Bernard of Clairvaux, in her godly yet practical concern for her children. She gave her brood of nineteen children a good religious as well as elementary education. The family learned obedience without whimpering. She held services for up to two hundred parishioners in the kitchen during Samuel's absence in 1712, much to his chagrin when he returned. (It was not considered proper at the time for a woman to lead a religious service.)

John narrowly escaped death when the manse burned. Rescued from a second-story window by one man standing on another's shoulders, he often referred to himself as a "brand plucked from the burning."

He prepared for college at Charterhouse, where he often went hungry because larger boys took his food. He went to Christ Church, Oxford, where he received an M.A. in 1727. In 1728 he was elected a fellow of Lincoln College, a position he held until 1751. From 1727 to 1729 he served as his father's assistant at Wroote near Epworth. He was ordained in 1728.

When he returned to Oxford as a fellow in 1729, he assumed leadership of the Holy Club, which Charles, along with Robert Kirkham and William Morgan, had begun about a year earlier.

When James Oglethorpe wanted ministers for Georgia, the Wesleys and Whitefield responded. John was in Georgia from 1735 to 1738, but his tactless ways and High Church views did not set well with the colonists. He fell in love with Sophia Hopkey, a catechumen whom he was instructing. He finally cast a lot, a typical Wesley practice, as to whether he should marry her, and the lot was negative. When she married another man and did not appear for instruction, Wesley excluded the two from Communion. This and other tactless acts forced Wesley to leave the colony.

He had been impressed on the ship going to the colony with the bravery of the Moravians in a terrible storm. When he arrived in Georgia, August Spangenberg, another Moravian, challenged him as to whether he knew that Jesus Christ was his Savior. At this time Wesley felt he lacked saving faith. Peter Böhler had many talks with him on his return to England and urged him on to justification by faith. On May, 1738, he "unwillingly" attended a religious society meeting in Aldersgate Street, London. When the preface to Luther's *Commentary on Galatians* was being read, he felt his heart "strangely warmed" and he trusted in "Christ alone" for salvation. Charles had been converted three days earlier. William Law's writings, the Moravians, the Holy Club, and Whitefield had been helpful influences in the Wesleys' development.

He visited the Moravian center at Herrnhut, and was with them from mid-June to mid-September of 1738, but he was disturbed by

JOHN WESLEY (1703-1791) preaching on his father's grave in the churchyard at Epworth, England, 1742. Wesley preached to thousands and began the Methodist movement, which later separated from the Church of England. *(Courtesy of the Billy Graham Center Museum)*

their mysticism. He did worship with the Moravians after return-ing home, though he broke with them in 1740.

When George Whitefield went to America in 1739, he invited John to look after his work in Bristol while he was gone. White-field persuaded him to begin open-air field preaching on April 2, 1739. Wesley took to this new procedure, despite his initial distaste for it. On one occasion, when the rector closed the pulpit of Epworth Church to him, he preached on his father's tombstone in the churchyard. (Since the grave was considered family prop-erty, the rector could not order Wesley to stop preaching on this site.) He completed Charles's Kingswood School, but dismissed John Cennick as the schoolmaster and opened the New Room meeting place. He put titles to those places in his own name. He also preached against the doctrine of election even though Whitefield had urged him not to.

Wesley was active in London and renovated "the Foundery" (an old cannon factory) for his first society in 1739. He broke with the Moravians on July 16, 1740, when he and several others with-drew because of the quietism and mysticism of the Moravians. In 1741 he and Whitefield parted company in a dispute over predesti-nation and perfectionism. Wesley held to Arminianism and his brand of perfectionism. He and Whitefield later became good friends.

Wesley reluctantly approved lay preachers in 1741 after Thomas Maxfield, with Lady Huntingdon's encouragement and support, began preaching. Wesley's mother also told him that Maxfield was as much called of God as he was. Eventually he had seven thousand lay preachers.

Wesley fell in love with Grace Murray; one of his preachers, named Bennett, also loved her. She married Bennett through Charles's interference, and for a time the two brothers were separated. John finally married Mrs. Mary Vazeille, a banker's widow, on February 17, 1751. It was an unfortunate marriage, for she was jealous and short-tempered and rebelled against her hus-band's constant travel. She left him in 1776.

John had earlier adopted the idea of the Moravian "bands," a few people meeting for their mutual religious edification. He began class meetings at Bristol in February 1742. Captain Foy, a Wesleyan convert, suggested that collecting a penny a week from each member of the class was a good way to pay for the New Room chapel. The class had about eleven people and a leader. Classes were part of the society, and the local-level societies were grouped into circuits and circuits into districts under the annual conference.

He held his first annual conference from June 25 to 30, 1744, with six Church of England clergymen and four laymen present. The system of lay preachers traveling on circuits was later used to advantage by Francis Asbury in America.

Although the Methodists met in chapels, they were not a separate denomination; rather, they were part of the established church and usually took the sacraments in the parish church. But on February 28, 1784, Wesley's Deed of Declaration registered his chapels under the Toleration Act and put them in control of one hundred preachers who held the property. This was a virtual separation from the Church of England. Wesley, moreover, in early September of 1784 ordained Whatcoat and Vasey and consecrated Coke as the superintendent of the American work. He was thus taking to himself the power of a bishop (since only a bishop could officially ordain ministers in the Church of England). The Plan of Pacification in 1795 after his death brought the final separation and the emergence of the Methodists as a denomination numbering over seventy thousand.

Earlier (1784) the Methodists in America had created a national organization with Thomas Coke and Francis Asbury, elected by the American clergy, as superintendents. Later the two were called bishops. There were fifty-seven thousand in the Methodist Episcopal Church in America at this time. Their Articles of Faith were modeled on the Twenty-four Articles drawn up by Wesley. The constitution of the church was like that of the Anglican Church. Thus had the revival of 1739 prospered.

Wesley may have had High Church tendencies in ritual, but he was evangelical in theology. He believed that man was depraved and unable to save himself and that he must be justified by faith through the blood of Christ. To him the Scriptures were the final inspired rule for faith and practice. He also believed in Christian perfection. He held that the love of God would so fill the heart that one would not sin consciously, although "mistakes" might be made. This doctrine, set forth in his book *Christian Perfection*, is different from the "entire eradication of the old man" doctrine of some holiness groups and from the instantaneous and progressive sanctification of the later Keswick movement. Wesley also departed from most of the revivalists in taking a strong Arminian position. (Most of the early revivalists had been staunch Calvinists.)

John Wesley's main contribution may have been the Methodist Church, but he was influential in many other activities. His writings, including his *Journals* and *Letters*, comprise seventeen volumes. He wrote 233 books and pamphlets.

To Wesley the soul of reform was regeneration of the soul. He felt that the gospel knows only "social holiness." For him, Christianity was "essentially a social religion." His abomination of liquor was second only to that of the slave trade, which he described in February 1772 as "that execrable sum of all villainies." In his last letter, which was addressed to William Wilberforce, he urged him to stand against the world. He wrote a tract called *Thoughts Upon Slavery*. About 1787 he had it reprinted and distributed to the societies; he urged them to support the work of the Clapham Sect against the slave trade. Methodists by the tens of thousands signed petitions to Parliament, which were influential in helping to end the slave trade.

He encouraged John Howard, whom he described as a "great" and "extraordinary" man, in his work of prison reform. Wesley himself visited prisons and urged his Methodists to do so. His sermon at Bristol on the needs of French prisoners resulted in the giving of blankets and clothes to them.

In a letter to James Hervey, who had criticized him for itinerancy, Wesley said that he "looked upon all the world as [his] parish." Little wonder that with such a spirit he traveled about 225,000 miles. Most of his itinerating was done on horseback, for he had no carriage till friends gave him one when he was sixty-three. He preached over 46,000 sermons (some say 52,400) from 1738 to 1791. He was in Ireland about twenty-three times, in Scotland eleven times after 1751 and in Wales nine times from 1740 to 1746.

John had been a puny child and as an adult he was only five-foot-four in height and never exceeded 122 pounds. He dressed neatly, almost as a dandy. His life of horseback riding in the open air gave him a hardy constitution so that he overcame a tendency to consumption.

His recipe for long life was plain food, eight hours of rest per night, fresh air, exercise (which for him was riding horseback) and a contented spirit. His *Primitive Physic* in twenty-three editions was a Methodist doctor's manual. He liked to prescribe cures for illness himself.

Faith and love, profession and practice met in him. Little wonder that Methodist leaders following these rules and learning to speak in exhorting later became successful trade union leaders.

Wesley was quick-witted. On one occasion Beau Nash, the dandy at Bath, is said to have forced Wesley off the walk and commented, "I never make way for fools." Wesley, stepping aside, said, "I always do."

He was extremely generous, living on £28 a year so that he gave £30,000 away in profits from his books over a fifty-year period. He urged the Methodists to gain all they could, to save all they could, and to give away all they could.

The evening before he died, he said, "The best of all is God is with us." It was with God he lived and died.

His brother, Charles Wesley (1707–88), the eighteenth child, was more urbane than John. Born two months prematurely, he never cried or opened his eyes for two months, but was kept by the fire wrapped in wool. When the parsonage was burned, his nurse rescued him. In 1716 he went to Westminster School, where his brother Samuel was a tutor. He became captain of the school and a fighter. When an Irish relative, Garrett Wesley, wanted to adopt him and leave his fortune to him, Charles refused.

Charles was given a scholarship at Christ Church College, Oxford, for £100 a year. Here he went astray for a time. When he became more serious, he and some friends founded the Holy Club. His befriending of George Whitefield and loan to him of books in 1732 led to Whitefield's conversion. Charles received the M.A. in 1733 and was ordained in 1735.

Heeding Oglethorpe's call for help, Charles went to Georgia in 1735 as Oglethorpe's secretary. He soon found himself opposed to Oglethorpe because a woman falsely gossiped about her supposed affair with Oglethorpe. He resigned in April 1738 and returned to England ill and discouraged.

He was cared for in the home of John Bray, who later became a Moravian. Bray's sister, Mrs. Turner, was led by a dream to say at Charles's door, "In the name of Jesus of Nazareth, arise and believe, and thou shalt be healed of all thine infirmities." He believed and was converted on May 21, 1738, three days before his brother John.

Charles had himself locked in Newgate prison in July 1738 to give spiritual help to those slated for execution and to ride with them to Tyburn where they were to be hanged.

He was curate at St. Mary, Islington, for six months. He began field preaching in a farmer's field at Broadoaks on May 29, 1739, and later spoke to ten thousand at Moorfield on June 1, 1739, in the open air. He then helped John at the Foundery. From 1739 to 1771 he engaged in itinerant preaching. He went through the period of bitter persecution of the Methodists from 1739 to 1741.

He married Sarah Gwynne of Wales in April 1749 and they made their home in Bristol from 1756 till 1771, when they moved to London. Here he helped John in the City Road Chapel from 1771 until his death. Sarah had a severe case of smallpox during which Lady Huntingdon nursed her. Charles mourned the marring of her beauty. When Charles died, Wilberforce and two friends gave her an annuity of £60 a year for years. Charles's two sons, Charles and Samuel, became musicians.

Charles's greatest work was composing hymns and translating others from German, French, and Spanish. He is credited with composing 6,500 hymns (some say 7,200), including "O, for a Thousand Tongues," "A Charge to Keep I Have," "Hark, the Herald Angels Sing," and "Jesus, Lover of My Soul." His hymnal, *A Collection of Hymns*, was used by Methodists until 1904. He taught the Methodists to sing and left an enormous legacy to English hymnody.

We have traced the course of the Great Awakening from Germany, the thirteen colonies, and England and noted the many able leaders. We noticed unity of doctrine and similarity in methods of itineracy, extemporaneous preaching and prayer, use of the laity and organization with settled congregations in the state church until they became independent denominations. Multiplied thousands of Christians were renewed and sinners brought to salvation. Faith in Christ was made practical in loving service to man.

3. THE SECOND
AWAKENING, 1776–1810

THE Second Awakening, like the Great Awakening, was Protestant, transatlantic, and Anglo-Saxon, except for the revival in Scandinavia under Hauge. Revivals in such colleges as Hampden-Sydney and Yale occurred in the South and East. The Methodists in the South, aided by Devereux Jarratt, profited most from the itinerant revival. In the South the camp meeting provided still another type of revival.

The flood of deism from England during the French and Indian Wars threatened to inundate America religiously after 1756, posing a threat to orthodox Christian teaching. But alarms of the French Revolution and the Napoleonic Wars forced Christians to rethink their values and see the need for concerted prayer to meet material and spiritual needs. From about 1785 the first Monday evening of each month was set aside in Great Britain as a day of prayer for revival. In the 1790s Isaac Backus led in starting a Concert of Prayer in New England for revival.

THE SECOND AWAKENING

UNITED STATES   CANADA

East   *South*   *Nova Scotia*
Yale revival   Jarratt   Alline
Congregations   Williams   Black
in New England   Asbury
                    Dow
                    Circuit riders (Methodist)
                    Hampden-Sydney revival
                    Camp meetings
                        Kentucky
                        McGready
                        Cane Ridge

THE SECOND AWAKENING IN CANADA

Because Henry Alline began his itinerant revivals in the Maritime provinces of Canada in 1779, that work will be considered first. When Pepperell and his New England men had taken Louisburg in Acadia (now known as Nova Scotia), New England settlers migrated there, taking with them New England Congregationalism. By 1776 there were ten Congregational churches in Nova Scotia. It was this group that Alline disturbed with his New Light (prorevival) ideas and William Black with Methodist revival.

Henry Alline (1748–84) was born and received his early education in Newport, Rhode Island. His family moved to the Minas Basin in Nova Scotia in 1760 and was given land by lot in Falmouth. They survived the winter of 1760–61 in spite of their fear of Indians and a diet of mackerel, corn, and flour. Henry

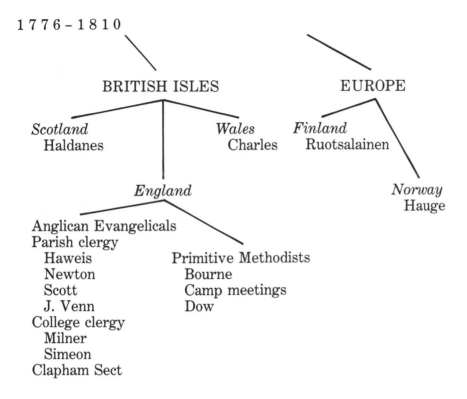

1 7 7 6 – 1 8 1 0

BRITISH ISLES   EUROPE

Scotland   *Wales*   *Finland*
Haldanes   Charles   Ruotsalainen

England   *Norway*
                       Hauge

Anglican Evangelicals
Parish clergy
   Haweis   Primitive Methodists
   Newton   Bourne
   Scott   Camp meetings
   J. Venn   Dow
College clergy
   Milner
   Simeon
Clapham Sect

looked after the farm and even served one term as the local constable.

He was especially fearful of hell, and from the time he was about eight until he was in his mid-twenties he gave much thought to how he could be saved. He read books by Law and Fletcher and became somewhat mystical. He was converted and experienced a call to the ministry on March 26, 1775. On April 19, 1776, after his final decision to preach his major emphasis was on the New Birth. His meetings were to disrupt Congregationalism by organizing New Light Congregational churches.

From 1776 until his death he was an itinerant preacher in Nova Scotia and Prince Edward Island, often preaching twice a day. He had the laity participate in meetings, which were often emotional. He preached in the Minas Basin from 1776 to 1778. In 1778 he began work in Prince Edward Island. When Congregationalists refused to recognize his right to preach, he spoke in barns, houses, or the open air. New Light Congregational churches were formed in Newport in late September 1776, in Cornwallis in 1778, and in Horton (now Wolfville) in 1779. He was ordained on April 5, 1779, by these churches as an "Itinerant or Traveling Pastor and Teacher." Most of his New Light churches became part of the Baptist Association of Nova Scotia by 1800. In 1783 he went back to New England, where he died in Northampton, New Hampshire.

He wrote a doctrinal treatise, *Two Mites Cast into the Offerings of God*. He also did an autobiographical work, *The Life and Journal of Henry Alline*. An element of mysticism (picked up from his reading of William Law) pervaded both books.

William Black (1760–1834) was born in Huddersfield, the town where Henry Venn had been pastor, and migrated to Nova Scotia in 1775. He became a Christian in an Alline meeting in the spring of 1779 and began to preach as a Methodist itinerant. By 1784 he had preached in nearly all of Nova Scotia and in Prince Edward Island.

The Methodists' Baltimore conference, which he attended in 1784, sent Freeborn Garretson and James O. Cromwell to work in Nova Scotia for two years. From 1786 to 1806 revivals came in many towns. Converts were cared for by local lay farmer preachers. The annual Methodist conference formed in 1796 was led by Black. For a time Black was general superintendent of all Methodist work in America.

Methodism also spread in Ontario and Quebec through the efforts of William Losee, who went to Canada in 1790 and set up the first Methodist class in Ontario in February 1791. Revival occurred in the Niagara Peninsula in 1801 and 1810. William Case helped to organize the itinerant system, lay preachers, protracted meetings, and camp meetings. There was a Canadian Annual Conference, which separated from Methodism in the United States in 1824.

THE SECOND AWAKENING IN THE UNITED STATES

The awakening in the East occurred in colleges and local congregations, was Calvinistic in theology, and was primarily an upper-class movement. The revival in Kentucky was mainly a lay movement and more Arminian in theology. The eastern meetings were fairly rational in outlook while the southern and western awakenings tended to be more emotional. Some camp meetings were marked by extreme physical manifestations.

Revivals in New England. Religion in New England was in decline by 1776. The New England Congregational churches split into two groups: those who followed Edwards's theology (New Light) and those who followed the lead of Charles Chauncy (Old Light). Conflicts over the writing of the Constitution and the earlier French and Indian Wars, when British officers had brought deism to the colonies, distracted from spiritual concerns. College students much admired the French deists' ideas. Few professed to be Christians, and many were guilty of gambling, drunkenness, swearing, and immorality, according to Lyman Beecher's account of conditions in Yale.

COLLEGE REVIVAL AT YALE. George Whitefield had spoken at Yale on five previous occasions, with about one hundred of the students and some faculty in his meetings. When he again spoke at the college in March 1741, some were converted. In 1757 the college chaplain, Naphtali Dagget, led a small awakening. In 1783 a revival brought eighteen students into the college church in one month.

Not one in ten students professed religion in the 1780s and 1790s. Many professed to be infidels or deists, some of them adopting French names. When Timothy Dwight (1752-1817) became president of Yale in 1795, spiritual interest was at a low ebb.

Forbears of Dwight had been pillars of the church and community for five generations. His merchant father, standing six-foot-four, was a strong man, and his mother was a daughter of Jonathan Edwards. Timothy, born in Northampton, was a preco-

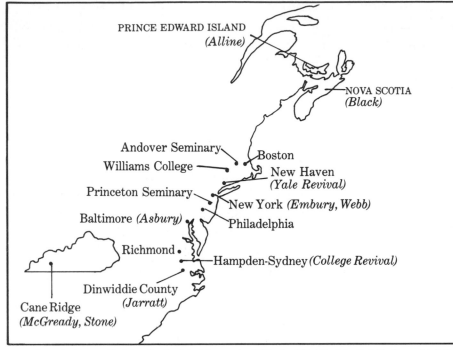

PRINCE EDWARD ISLAND
(Alline)

NOVA SCOTIA
(Black)

Andover Seminary
Boston

Williams College
New Haven
(Yale Revival)

Princeton Seminary
New York *(Embury, Webb)*

Baltimore *(Asbury)*
Philadelphia

Richmond
Hampden-Sydney *(College Revival)*

Dinwiddie County
(Jarratt)

Cane Ridge
(McGready, Stone)

THE   SECOND   AWAKENING   IN

cious, serious child. At four years of age he could read the Bible
and at six he learned Latin grammar unaided. He was ready for
college at eight but was thirteen when he went to Yale in 1765. He
wasted time at cards until his tutor, Stephen Mitchell, influenced
him to study more. He began to study fourteen hours a day and
nearly ruined his eyesight by studying by candlelight long after
dark. He graduated at the top of his class.

After teaching at a grammar school in New Haven for two
years, he became a tutor and graduate student of theology at Yale
in 1771. He earned his M.A. in 1772. Although he swam for exercise, his poor diet and poor sleeping habits forced him to go home
to regain health in March 1774. Horseback riding and good food
restored his health, but he could not study by candles at night any
longer. He made a public profession of Christ in early 1774 and

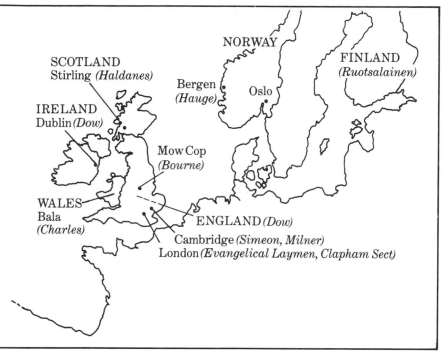

SCOTLAND
Stirling *(Haldanes)*

IRELAND
Dublin *(Dow)*

NORWAY

Bergen
(Hauge)

Oslo

FINLAND
(Ruotsalainen)

Mow Cop
(Bourne)

WALES
Bala
(Charles)

ENGLAND *(Dow)*

Cambridge *(Simeon, Milner)*
London *(Evangelical Laymen, Clapham Sect)*

AMERICA & EUROPE 1776-1810

joined the church. He continued to tutor at Yale until 1777.

In October of that year after licensure he was appointed as chaplain to the First Connecticut Brigade, to which he preached and lectured on morals. His unit had a difficult time during the winter.

After thirteen months in the army, he went home to run the farm from 1777 to 1783 and to do supply preaching. He also served as a Massachusetts legislator in 1781 and 1782.

He was called to the Greenfield Hill Church in Fairfield in May 1783 and was ordained. Exercise here consisted of gardening. He also founded an academy where he educated both boys and girls.

When Ezra Stiles, the president of Yale, died in May 1795, Dwight was chosen as his replacement. He held that position until 1817. He taught the seniors himself, added law and chemistry to the curriculum, and hired Benjamin Silliman to teach science and medicine.

Students who were to dispute before him chose as one of their topics, "Are the Scriptures of the Old and New Testament the Word of God?" He listened to the students as they propounded the negative and deistic ideas. For six months in fifty talks he spoke on the divine origin and authority of the Bible.

In the fall of 1796 only one freshman, one junior, and eight seniors were professing Christians, but in 1797, 25 students founded a secret Moral Society pledged to follow biblical conduct and not swear or gamble. By the spring of 1802, Dwight's steady barrage of scholarly talks and student prayer demolished deism at the school. A revival began in which about a third of the 230 students in the college became Christians. Over 60 joined the college church; of those, over 30 became ministers later. Dwight spoke daily and twice on Sunday in chapel and at evening prayers. One late spring day, 50 "serious inquirers" came for counseling. The revival spread to Dartmouth and Princeton. Nearly 80 of the 105 students at Princeton were saved and 25 of them became ministers.

Revival again came in 1808 when 30 were converted, and in 1812 and 1813 when about 180 students were moved by a student prayer revival. Revivals again occurred in 1831, when Horace Bushnell was converted, in 1841 with 75 converts under the preaching of Jacob Knapp, and in 1878 under the preaching of Dwight L. Moody.

Timothy Dwight's health gave way in February 1816, and a year later he died. If he had a motto, it surely was, "For God, for country, and for Yale." He strongly supported missions and the American Bible Society. He wrote the hymn, "I Love Thy Kingdom, Lord." He trained such able men as Lyman Beecher and Moses Stuart.

LOCAL CHURCH AWAKENINGS. About 150 New England churches had "times of refreshing" from 1797 to 1798. In Somers, Connecticut, in 1797, an awakening under Charles Backus began with the young people. Fifty-five joined the church over a two-year period. At Torringford, Connecticut, on December 26, 1798, Alexander Gillet spoke on Proverbs 8:14. By June, forty-five were converted. In the spring of 1798, in Granville, Massachusetts, Timothy M. Cooley invited people under conviction to come to his study for counsel. That year fifty people were added to the church. Samuel Shepherd's parishioners in Lennox, Massachusetts, asked for prayer meetings in April 1799, and by October more than twenty were converted. A total of fifty-three were won. These samples of renewal, mostly in Connecticut, demonstrate the vitality of faith in New England.

Park Street Church in Boston was founded in February 1809 and became a center of missionary activity and renewal in Unitarian Boston. Most revivals occurred in the period from 1813 to 1846. One was under Sereno Dwight in 1826 and 1827. In 1831, Charles G. Finney preached a series of sermons to awaken Christians in Park Street Church, and again in 1857 his work brought two hundred into the church.

Revival in the South.

DEVEREUX JARRATT AND THE METHODISTS. Jarratt's work in awakening Christians and the rise of Methodism are usually linked with the Great Awakening, but the Great Awakening was in decline by 1747, and Jarratt's real ministry started in 1763. The Methodist churches were few in number when Asbury arrived on the scene in 1771.

Methodism began unofficially in the United States in the 1760s with Philip Embury and Robert Strawbridge. Strawbridge (1732–81), who had been converted under the ministry of John Wesley, came to America from Ireland about 1760. He purchased a farm at Sam's Creek, Maryland, and preached as a lay preacher in his home. This meeting soon grew into a society meeting in a twenty-foot-square log church. Later a second society was added.

Philip Embury (1728–73) and Barbara Heck (1744–1804) were descendants of German Palatinate refugees who had settled in

Ireland. After he was saved, Embury became a local preacher and a carpenter. He moved to New York about 1760. In October 1766, Barbara Heck, his cousin, became spiritually distressed with a group playing cards in a house. She asked Philip to preach to them or they would all go to hell. He did so, and in 1768 a forty-two-by-sixty-foot chapel was built in John Street.

Embury was aided by Captain Thomas Webb (1724–96) who, dressed in full regimentals, came to his church in February 1767. At first the people were dismayed by this portly military figure with a green patch over his right eye, which he had lost in the battle to take Quebec. Webb got the lots and gave £30 for the church. He later went to England to ask Wesley to send preachers to America. He preached with great success in Pennsylvania, New York, New Jersey, and Delaware.

Because of her Tory sympathies, Barbara Heck went to Canada during the American Revolution and helped to build Methodism there. When Wesley's missionaries arrived, Embury moved to his brother's farm at Camden, New York, but kept on preaching until his death.

Robert Williams (1745–75) came to America in 1769 and became pastor of the John Street Church. He was the spiritual father of Jesse Lee. Lee is credited with winning 4,200 to renewal or salvation in a revival in 1787. Williams worked with Devereux Jarratt in Virginia for a time.

During the period from 1760 to 1769, these unofficial Methodist preachers served until official missionaries were sent by Wesley. Richard Boardman (1738–82) was sent with Joseph Pilmoor (1739–1825) in 1769 by the Leeds Conference after they volunteered for that duty. They were welcomed in 1769 by Captain Webb in Philadelphia. Boardman worked in the John Street Church and Pilmoor in Philadelphia. Boardman and Pilmoor returned to England in 1774.

Francis Asbury was sent in 1771, and Thomas Rankin and George Shadford arrived in 1773. Rankin was to be superintendent of Methodist work and called the first American conference in that year. He traveled widely in the South, but his stern ways and inability to compromise kept him from being a good leader. He returned to England after only five years.

Francis Asbury (1745-1816) was America's greatest Methodist leader. He was born near Birmingham, England, and had become a Christian by 1759. After working as a blacksmith from 1759 to 1765, he became a local preacher about 1766. After serving on several circuits during the period from 1776 to 1771, he came to America in 1771 at his own request. He became Wesley's general assistant in America. He preached all through the middle and southern colonies. He set up a system of circuit riders to spread Methodism swiftly and widely. In 1784 the Methodist Episcopal Church was organized. Thomas Coke, consecrated by Wesley, and Asbury were elected by the church as superintendents. (After 1787 they were called bishops.) On three successive days, December 25-27, Asbury was ordained deacon and elder by Coke and consecrated as superintendent. Asbury traveled 300,000 miles, preached tirelessly, and received several thousand preachers into the American Methodist church. He and Coke founded Cokesbury College in 1785; it closed after a fire in 1795. The Methodists in America numbered over 200,000 by the time of Asbury's death. He did this work even though he was often ill with many ailments.

The South was very receptive to revival, and Methodism made great gains there through the efforts of Devereux Jarratt, who lost many of his Anglican converts to Methodism. The foundation laid by Jarratt and the unofficial and official Methodist leaders from England made great growth possible between 1770 and 1776 and in the Second Awakening.

Devereux Jarratt (1733-1801), although an Anglican, laid the foundation for Methodism's greatest growth between 1763 and the Second Awakening. He was born in New Kent, Virginia, twenty-five miles from Richmond. His father taught the children reading and writing and the catechism. Devereux had an excellent memory. When his father died, he helped his brothers by exercising race horses, teaching gamecocks to fight, and doing general work on the plantation. In this period he had no religious influence and indulged in racing, cards, and dancing.

About 1751 he moved to Albemarle, two hundred miles away, as a teacher. He came across and read eight of Whitefield's sermons. When he moved to the home of John Cannon to board, Cannon's wife, a New Light Christian, read Flavel's sermons each night. When Jarratt heard the words "Then opened he their under-standing" in one of the sermons, he was convicted of sin and he tried to be moral. A Presbyterian minister gave him books by Richard Baxter, Isaac Watts, and Philip Doddridge. He finally trusted alone in Christ.

As "chaplain" in the Cannon home, he learned to pray extempo-rancously, to sing hymns, and to read sermons. After some time John Cannon and John Hunter offered to finance more schooling, and at the age of twenty-five he went to Abel Martin's school. Within a year he read Latin and soon took over Hunter's school for a year and a half.

By 1762 he quit teaching and studied for ordination in the Church of England. He obtained title to a parish and the neces-sary papers from the bishop's commissary and the governor. This meant cutting his ties with the Presbyterians. With the money from selling three hundred acres of land he inherited, he went to England in the fall of 1762. On the voyage he twice saved the ship, first by suggesting the use of ropes to attach the ship to other boats when it ran aground, and later by cleverly talking the pilot into ignoring the captain's temper. They arrived safely in Liver-pool.

Jortin, the chaplain of the bishop of London, examined him in theology, and Jarratt was ordained in January 1763. He heard John Wesley and George Whitefield preach in London and com-mented that they "spoke well and to the purpose."

He contracted smallpox and had a fever which hurt his eyes, but neither the druggist nor the doctor would charge him for their services. He collected the £20 of Queen Anne's Bounty for clergy-men ordained to Virginia and gave it and an additional £50 to Lewis, his landlord, for safekeeping. Lewis spent the money on his family, leaving Jarratt penniless, but John Tabb from Virginia loaned him £10. He arrived home in early July 1763.

He learned of a vacancy in a three-point parish in Dinwiddie County. He preached on a Sunday and Thursday for the churches and was given the position on the following Monday. He served this church from 1763 to 1801.

His preaching emphasized man's depravity by the Fall and his inability to be saved by works. He taught that complete salvation was in Christ's redemptive work, to be received by faith. He exhorted believers to good works and the holiness of perfection. He spoke and counseled in homes and had classes for teaching the catechism.

His parish experienced revival under this preaching from 1764 on and was at its peak in 1776. He itinerated over a five-hundred-mile circle. When clergy closed their churches to him, he spoke in the open air. He preached 275 sermons a year, often preaching five times a week. By 1773 he had nine hundred to one thousand regular communicants in his churches.

He described Robert Williams, the first Methodist he met, about 1772, as a "plain simple-hearted pious man." Williams assured him that the Methodist preachers did not administer the sacraments but encouraged their religious societies to be in the Church of England. He claimed that those "who left the church (Anglican) left the Methodists." Jarratt helped the Methodists by administering the sacraments in many counties from 1776 to 1783. In the spring of 1784 Asbury urged Methodists in Virginia not to ordain ministers or dispense the sacraments. When the Methodists did set up a separate American denomination in December 1784, many of Jarratt's converts went with them. Jarratt, who had worked so hard to help them and suffered abuse from the clergy for it, was deeply hurt. Like many other godly Evangelical ministers, Jarratt wished that renewed Christians would remain within the Church of England.

Methodists gained the most in the South thanks to Jarratt's revival preaching, which brought thousands into the church, and to Asbury's circuit riders, lay preachers, and class meetings. The diligence of the Methodist circuit riders was attested to by the common saying about foul weather: "There is nothing out today but crows and Methodist preachers." The Baptist farmer-preacher was equally diligent. While the Methodists grew about 300 percent, the Baptists in the South multiplied by almost 400 percent in this period.

THE HAMPDEN-SYDNEY COLLEGE REVIVAL, 1787. Hampden-Sydney College had been founded in 1776 as a result of the Great Awakening. In 1787 it had eighty students. One student, Cary Allen, was saved during vacation in 1777 in a Methodist revival under Hope Hull, an Anglican follower of Wesley. Another student, William Hull, was reading Joseph Alleine's *Alarm to the Unconverted*. James Blythe, who saw him reading it, read it and was converted through it. Later Clement Read joined the three in prayer meetings in the forest and in their room on Saturday afternoons. Rowdy students swore at them, objected to the meetings, and complained to the president, John B. Smith. He invited the four to meet in his parlor and later in the college hall.

Revival resulted from all the prayer, and more than half the students were converted. More than thirty went into the Presbyterian ministry. Archibald Alexander, who rode over from Liberty Hall school with Dr. Graham, was deeply influenced and converted later at a sacramental meeting. Alexander became the first professor and president of Princeton Seminary. Union Theological Seminary at Richmond owed much of its inception to the Hampden-Sydney revival. James McGready, who visited the college in 1788, owed much of his spiritual development to the revival he observed there. The revival spread to Washingon College (now Washington and Lee University) and to Prince Edward, Charlotte, and Cumberland Counties. Hampden-Sydney later

This *Harper's Weekly* depiction of the dedicated circuit-riding preacher was inspired by such Americans as the Methodist preacher Peter Cartwright. *(Courtesy of the Billy Graham Center Museum)*

gave a doctor of divinity degree to Asahel Nettleton.

THE GREAT WESTERN REVIVAL IN KENTUCKY, 1799–1803. The Methodist expansion under Jarratt and the circuit riders, such as Jesse Lee, was later augmented by the technique of the camp meeting, which the Methodists and Baptists borrowed from the Presbyterians. The camp meeting revival won about twenty-thousand in Kentucky and Tennessee.

The camp meeting emerged from the sacramental weekend meeting imported from Scotland by the Presbyterians. James McGready (1758–1817) was born in western Pennsylvania of Scotch-Irish extraction and studied theology in John McMillan's "log college" in Canonsburg, Pennsylvania. He was converted in 1786 in a Presbyterian sacramental meeting. His visit to the Hampden-Sydney revival renewed his spiritual life. He ministered from about 1790 to 1796 with much success in North Carolina, but opposition to his fiery preaching of revival drove him out. From 1797 until 1811 he served three churches in Logan County, known as "Rogues Harbor" for its denizens.

McGready's fervent preaching, congregational prayer meetings at sunrise and sunset, and open-air sacramental meetings brought awakening. Revival broke out at Red River when William McGee, a Presbyterian and one of McGready's converts, and his brother John, a Methodist, stopped on their way to Ohio to help with the sacramental meeting in June 1800. John later wrote *A Short Narrative* telling of these revivals in Kentucky and Tennessee from 1797 to 1800. Many were renewed and saved. Another meeting held at Gasper River in the end of July 1800 was the first camp meeting. Services were held in the open air and people lived in thirteen "wagons" over the weekend. These meetings at McGready's churches were the beginning of the Kentucky revival.

Barton Stone (1772–1844), a Presbyterian pastor who later founded the Christian Church, was pastor at Cane Ridge in 1798. He organized a large sacramental meeting at Cane Ridge near Paris, Bourbon County, Kentucky. He and Richard M'Nemar were the main speakers from August 6-12, 1801. Estimates of the attendance vary from 10,000 to 25,000 present, but 12,500 is probably more accurate. Three dozen Methodist, Presbyterian, and Baptist preachers were there. At least 125 wagons (some accounts report 500) bearing Presbyterians and Methodists came from Kentucky, Ohio, and Tennessee.

The camps were arranged in a circle, rectangle, or horseshoe with a brush fence having two gates. Plank seats were set before covered raised platforms for preachers. A pen for "seekers" was set off by rails in front. Boys called "runners" chased out the hogs and dogs. Sermons, delivered at 11:00 A.M., 3:00 P.M. and 7:00 P.M., were preceded by the singing of simple folk hymns—some of them doggerel—with an oft-repeated refrain. There was a prayer meeting at 7:00 A.M. People brought their own food and slept in wagons or on the ground.

The camp meeting was accompanied by emotional and physical phenomena, such as "falling," "rolling," "jerks" (of the head from side to side or back and forth), "barking" on all fours (like dogs), dancing, singing, or laughing. In discussing these physical phenomena, one should remember that these people lived in isolated cabins, often in danger from Indians, and in close touch with nature. Their religious experience, compressed into the few days of the camp meeting, often became intense. The wonder is that there was so little emotion, and the preachers did oppose excess emotionalism. M'Nemar said camp meetings were preceded by "praying societies," generally in Calvinistic churches.

The Presbyterians had generally abandoned the camp meeting by 1805, but the Baptists and especially the Methodists continued to use it. The camp meetings were termed the "Methodist harvest time." Francis Asbury, in his journal, said that four hundred to five hundred camp meetings were held in 1811. It is estimated that about a thousand were held in 1820. Camp meetings were not used much after the 1840s. But during their heyday they greatly improved the moral tone of society in Kentucky and Tennessee and added new members to the churches.

REVIVAL IN THE BRITISH ISLES
Revival in England.

EVANGELICAL CLERGY IN THE PARISHES. Evangelical clergy were as prominent in this era of revival as Walker, Grimshaw, and Romaine were earlier. Thomas Haweis (1734–1820) was born in Cornwall. He read the Bible at three and learned Latin at four and five years of age. A sea captain who liked him offered to educate him, but he refused. He was converted and called to preach under the preaching of Samuel Walker of Truro and met with Walker's religious society. An uncle who had financed him in training for medicine agreed to let him enter the ministry. Joseph Jane financed his training at Christ Church, Oxford. Haweis went to Oxford in 1755 and started a study group to read the Greek New Testament, study theology, and pray.

He was disliked by church leaders for his "enthusiasm" and passion for souls, but was ordained in 1758. Later, when he was expelled from the church, he assisted Martin Madan from 1762 to 1764 at Lock Hospital in London. He helped John Newton study for the ministry and get ordination.

He went to All Saints, Aldwincle, Northampton, in 1764 and ministered there for forty-four years. He spoke three times each Sunday, held open-air services, and did house-to-house visitation. He served as one of Lady Huntingdon's chaplains for twelve years and was one of the executors to carry out her will.

Haweis was greatly interested in missions in general and Tahiti in particular. He published a review of Melville Horne's book on missions in *The Evangelical Magazine* and in it called for a missionary society and said he had £500 (his own gift) to give. He was partly responsible for the founding of the London Missionary Society and the choice of the South Seas for its first mission field. He helped to raise money for the ship to take missionaries out to Tahiti.

By 1757 he published a commentary on the Bible called *The Evangelical Expositor*. His *Carmina Christi*, a collection of 256 hymns, sold widely. This godly scholar helped in many revivals in northern England.

John Newton and Thomas Scott were leaders among the Evangelical clergy in the English Midlands. Newton (1725–1807) was born to a pious mother and a sailor father. He went to sea with his father at the age of eleven and was in Spain and Venice. When he met his thirteen-year-old cousin Mary Catlett in 1742, he fell in love with her. He was pressed into a warship but deserted, was caught, and finally discharged.

After deserting a second ship in Sierra Leone, he became the slave of his master's black mistress, who mistreated him for a year. His father freed him and he returned to England in 1749, marrying Mary Catlett in 1750 after he had been soundly converted.

As captain of a slave ship from 1751 to 1754, Newton got to know the slave trade firsthand. He retired to a position as surveyor of tides at Liverpool and, with much spare time, he began to read his Bible and pray. He learned Greek and Latin. He talked with Whitefield, Romaine, and Grimshaw about entering the ministry.

Through the Earl of Dartmouth and Haweis, to whom Dartmouth had originally offered it, Newton was granted Olney parish. Here he served from 1764 to 1779. John Thornton gave £200 a year for hospitality. He raised it to £400 to enable Newton to help the poet William Cowper in the sixteen-year period Cowper lived near Newton. Through John Thornton's aid, Newton was granted the parish of St. Mary Woolnoth in London, where he served from 1779 to 1807.

He wrote *Thoughts on the African Slave Trade* in 1787 to expose its evil. He wrote the much-loved hymns, "Amazing Grace," "How Sweet the Name of Jesus Sounds," and "Glorious Things of Thee Are Spoken." Newton led William Wilberforce to Christ in 1785. Thomas Scott, the Bible commentator, was won from Unitarianism in 1777 by Newton's walking to visit a sick parishioner of Scott in 1774 and by his gentle correspondence. Scott said that God's working in his soul was mainly because of Newton's preaching.

Thomas Scott (1747–1821), born in a farm family in Lancashire, was apprenticed to a surgeon but turned to theology after a time and specialized in Greek. He became curate at Stoke and at Weston from 1772 to 1780, when Newton helped him to become a believer. From 1780 to 1785 he was curate at Olney and then worked in Lock Chapel at Lock Hospital in London from 1787 to 1792. Here he opened a shelter for prostitutes.

Scott wrote a commentary on the Bible between 1787 and 1792. The commentary was first published weekly, and Scott was given twenty-five copies and one guinea a week in payment. He advanced £800 to the publisher but lost on the venture. The publisher sold 37,000 sets at a profit of £200,000. Scott finally sold the copyright in 1810. In all he spent thirty-three years in writing and revising it. He was made pastor at Aston-Sandford from 1802 to 1821.

His great contribution was his commentary, but he should also be remembered for helping William Carey. Carey claimed that God's working in his soul was due to Scott.

John Venn (1754–1813), the son of Henry Venn, was born at Clapham. He earned his M.A. at Sidney Sussex College, Cambridge. After ten years as rector at Little Dunham, he became rector of Clapham in 1792. Until 1813 he was the spiritual advisor of the Clapham Sect, who lived in his parish. He was one of the leading founders of the Church Missionary Society in 1799.

EVANGELICAL CLERGY IN UNIVERSITIES. While Cambridge became the later center of Evangelical revival, some colleges in Oxford had supported the Great Awakening. The Holy Club was founded in Oxford and functioned well for some years. Joseph Jane, the godly Evangelical minister of St. Mary Magdalene Church, supported Evangelical students financially. William Romaine frequently preached in Oxford until his declaration of salvation by faith led to a ban on his preaching there. Six Evangelical students were expelled from Oxford in 1768 for attending Methodist meetings. From this time on Cambridge became the main center of Anglican Evangelicalism, with Isaac Milner as a college president and Charles Simeon as a preacher there.

Isaac Milner (1750–1820), a large man physically, was born in Leeds and graduated from Queen's College, Cambridge, with financial aid from his brother Joseph. He did so well that his final examination was graded *Incomparabilis*. He became a fellow of his college in 1776 and was ordained in 1777. He became professor of natural philosophy in 1783. The office of president of Queen's was given to him, and he transformed Queen's into a center of Evangelicalism. In 1792 he received the high honor of becoming vice-chancellor of Cambridge. He completed the church history for which his brother Joseph was famous. William Wilberforce was greatly helped in his religious pilgrimage on two trips to Europe with Isaac Milner in 1784 and 1785.

While Milner helped Queen's College to become a center for Evangelical students, Charles Simeon (1759–1836) helped to train them for the ministry. Simeon was born at Reading and educated at Eton by his rich lawyer father. Here he only learned Latin well. He loved sports, such as swimming and horseback riding. He was always well dressed with black umbrella, coat, breeches, gaiters, a white ruffled shirt, and white gloves. He went to King's College, Cambridge, in 1799 as one of the fifteen undergraduates there, all of them from Eton. He, too, received the grade *Incomparabilis* on his final examination.

On February 2, 1799, he was told that he would have to take Communion in three weeks. In preparation he read *The Whole Duty of Man* and Thomas Wilson's *Instruction for the Lord's Supper*. He still felt unworthy and became ill with study, prayer, and fasting. He experienced conversion on Easter Sunday, April 4, 1799. That summer he spent time with Henry Venn, who taught him to "let the Bible speak" in his sermons.

Simeon became a fellow at King's College in 1782. He held this position for the rest of his life and was dean of arts and dean of divinity for seven years. His father influenced the bishop of Ely to suggest his name as minister for Holy Trinity Church, Cambridge. He was opposed by some in the church from 1782, when he obtained the position, until 1794. On one occasion he was even locked out of the church. In 1790 he started an evening service and weeknight meetings for prayer, Bible study, and fellowship. By 1794 he also got control of the Sunday afternoon lectureship in his church. He arose at 4:00 A.M. to have four hours of prayer and Bible study. His generosity was shown in the hard winter of 1798–99 in his efforts to raise £1,000 for food, coal, and blankets for the poor.

His 2,536 sermon outlines were published in the twenty-two volumes of the *Horae Homiletica*. He gave away the royalties. His aim in preaching was to humble the sinner, exalt the Savior, and promote holiness. He spent at least twelve hours on each of his sermons.

Simeon was interested in helping poor Evangelicals prepare for the ministry. When Henry Venn and his friends organized the Elland Society in 1767 to raise money to educate poor men for the ministry, Simeon gave £3,700 to it. He also helped to found the Simeon Trustees in 1817 to raise money to buy up livings to which Evangelical ministers could be named as pastors. At his death in 1836, 21 had been bought, and 150 had been bought by 1842.

Simeon was also interested in informal training of ministers. Beginning in 1792 he held informal sermon classes in his quarters each Sunday evening for fifteen to twenty undergraduates. The classes focused on how to build sermons and to preach. Beginning in 1813 he held Friday evening "conversation parties" with 6:00 P.M. tea and opportunities for questions. His students led twenty-six classes in a Sunday school at Barnwell near Cambridge. Over the years sixty of the teachers became Church Missionary Society missionaries. In 1796 he began to hold annual house parties of two days for twenty to thirty ministers at a time to study religious books. Separate sessions were held for their wives. He also counseled people in seven thousand letters by 1829.

Simeon was deeply interested in missions. Samuel Marsden, apostle to Australia and New Zealand, was one of his students. Simeon rode with James Haldane on a preaching holiday horseback trip to Scotland. Revival came at Moulin where he preached. Alexander Stewart was renewed and in turn won Alexander Duff. Duff later spent fifty years in India as an educator who gave the Bible a major place in the college curriculum. As a friend of Charles Grant, influential in the British East India Company, Simeon was able to obtain chaplaincies in India for David Brown and Henry Martyn, who also did missionary work. Simeon played an important role in the founding of the Church Missionary Society. He asked the group on March 18, 1799, "What can we do? When shall we do it? How shall we do it?"

His whole life was one long labor of love. His fellowship brought in £400 a year, but he lived and ate sparingly on £50 a year. When his brother left him £15,000, he used it for charitable works. His life was of tremendous service to the cause of Evangelicalism in the town and university. Under him Cambridge became a center of Evangelicalism and Calvinistic theology. When dying, he said, "I cannot have more peace."

THE CLAPHAM SECT. Cooperating with the Evangelical clergy in parish and university were the lay leaders of the Clapham Sect. These upper-class men, all Evangelicals, were leaders in social reform for more than two generations, from 1771 to 1846. They used their social position and influence for the betterment of social conditions in Britain. The efforts of the Clapham Sect are discussed in Chapter 10.

THE PRIMITIVE METHODISTS AND CAMP MEETINGS. The origin of the Primitive Methodists in England can only be understood by a look at the life of Lorenzo Dow (1777-1834). A powerful preacher both in the United States and England, he introduced the camp meeting to England. Disputes over the use of camp meetings led to the expulsion of the Primitive Methodists from the Methodist Church.

Lorenzo Dow was born in Coventry, Connecticut. Because of a

serious illness at the age of twelve, he was asthmatic for the rest of his life. He was a morbid child who feared death. At age twelve he promised God to serve him if he won a lottery. He won nine shillings but forgot his promise. He had dreams while under conviction and all during his life. Hope Hull, a Methodist preacher, won him to Christ in his late teens. He felt called to preach when he dreamed that John Wesley wanted him to preach, and on April 3, 1796, he gave his first sermon.

Dow bought a horse on credit and was allowed to travel with a licensed itinerant preacher for about three months in the spring of 1796. He was ordered home but passed the Methodist conference examination. He was not licensed because of his enemy Nicholas Snethen. He was sent home for the fourth time when Jesse Lee refused to issue his credentials. He got the name of "Crazy Dow."

He was finally granted a license on trial in 1798 because of the large number of converts in his meetings. On the circuit he had about twelve hundred converts in twelve months. He visited from house to house along with his preaching in meetings.

He had Ireland on his mind and went there by way of Quebec, Canada, arriving in Dublin in December 1799. While in Dublin he contracted smallpox and was befriended and nursed for forty-four days by Dr. Paul and Letitia Johnson. Johnson sent him home with a library of books and money in January 1801.

When Francis Asbury gave him a license to preach in America, he traveled on circuits in New York and New England. He claimed to have experienced sanctification in Canada in April 1802.

He met Peggy Holcomb (1780–1820), who lived with her sister Hannah Miller and brother-in-law Smith Miller. Hannah told Dow that Peggy had said she would sooner marry a preacher than any other man. Dow proposed the next morning, but then went off to the South. He married Peggy on his return in 1804. He called her his "rib." She called him "Lorenzo," "my companion," or "my precious Lorenzo." In spite of this devotion, he left the morning after their wedding for a four-thousand-mile trip to Mississippi.

He usually held five hundred to eight hundred meetings a year with crowds of up to two thousand to five thousand at camp meetings.

His writings numbered twenty-five. His *Chain*, a book against deism, brought in $500. He gave this to the Methodist Church. He wrote a *Defense of Camp Meetings* and his *Journal*. Peggy also wrote a book telling of her life with "my dear Lorenzo."

He returned to Ireland, this time with Peggy, and also visited England and Holland from December 1805 to the spring of 1807. A baby girl was born to them in Dublin but died in England. They spent a good amount of time in northwestern England. Dow was a guest of Bible commentator Adam Clarke, but Thomas Coke snubbed him when he went to see him in London. It was on this trip that Hugh Bourne heard him speak and read his book on camp meetings. Dow held more than two hundred meetings and traveled seventeen hundred miles by land on this trip. He returned to England alone in 1818 and 1819.

When he got home in 1819, he had to assume Smith Miller's debts. He also discovered that Peggy's sister Hannah had committed adultery, a severe blow to Peggy. He had earlier incurred heavy expenses in buying over forty-five thousand acres in western Wisconsin when he proposed to set up his City of Peace, or Loren. This venture cost him $90,000, which his writings had brought in, but it never amounted to anything.

When Peggy died early in January 1820, he described his loss as "a sword through my soul," but he remarried in April. By the time of his death, he had spent thirty-seven years in the "public field of battle" in his "wanderings through the world." Dow was a stoop-shouldered, long-legged, long-armed man. Long brown hair and a long beard set off a pallid face with a thin nose and small light blue eyes. He had a harsh voice. His clothing, ragged and not too clean, was covered with a long black cloak. Yet this man had great power in preaching and thousands were converted by his ministry.

Hugh Bourne (1772–1852) learned of the camp meeting technique from Dow and used it effectively, but the Methodist Church expelled him. He then founded the Primitive Methodist Church.

Bourne was born on a farm in Staffordshire. His father was a drunken, domineering, bad-tempered man. Hugh was converted in the spring of 1799 by reading religious books and the Bible.

His written and oral testimony helped Thomas Maxfield, the first Methodist lay preacher. Bourne had talks or "conversations." Many were won, and revival came. On July 12, 1801, he preached his first sermon in the open air. He built a chapel in 1802 at Harrishead for his society. Three hundred were saved in 1804.

In April 1807 at Harrishead he heard Dow speak about the American camp meetings. He bought Dow's book on the why and how of camp meetings. He held his first camp meeting on May 31, 1807, at Mow Cop. Dr. Paul Johnson, Dow's doctor friend, spoke at one of the preaching stands. Four to five thousand were there. A second meeting was held at Mow Cop from July 19–21, 1807, and over sixty were saved.

The Methodists expelled Bourne on June 27, 1808, when he refused to end the camp meetings. The Primitive Methodist Connexion came into being in the fall of 1808. Bourne edited a hymnal for the movement in 1809 and on May 30 of that year he began to issue quarterly membership tickets. The church adopted the name of Primitive Methodists on February 13, 1812. By the first annual conference in May 1820, there were 7,842 members, 207 local preachers, and 48 itinerant preachers. The membership had grown to 110,000 members, 9,350 local preachers, and 560 itinerants by 1852.

Bourne was a round-shouldered, red-haired man who walked twenty to thirty miles a day to preaching appointments. His diet was usually bread, figs or raisins, and boiled eggs. He talked a lot to himself and was often hasty and overbearing. In addition to his work in England, he traveled in the United States and Canada from August 1844 to May 1847. His "conversation" gift was exercising faith in personal talks to lead men to Christ. He had an able helper in William Clowes (1780–1851) whose uncle was Josiah

Wedgwood of the fine china firm. Clowes too was expelled from the Methodist church in 1810 over the issue of camp meetings. The Methodists thus missed out on revival in this era.

The Revival in Scotland. The Haldane brothers, Robert (1764–1842) and James (1768–1851), were born into a wealthy sea captain's family on an estate named Airthrey near Stirling. Their mother taught them to love the Bible. They were sent to High School, located in Edinburgh, in 1777.

Robert joined the navy in 1780 and was assigned to the *Monarch.* When he was transferred to the *Foudroyant,* he attended the independent church at Gosport which David Bogue served from 1777 to 1825. Robert left the navy in 1783, studied a few months under Bogue, and made a tour of France and Holland. He married in 1786 and settled down to a country gentleman's life at Airthrey.

Robert was converted in 1795 and sold Airthrey about 1798. He wanted to use the money for a mission to India with Bogue, Grenville Ewing, John Ritchie, and himself as missionaries. He set aside £25,000 for this purpose, but the opposition of the British East India Company killed the venture. He did, however, in December 1797, organize the Society for the Propagation of the Gospel at Home, which sent out 114 catechists and missionaries.

When Rowland Hill spoke in Edinburgh in July 1798, Robert went back to England with him. He decided to use his money to build Congregational churches when he left the Kirk of Scotland.

In 1799 he bought a circus building in Glasgow for £3,000 to house 120 converts. The number soon grew to 300. He later built a tabernacle in Edinburgh that seated 3,000. His brother, James, ministered there for fifty years. Robert built a total of eighty-five chapels.

He sponsored a Ministerial Training Institute from 1799 to 1808 under Grenville Ewing, a pastor in Edinburgh. The school opened with 24 students. He personally financed the education of 300 students at a cost of £100,000 in order that they might become

Congregational ministers. He had Zachary Macaulay bring 24 black boys and 4 black girls, children of African chiefs, to England in 1799 to be trained as missionaries to Africa; but the Church of England took them over. He spent a total of £350,000 on the Africans, chapels, seminaries, and Bible distribution.

The brothers left the Kirk of Scotland about 1799; they founded the Congregational Church of Scotland when the moderates or liberals in the Kirk of Scotland rejected them. They were immersed in 1808 and became Baptists.

Robert was in Switzerland and France with students from 1816 to 1818. Those whom he won to Christ became leaders in the French and Swiss *Réveils* (awakenings). He wrote *Exposition of the Epistle to the Romans* and *Evidences and Authority of Divine Revelation.* Robert's seminary and chapels helped the Congregational cause especially. He was interested in and supported missions at home liberally from his fortune which he consecrated to Christ.

James Haldane attended the University of Edinburgh and at eighteen entered the service of the East India Company. He made four trading voyages to India and China from 1785 to 1794. He left the business upon his conversion in 1794. He preached his first formal sermon at Gilmerton near Edinburgh on May 6, 1797, and became an itinerant evangelist in northern Scotland, the Orkney Islands, and Ireland, with crowds of two thousand to four thousand. His riding tour with Charles Simeon in 1794 and 1795 in Scotland, consequent renewal at Moulin, and a trial at open-air preaching at Kintyre led him into itinerant work in 1797.

James settled in Edinburgh for fifty years as pastor of the tabernacle which Robert had built for him. He was immersed in 1808 and became a Baptist.

The Scottish Congregational and Baptist churches emerged largely through Robert's preaching, teaching, and philanthropy and James' preaching. They firmly believed that Congregational government by elders and baptism by immersion were biblical.

The Revival in Wales. Thomas Charles (1755–1814) was born at Point Dwfm in Carmarthenshire in a farm laborer's home. He was educated at Carmarthen Academy and earned his B.A. in 1779 at Jesus College, Oxford. He was converted on January 20, 1773, after conviction under a sermon by Daniel Rowland at Llangleitho. He was ordained in 1780 and married in 1783. He served as curate in several churches from 1778 to 1783.

He made Bala in northern Wales his home in 1783 and did much itinerant preaching. After 1793 he spoke three months each year in Lady Huntingdon's Spa Fields Chapel. He helped in a great revival at Bala and other places in 1791. His wife's successful millinery shop in Bala made him financially independent.

Charles carried on the earlier work of Griffith Jones's circulating schools after 1785 with his own charity schools. A Mrs. Jones, hearing of Griffith Jones, had left £10,000 for his schools. When her will was released about 1809, over £30,000 was available for schools and Sunday schools which Charles also promoted.

He saw the need for a Welsh Bible in 1799 or 1800 when Mary Jones walked twenty-five miles over mountains to get a Bible after saving enough to buy one. He had sold his supply but gave her one anyway. This may have influenced him to help in the founding of the British and Foreign Bible Society in 1804. The society printed twenty thousand Welsh Bibles in 1806. While editing the Bible, Charles drew up the rules for Welsh orthography. He also edited a Welsh Bible dictionary from 1805 to 1808.

Charles was asked to draw up rules for the Welsh Calvinistic Methodist Church in 1801. In June of 1811, as the only clergyman, he examined and ordained eight men to the ministry. John Elias (1744–1841) was one of this group. This was the origin of the Welsh Calvinistic Methodist Church, now Presbyterian. Charles's preaching, which promoted revival, schools, Sunday schools, and the securing of Bibles in Welsh, greatly helped the cause of Christ in Wales.

REVIVAL IN SCANDINAVIA

Hans N. Hauge (1771–1824) was instrumental in a revival that led lay people to live righteously, to witness, to promote education, to practice charity, and to turn the tide against a liberal intellectualism in Norway. This revival was led by laymen and opposed by the clergy.

Hauge was the son of a farmer in the parish of Tune, fifty miles from Oslo. He was confirmed in the Lutheran church in the fall of 1787 with little change of life. On one occasion he promised his father he would read one of Luther's sermons; when he failed to do so his father reproved him. He nearly drowned on one occasion when a hay boat capsized. This narrow escape, when he was about thirteen, made him think fearfully of death and hell.

As a boy he learned to make his own tools and to make cabinets which he sold. In 1795 he went to Frederikstadt and saw the coarse life-style of the world. On April 5, 1796, this moral farm lad became certain of salvation when his soul was lifted up as he sang a hymn at his farm work. He began testifying to family and friends. In 1796 he wrote a tract titled "Meditations on the Folly of the World" and *Career*, in which he blasted careless clergy. He walked fifty miles to Oslo to get *Career* published and while there learned book printing and binding. He wrote a total of thirty-nine books. His major work, *Christian Doctrine*, sold over ninety-five hundred copies.

Hauge traveled ten thousand miles on skis and on foot during his period of active ministry (1796–1804). In Urdal the parish priest read the Conventicle Act of 1741 which forbade laymen to preach. Later a sermon in Glemmen led to Hauge's arrest and imprisonment, but this treatment only attracted attention to his work. He was later arrested twice in Oslo in 1798.

From Tune he made eight major trips all over Norway. Bergen became a main center of revival about 1800 because there was less persecution. Hauge soon had many lay preachers, such as Lars Hemstad. Although the clergy used the Act of 1741 against him, the lay people backed him against the clergy. By 1800 thousands had been converted in spite of persecution.

He set up a printing press to print his book. He bought the Eker paper mill to have paper for his Christian books. He also purchased a stamping mill and foundry, plus ships to engage in buying herrings. These businesses were not for his own profit but to finance the printing and distribution of Christian literature.

Hauge was arrested in Eker on October 24, 1804, and put in irons. Except for a short time during the Napoleonic Wars when he was set free to set up a salt plant, he remained in prison until 1814. The prison in Oslo was a damp room with a dirt floor. He was refused writing or reading materials and spent his time knitting socks and mittens. He was given hearings in 1805 and 1806. On December 13, 1813, he was sentenced to two years of hard labor and the cost of his trial under the Conventicle Act. Friends paid his fine, and he was finally released in December 1814.

He went to his farm at Bakke, but his health was poor. He married twice and had three children. Bakke became the center of revival leadership until 1817 when he moved to Bredvet. He was a patriot, benefactor, and revival leader.

Hauge wore the everyday jacket and knee trousers with long woolen socks which he knitted as he skied or walked. He learned local ways and customs by careful observation, was friendly, and used the peasant dialect in his preaching. His uniform greeting was, "Do you live so well here?" He would then ask if one wanted "to become a brother in Christ." For eight years this godly man led a national revival through his writings and preaching. His preaching stressed faith, conversion, a pious daily life, righteousness in deed, and denial of worldliness. His revival was exported to the prairies of the United States by Norwegian Lutheran settlers of the Haugean Synod. His revival was predominantly a lay revival, but university-trained pastors participated in later revivals. Hauge's societies remained within the Lutheran church as Pietism did in Germany.

Finland also experienced revival in this era. It was led by Paavo Ruotsalainen (1777–1852). He was convicted in 1796 when a blacksmith told him that because he lacked the "inner knowledge of Christ" he lacked everything. He was converted through the reading of his Finnish Bible. Large numbers of people won by his itinerant preaching were organized into societies which laymen led in services marked by hymn singing and Bible reading.

New techniques of revival came in this era with college revivals and the camp meeting. Laymen were used as preachers of revival and as promoters of social reform. God renewed his people and brought many into the church by the power of the Holy Spirit.

4. PROTESTANT TRANS-ATLANTIC REVIVAL, 1813–1846

MOST scholars writing on revival combine the movements of 1776–1810 with those of 1813–46, referring to the movements as the Second Awakening. Although some of the leaders of revival, such as Robert Haldane, were active in both periods, the era from 1813 to 1846 should be considered as a distinct movement.

The era marked the fruition of second-generation Evangelical reform in England under James Stephen, Jr., T. F. Buxton, and Lord Shaftesbury and the *Réveil* in Switzerland, France, and the Netherlands through the efforts of Robert Haldane. Lyman Beecher, Asahel Nettleton, Charles Finney, and James Caughey brought renewal to the church and salvation to souls. Revival in South America came through the Englishman, Thomson.

In the United States the era was marked by the rise of voluntary societies modeled after the earlier British societies in the preceding era. These societies were financed in the United States by the "Benevolence Empire" or "United Front" of bankers, lawyers, merchants like the Tappans, and manufacturers like Colgate (of soap fame). Together with the clergy, these people formed

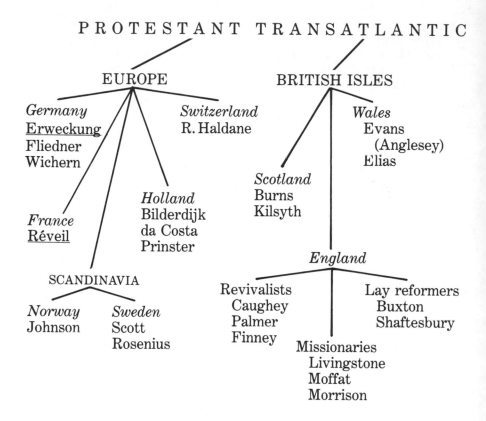

PROTESTANT TRANSATLANTIC

EUROPE

BRITISH ISLES

Germany
Erweckung
Fliedner
Wichern

Switzerland
R. Haldane

Wales
Evans
(Anglesey)
Elias

France
Réveil

Holland
Bilderdijk
da Costa
Prinster

Scotland
Burns
Kilsyth

SCANDINAVIA

England

Norway
Johnson

Sweden
Scott
Rosenius

Revivalists
Caughey
Palmer
Finney

Lay reformers
Buxton
Shaftesbury

Missionaries
Livingstone
Moffat
Morrison

interlocking directorates of the voluntary societies.

Their efforts took on a postmillennial evangelical tinge. They believed that regenerated Christians active in society could bring about a more and more perfect millennial society to which Christ would return. Premillennialism did not become an issue until the revival of 1857 to 1895.

Evangelicals felt the need of revival as they faced transcendentalism in England and the United States. Transcendentalism emphasized the inner emotions of man in contrast to reason. Stress was upon subjective mystical experience and not upon the Bible. It was fostered by the idealistic philosophy of Kant and Hegel in Germany.

In America the frontier was still a rough area in need of revival.

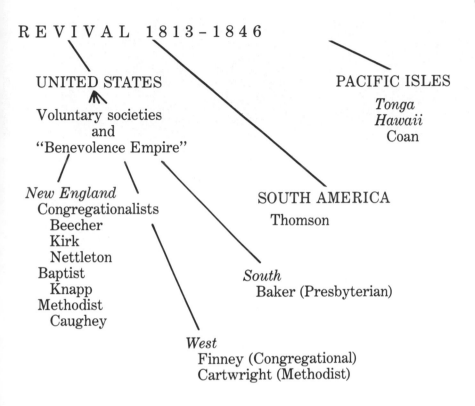

REVIVAL 1813-1846

UNITED STATES

Voluntary societies
and
"Benevolence Empire"

New England
Congregationalists
  Beecher
  Kirk
  Nettleton
Baptist
  Knapp
Methodist
  Caughey

West
  Finney (Congregational)
  Cartwright (Methodist)

South
  Baker (Presbyterian)

SOUTH AMERICA
  Thomson

PACIFIC ISLES
  Tonga
  Hawaii
  Coan

The Napoleonic Wars in Europe and the War of 1812 in the United States led to a decline of religion. Many people again began to pray for revival.

VOLUNTARY SOCIETIES IN THE UNITED STATES

The wave of voluntary societies in England, supported by such wealthy men as the Thorntons and Haldane, became the model for those in the United States. These societies were formed as the need for their existence arose and were usually dropped when the temporal function was fulfilled. They were usually initially organized on a city, state, and/or regional basis and later became national. Many were nondenominational or interdenominational in scope. Their directors were clergy and wealthy men who served on several of the boards and often were related to each other, either by blood or marriage, or had denominational ties.

Societies were organized to promote religious literature. The American Bible Society (1816) and the American Tract Society (1825) provided Bibles, books, and Christian tracts for the West and South on the frontier. The American Sunday School Union (1824) provided information on methods of teaching, Sunday school papers, and coordination of Sunday school activities. The American Education Society (1815), at first organized to help poor New England theologues, raised money to subsidize the ministerial education of needy ministerial students who could then serve churches on the frontier. Its function was similar to that of the Elland Society of England.

The American Home Missionary Society (1826) was formed to raise money for support of Southern and Western frontier missionaries such as the Iowa or Illinois Bands. The American Board of Commissioners for Foreign Missions (1810) was formed to promote missions abroad.

Other societies were set up to promote reform. Most of these are discussed in Chapter 10.

The activities of these societies growing out of revival were financed by wealthy men who had been renewed or saved in revival. They adopted the biblical idea that they were stewards of the wealth God had given them and should use it for man's good and God's glory. Thus they gave liberally to the above societies and served them as directors and officers. Among these men were many wealthy merchants, such as the Tappan brothers, plus many financiers, landowners, manufacturers, publishers, and lawyers. They were the American equivalent of the British Clapham Sect. During 1826 and 1827 nearly $369,000 was given by them to the societies. About $2.8 million was given between 1789 and 1828.

The activities of the Tappan brothers best illustrate the activities of these supporters of societies. Arthur Tappan (1786–1865) started his business career as an apprentice in a dry goods store in Boston. He became a silk merchant in Portland, Maine, in 1807 and by 1826 had a wholesale silk firm in New York. He published the *New York Journal of Commerce* from 1827. By the 1830s he and his brother were earning $1 million a year from their firm.

He served as an officer and director of many societies and gave generously to religious and reform activities. He built Broadway Tabernacle for Finney and helped support Lane Seminary and Oberlin College. He was the major founder and president of the American Anti-Slavery Society in 1833. He helped Theodore Weld financially in his propaganda for manual labor colleges and later for abolition. His more cheerful brother Lewis Tappan (1788–1873) seconded his giving.

REVIVALISTIC PASTORAL EVANGELISM IN THE UNITED STATES

These philanthropists also supported financially the revivalists of the era. Although revival was still promoted by pastors such as Lyman Beecher, other pastors—Asahel Nettleton, Charles Finney, Daniel Baker, Peter Cartwright, and others—itinerated in the churches without a fixed pastorate and held "protracted meetings" for periods of a week or more. While still recognizing the work of the Holy Spirit in bringing revival, Finney especially believed that revival would come with the use of proper measures (the "New Measures"). In this he and others like him were forerunners of the professional organized mass urban revivals of Moody and his successors. Most of these men supported reform measures against alcohol and slavery, but their main work was renewal and evangelism. One scholar estimates that two hundred thousand were added to the churches between 1826 and 1832 through their efforts.

The East. Sereno E. Dwight, pastor of Boston's Park Street Church from 1817 to 1826, led his church in a revival. He received a note from one person requesting a prayer meeting on September 7, 1817. This request resulted in a Monday night prayer meeting for revival and days of fasting and prayer. In 1823 and 1824 revival came to the church, with several inquirers each week. In a meeting for Christians in May 1827, the deacons made confession and began to pray and witness. In all, 348 decided to serve Christ in four churches, about 120 of them in Park Street Church. When E. N. Kirk spoke in June 1840, 100 were added to the Park Street Church and a new Congregational church was founded.

Lyman Beecher (1775–1863) was an eccentric, activistic, evangelistic, and sometimes hypochondriac minister. He studied at Yale and was converted under Timothy Dwight's preaching. He went to East Hampton Presbyterian Church in 1798 after ordination. From there he moved to Litchfield, Connecticut, and from 1810 to 1825 renewal and reform were his major emphases. His six sermons on intemperance in 1825 were published and translated later into many languages, including Greek. He was called to Hanover Street Congregational Church and from 1826 to 1832 championed the cause of orthodoxy against Unitarianism in Boston.

The Presbyterian Lane Seminary was established in Cincinnati on land given by James Kemper and money from Ebenezer and William Lane. Arthur Tappan promised the school $6,000 if Beecher became president. Beecher agreed to go there as president, feeling that there he could train men to win the West and "to regenerate society through Christianity." He served as president of Lane from 1832 to 1851.

Slavery became an issue with the students in the winter of 1834–35 when Theodore Weld, one of Finney's converts and Tappan's protege, led debates (which were mixed with prayer meetings) on slavery. After the trustees banned debate, thirty-seven theology students and fifty-five literary students left Lane in October 1834. Most of them went to Oberlin College with Asa

Mahan, a professor at Lane, who became president of Oberlin, and with Charles Finney, who became professor of theology. Free speech and the admission of blacks to the school were set down as conditions to be met for those who enrolled in Oberlin.

In addition to the loss of students, Beecher was put on trial before the presbytery and accused of heresy by Joshua L. Wilson for preaching "free will." He was exonerated and allowed to continue as pastor of the Second Presbyterian Church of Cincinnati. Here he served eleven years and witnessed 450 additions to the church, with 240 of them by profession of faith.

Harriet Beecher Stowe and Henry Ward Beecher were the most famous of Lyman Beecher's eleven children. Harriet wrote *Uncle Tom's Cabin*, which inflamed the North against slavery. Henry became a famous preacher and social reformer.

Beecher and Asahel Nettleton (1783-1844), who was born in North Killingworth, Connecticut, later bitterly opposed Finney's New Measures and itinerancy without permission from the local pastor. After ten months under conviction in a local revival, which ran from 1800 to 1802, Nettleton was converted in September 1801. When his father died the same year, he worked the family farm.

Nettleton decided to be a missionary through reading about the founding of missionary societies in England in the *Connecticut Evangelical Magazine*, Melville Horne's *Letters on Missions*, and through the influence of Samuel Mills. His cousin, Titus Coan, was also greatly used as a missionary in Hawaii from 1837 to 1839.

Nettleton taught school by day and studied theology at night with his pastor. When he entered Yale in 1805, he found chapel, Dwight's sermons, and Bible study the most attractive part of college. In a revival at Yale in 1807 he counseled students; on one occasion he stayed up all night to help a student. During his junior year he met Samuel Mills, who had gone to Yale to see him. These two men had many things in common: Both were born on the same day, both were converted in the fall of 1801, both were

*Cities which hosted Finney meetings

PROTESTANT TRANS

farmers, and both wanted to be missionaries but were hindered by other responsibilities.

Nettleton stayed on a year to study theology at Yale, working as a butler to pay his debts. When he left Yale, he studied with Bezaleel Pinneo, a pastor, from 1810 to 1811. He was ordained as an evangelist in the summer of 1817, but he clung to his vision of being a missionary until 1822, when his success in many revivals led him to direct his life to an itinerant revivalist's career, mostly in pastorless churches, until 1816. A major revival under him at Stonington, Connecticut, launched him into that career.

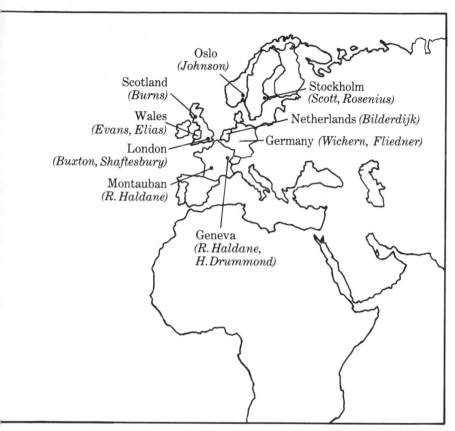

Oslo
(Johnson)

Scotland
(Burns)

Stockholm
(Scott, Rosenius)

Wales
(Evans, Elias)

Netherlands (Bilderdijk)

London
(Buxton, Shaftesbury)

Germany (Wichern, Fliedner)

Montauban
(R. Haldane)

Geneva
(R. Haldane,
H. Drummond)

ATLANTIC REVIVAL 1813-1846

He cooperated with pastors in meetings or stayed for prolonged
periods at churches with no minister. His Calvinistic doctrinal
sermons had pointed practical action. People who were convicted
came to his house or he visited from house to house, or he held "inquiry meetings" at which he would help people to salvation by an-
swering their questions and giving wise counsel. These meetings
followed his Sunday service, two weekly meetings and prayer
meetings. He also used hymns in his meetings. His converts were
known for their stability.

At an awakening at Waterbury where Nettleton worked with

Beecher in the summer of 1816, 110 were won. Over one hundred were saved in a meeting at Malta, New York, in August 1819. Over one hundred were converted and two hundred went to the inquiry room at an awakening in Union College, Schenectady, during the following winter. During the fall of 1820 Nettleton had over fifteen hundred converts in New Haven, many of whom were Yale students. When he held a meeting in his hometown of North Killingworth from September 1821 to January 1822, 162 responded. So it went in all his meetings.

He contracted typhus in October 1822 and preached infrequently until 1824. In 1824 he published his revivalistic *Village Hymns* and gave the royalties to the American Board of Commissioners for Foreign Missions and to the New Seminary, later Hartford Seminary, at East Windsor, Connecticut.

Continued ill health led him to Virginia in the fall of 1827, where he held several meetings. From then on he alternated between the North in summer and the South in winter, except for a visit to the British Isles from the spring of 1831 to August of 1832. Wherever he went, he taught people to depend upon God, not him, for revival. Nettleton is credited with having won twenty-five thousand people to Christ.

When Hartford Seminary was founded in 1833 at East Windsor, Connecticut, Nettleton contributed $2,500 but refused to become a professor. He did, however, serve as adjunct professor and gave lectures each year on revival. He made his home near the seminary for the last ten years of his life. The seminary moved to Hartford in 1865. Hartford Seminary ceased training ministers in 1972, but the Hartford Seminary Foundation continues.

The dispute with Finney over his New Measures caused Nettleton much concern for several years. He met Finney at Albany in 1826 or 1827 but did not want to be seen in public with him. Finney and the western revivalists met with Beecher, Nettleton, and other eastern ministers at New Lebanon, New York, from July 18 to 26, 1827. Both Nettleton and Beecher opposed Finney. In an earlier letter dated January 1827, and published as a pamphlet in

1828 in New York, Nettleton had expressed his dislike of the New Measures.

Nettleton believed that preaching correct doctrines of depravity (which Finney, he thought, denied) and justification through Christ's blood would be used by the Holy Spirit to convict and save. Though he loved the souls of men, he was a New England Calvinist opposed to excitement and to dependence on human effort in revival. Unlike Finney, his work was mainly in small towns in the Northeast and South. He and others introduced protracted meetings into American revivalism in the period between 1813 and 1895.

Edward N. Kirk (1802-74) was born in New York and educated at Princeton University and Princeton Seminary (1822-25). He had been converted in 1822 after two years of legal activity. He served two years in the middle and southern states as a missionary of the American Board of Commissioners for Foreign Missions. His preaching brought revival to the Presbyterian church in Albany, which he served from 1828 to 1837. He preached in England from April 1837 to 1839. He was a successful itinerant preacher until 1842, when he became pastor of Mount Vernon Congregational Church in Boston. About one thousand were added to his church. Dwight L. Moody was led to Christ by one of Kirk's Sunday school teachers. During this time Kirk also conducted thirty protracted meetings in other churches and colleges. He participated in the formation of the Evangelical Alliance in England in 1846 and was partly responsible for the organization of the first YMCA in Boston.

Jacob Knapp (1799-1874), born in New York state, was converted about 1816 and became a Baptist. He graduated from the academy at Hamilton, New York, in 1825 and was ordained in the same year. He served churches in Springfield and Watertown, New York, from 1825 to 1833. In Watertown two hundred were added to the church. He was active in revival meetings, mainly in New England and New York from 1833 to 1874. He made use of the "anxious seat" to help those under conviction. During his last meeting in Boston in the 1840s, two thousand were added to the church. He claimed to have won one hundred thousand during the 150 meetings of his career.

Jabez Swan (1800–73) was born in Stonington, Connecticut. His conversion experience came during a severe thunderstorm in 1821. Educated at Hamilton from 1825 to 1827 and ordained in 1827, he served churches in Connecticut and New York from 1827 to 1838. He then became a very successful leader in revivals among Baptists in New England and New York states. He had a keen sense of humor which he used to good effect in his sermons.

John N. Maffit (1794–?), a Methodist from Dublin, Ireland, came to the United States in 1819. Between 1820 and 1845 he held meetings in large cities from New England to Louisiana. He is credited with the conversion of Benjamin Harrison, later president of the United States, in a meeting in the winter of 1840–41. His ability as an orator, his dramatic presentation of the gospel, and his commanding presence won him a hearing before any congregation. In one meeting in New York he dramatically entered the church from a ladder through an opening above the pulpit. He was elected chaplain of the House of Representatives in 1841.

More noteworthy an evangelist was James Caughey (1810–97), born in northern Ireland and brought to the United States as a youth. He became a Christian at the age of twenty-seven, went into the Methodist ministry, and was ordained in 1836 as an elder in the Methodist Episcopal Church. Through reading of the need of the power of the Holy Spirit in preaching, he experienced in July 1839 a spiritual ecstasy which he felt would empower him to preach. He had already had successful meetings in Montreal in 1835. He felt led to preach in the British Isles from 1841 to 1847, mainly in the Midlands and North among the Methodists. In his meeting in Nottingham, William Booth was led to a deeper religious experience which led him to reach the lost in England. Methodists in England opposed Caughey's work because of his emotionalism and use of the "New Measures," but he claimed over twenty thousand converts in Britain. He used humor in his sermons but more often depicted the terrors of failure to accept Christ during his sermons and altar calls. He did, however, preach the law, sin, the Cross, repentance, faith, and regeneration. He, along with Walter and Phoebe Palmer, helped to introduce the doctrine of a second work of grace or entire sanctification in Britain. When he visited England for the second time from 1857 to 1859 he reported over eight thousand converts and three thousand who were "entirely sanctified." He had seventy-five hundred converts on his third tour in 1860, but did very little on his fourth visit because of ill health.

The South. Daniel Baker (1791–1857) was born in Georgia, studied at Hampden-Sydney College, and graduated from Princeton University. After three days of prayer with three other students during a revival at Princeton in 1815, Baker visited the rooms of every student and won forty-five to Christ. More than twenty-five of these later became ministers. He engaged in more theological study with William Hill while teaching in a female academy.

Baker served churches in Virginia, Washington, D.C., Georgia, Alabama, and Mississippi. In 1830 in Savannah, Georgia, a hundred people joined the church during a revival. In Washington he was the pastor of John Quincy Adams and Andrew Jackson.

His presbytery made him an evangelist in 1830 while he was still a pastor. Between 1831 and 1837 he held fifty meetings in Georgia, Texas, Florida, and South Carolina. About twenty-five hundred were saved in these meetings. For a time he used the anxious bench but gave it up in the 1830s for the inquiry room which he found to be more effective. It is estimated that he won about twenty thousand to Christ.

Baker helped to develop Austin College and served as its president from 1843 to 1857. In his last seven years he raised $100,000 for it. He was a godly educator, revivalist, and pastor.

The West and Midwest. During the eighteenth century, God used pastors in their own churches or itinerant pastors with permission of the local pastor in revival. They believed that revivals were "times of refreshing" from a sovereign God who sent revival in answer to prayer and biblical preaching.

A new era of revival may be linked with Charles G. Finney (1792–1875). He believed that, with the proper means, Christians would be revived and sinners would be converted. Jonathan Edwards and other preachers of the Great Awakening had seen revivals as "surprising works of God," inexplicable outpourings of God's Spirit. With Finney, a new attitude had arrived. According to Finney, "A revival is not a miracle, or dependent on a miracle in any sense." Rather, revival is a "result of the right use of the constituted means." These "constituted means" were the so-called New Measures advocated by Finney and others, who used such means as harsh accusations, protracted meetings, naming sinners in prayers, the "anxious bench" (familiar in frontier revivals), prayers and exhortations by women, the method of addressing congregations as if pleading with a jury, and "helpers" to urge the convicted to the "anxious bench." While Finney never assumed that these measures could in themselves save people (since only God could save a repentant sinner), he did assume that the revivalist must be a powerful and eloquent communicator, a popular figure who could do more than just wait upon the work of the sovereign God. And he assumed that any listener could, of his free will, repent and immediately obtain assurance of salvation.

The life of Charles G. Finney covers two eras of revivalism, but he was most active in revival and evangelism in the era ending in 1846. He was born in Warren, Connecticut, in the home of a Revolutionary War soldier. In 1794 the family moved by ox train to Oneida County, New York, and then further west. Finney grew to be a tall, slender man with piercing eyes and an exceptionally good voice. He loved music and learned to play the cello and violin.

Finney studied from 1806 and 1808 at the Hamilton Oneida Academy at Clinton, New York. He taught school from 1808 to 1812 and then continued his education in his home town of Warren

CHARLES GRANDISON FINNEY (1792-1875), revivalist and president of Oberlin College. He established the modern forms and methods of revivalism in America. *(Courtesy of the Oberlin College Archives)*

from 1812 to 1815. He again taught school until he entered the law office of Benjamin Wright Adams to study law in 1818. He bought a Bible because of references to the Mosaic Law in Blackstone's commentaries on law.

He began to attend George Gale's Presbyterian church. He became choir director of the church and often argued with Gale over Calvinism. The young people, and especially Lydia Andrews, who later became his wife, prayed for him. He decided on October 7, 1821, to settle the matter of salvation and read the Bible and pray. Alone in the woods on October 10, his conviction changed to joy. He felt he met Christ face to face as he was praying and received a call to preach. When a deacon asked him to plead his case Finney said that he had "a retainer from the Lord to plead his cause." He testified in the church and talked to his friends in town about their souls.

From 1821 to 1823 he studied theology with George Gale but opposed Gale's strong Calvinism. St. Lawrence Presbytery grudgingly licensed him to preach in March 1824. In the same month the Female Missionary Society appointed him to the rural area at Evan Mills and Antwerp in Jefferson County. It was in this period that he met "Father" Daniel Nash, a Massachusetts-born preacher who became his mentor, tutor, and prayer helper. Nash traveled with Finney from 1824 to 1827 as a prayer partner. He continued to pray for Finney in his own home and counsel him by letters until 1831. He taught Finney much about prayer, including the practice of praying for sinners by name in public. Nash would pray for three or four hours a day; sometimes, because he was deaf and prayed loudly, he could be heard half a mile away. Finney himself spent much time in prayer.

Finney's first appointment was in Evan Mills. While there, he spoke in a town called Sodom, where a man named Lot lived. Finney, not knowing of the man, spoke on the story of Lot and the destruction of Sodom and Gomorrah. The people were angered, but revival followed.

The presbytery ordained him in July 1824. On October 9 he married Lydia Andrews. From 1824 to 1827, together with Lydia and Nash, he held meetings in small towns in north central and western New York. When he was given newspaper publicity at a meeting at Western in October 1825, he received national attention. Theodore Weld was converted through the meeting in Utica when Finney spoke on "one sinner destroyeth much good!" Weld then traveled with Finney for a time as a helper just as Drummond later traveled with Moody in Britain. Girls, laughing at Finney when he toured a factory in New York Mills, were reduced to tears as he looked at them, and a revival came in the factory. In Rome there were five hundred converts.

Finney went from Troy to visit Asahel Nettleton, who was holding a meeting at Albany in late 1827. Nettleton, according to Finney, told him he did not oppose his doctrine but opposed his New Measures and said he "must not be seen" with Finney.

Finney's extemporaneous, logical, and conversational sermons were backed by much prayer and house-to-house visitation. Thomas Hastings sang solos and led the singing from 1832 in New York. Finney's meetings were planned by advance men and advertised, and his finances were audited. Lyman Beecher and Nettleton, who bitterly opposed his methods, headed a delegation of nine to meet with an equally large delegation of western revivalists in New Lebanon, New York. No results of note emerged from the meeting, but Beecher had ceased opposition by 1828, and Finney later preached in Beecher's church in Boston.

Five thousand were converted in a meeting in Philadelphia in 1828. At the the request of the Tappans, Finney conducted meetings in New York City from the fall of 1829 to midsummer of 1830. His campaign in Rochester from September 10, 1830, to March 6, 1831, was highly publicized and over one thousand were converted, among them many prominent people. He began to use the anxious bench regularly instead of just having sinners stand; he linked with it an "inquiry meeting" for counseling. From August

1831 to April 1832 he preached in Boston. Here he spoke to Christians first to win them from lukewarmness, worldliness, and neglect to witness.

His career of itinerant evangelism, which began in 1824, ended in 1832. Tappan had bought and remodeled the Chatham Theater in New York for Finney's meetings and he preached there beginning in April 1832. This became known as the Second (or Free) Presbyterian Church. When the Broadway Tabernacle was built in 1834, Finney became a Congregationalist. While his main recreation was hunting, he took a six-month Mediteranean cruise, beginning in January 1834, as a vacation.

When Joshua Leavitt, editor of the *New York Evangelist*, had a hard time financially because his antislavery stand had led to the loss of many subscriptions, he asked Finney to give lectures on revival in the Tabernacle. These Friday evening lectures, each almost two hours long, were published from Leavitt's notes. The twenty-two lectures were published in book form in 1835 under the title *Lectures on Revival*, and twelve thousand copies sold. The book was printed in France, England, Canada, Wales, and Germany. Eighty thousand copies were sold in England by the time of Finney's first visit there. It helped much in promoting his revivals. Finney's other main books were *Lectures on Systematic Theology*, published in 1846, and his *Autobiography*, published in 1868.

Meanwhile the Lane debates on slavery led to an exodus of students and Asa Mahan to Oberlin College. Oberlin was founded in 1835 with five hundred acres of land and one hundred students. At the urging of the Tappan brothers, who promised him financial assistance, Finney went to Oberlin and taught theology there from 1835 to 1875. Until 1837 he spent the summers at Oberlin and the winters in New York, but in 1837 he settled in Oberlin. Here it is estimated he taught a total of twenty thousand students. John Chapin of Providence supplemented his salary with $600 per year for several years. Finney was also pastor of the Congregational church in town from 1836 to 1872. He became president of the college in 1851 and admitted blacks and women on terms of equality with men. He made Oberlin a center of revivalism, perfectionism, and abolitionism.

He continued to hold meetings in the Midwest and the Northeast on a part-time basis. While in Boston in 1857 he participated in the newly formed businessmen's noonday prayer. In Boston in 1856 his first sermons were for "the searching of the church" to reclaim the backsliders. His lectures on revival brought an invitation to visit England from 1849 to 1851. When he spoke in Whitefield's Tabernacle in London, the inquiry room holding sixteen hundred was filled. He returned again to the British Isles from late 1858 to August 1860.

He is credited with having won five hundred thousand to Christ and bringing renewal to many others. Many lawyers were won because of his dignified, logical, conversational "reasoning" in extemporaneous preaching. His second wife, whom he married in 1848, held successful meetings for women in the United States and the British Isles. Group and private prayer, preaching, house-to-house visitation, and private counseling were integral parts of all his meetings.

Finney broke with the Calvinistic doctrinal stance of earlier leaders of revival. He focused on sin as the result of man's selfish choice in the exercise of his free will. He had little use for the typically Calvinistic ideas of original sin, the total depravity of man's nature, or man's resultant moral inability to seek God. Moral depravity to him was the voluntary state of selfishness of the will springing from the sinful heart. Man was "universally and morally depraved" with a propensity to sin, and it was by an act of free will that each man chose to sin.

His view of entire sanctification of the individual and postmillennial perfection of the race through Christians followed from this. Since selfishness is the basis of sin, it follows that benevolence and good works are the basis of perfection.

Finney's contribution to revivalism was his emphasis upon the use of means to bring about revival, but he did not neglect the necessity of the activity of the Holy Spirit in the process. He left his valuable *Lectures on Revival* as his heritage to the church. His theology of Arminianism and perfectionism was set forth in his *Lectures on Systematic Theology*. The latter influenced the holiness movement long after his death. He did not neglect social reform but advocated abstinence from liquor and abolition of slavery. Referring to social reform, he made the following statement: "Now the great business of the church is to reform the world—to put away every kind of sin. The Church of Christ was orginally organized to be a body of reformers."

Peter Cartwright (1785–1872), who for fifty years rode Methodist circuits from the Appalachians to the Mississippi, left the record of his life in his *Autobiography*. He was born in Amherst County, Virginia, into the poor family of a Revolutionary War soldier. His family moved by packhorse to Logan County, Kentucky. The area was known as "Rogue's Harbor" because of the violence and crime. It became the birthplace of the great western revival and the camp meeting.

Jacob Lurton, a circuit rider, visited the Cartwright home and organized a class which Peter's mother attended. When revival came in 1799, Ebenezer Church was built. Peter preferred dancing, horse-racing, and cards, at all of which he was very competent. In 1801 he came under conviction and let his mother burn his playing cards. He was converted in James McGready's sacramental meeting in May 1801 and joined Ebenezer Church in June. He saw one hundred men convicted by one sermon at a camp meeting.

He was given an exhorter's license by Jesse Walker in 1802. That same year he became a circuit rider. For a time he studied at Brown's Academy. In October 1804 he was appointed to a circuit in Kentucky, in 1806 to one in Ohio, and in 1810 to another in Tennessee. His quick wit helped him to confound a minister who used Greek to refute him. The man mistook Peter's respose in Dutch for Hebrew. Francis Asbury made him a deacon in the fall of 1806, and in 1808 Bishop William McKendree set him apart as an elder. He became a presiding elder in 1812.

Cartwright tells of how on one occasion he stopped at a place in the Cumberland Mountains where a dance was scheduled. Invited to dance by a pretty girl, he took her hand and, kneeling, said that, in keeping with his custom, he would ask God's blessing on the affair. The dance turned into a revival, fifteen were converted, and a society was organized.

During the Battle of New Orleans he was for some time a chaplain. In the fall of 1824 he left Kentucky and went to Illinois to be free of slavery and to get land for his children. When he settled in Sangamon County, he preached to the Indians through an interpreter.

Cartwright was a man of great physical strength which helped him to deal with rowdies in his meetings. He was dark-complexioned with high cheekbones, deep-set piercing eyes, and unruly hair. His commonsense prescription for life was "keep your feet warm, your head cool and your bowels well regulated, rise early, go to bed regularly, eat temperately . . . drink no spirits of any kind. . . ." Little wonder he was able to ride circuits for fifty-two years (1803–56), receive ten thousand into the church, baptize eight thousand children and four thousand adults, hold five hundred funerals, and preach in all about 14,600 sermons. He was also elected to the Illinois legislature in 1828 and 1829. In 1846 he lost the race for a seat in Congress to Abraham Lincoln. His contribution to the Methodist Episcopal Church was immense.

REVIVAL IN THE BRITISH ISLES

England. While there was no revival comparable to the Evangelical and Methodist revivals of the Great Awakening nor the scope of revival in the era from 1776 to 1810, there were some awakenings under such men as the Methodist James Caughey.

This was also the era when the missionary societies founded in the previous era began to send out some very notable missionaries. These included John Philip, who secured civil liberties for the Hottentots of South Africa by his Ordinance Fifty; Robert Moffat, who went to South Africa; and Robert Morrison who went to China and translated the Bible into the native languages; Krapf and Rebmann, the discoverers of snowclad mountains in Central Africa; and David Livingstone, whose explorations in Central Africa opened the road for missions and led to the abolition of the slave trade. The contributions of these men are discussed in more detail elsewhere in this book.

This period was the era of second-generation reformers, the successors of the Clapham Sect. T. Fowell Buxton in the House of Commons and James Stephen, Jr., at the colonial office, teamed up to abolish slavery in the British empire. Shaftesbury, the stepson of the Prime Minister Palmerston, got legislation to improve conditions for the insane and for workers in factories, mines, and brickyards. This godly man devoted his life to social reform at great cost to himself. His nurse and great friend, Maria Millis, a staunch Evangelical, taught him to read the Bible, pray, and serve Christ who had saved him. The life and work of these reformers will be given more attention later.

Scotland. The flames of revival burned brighter in Scotland through William C. Burns (1815–68). He was born at Dun and trained in the liberal arts at Aberdeen University and in theology at Glasgow University. He had committed his life to Christ at the beginning of his college career. He was appointed to Kilsyth in 1839. When he spoke on July 23, 1839, the people cried out for salvation. One Sunday he preached on the grave of James Robe, his predecessor in revival. He continued meetings in the churchyard and spoke in the market to crowds of over three thousand. A sacramental meeting on September 22, which drew a crowd of ten thousand, went on until 3:00 A.M. Many were renewed and saved.

When Robert Murray McCheyne went to Palestine, Burns supplied for him in his Dundas church. He described the Kilsyth revival to the people on August 10, 1839, in the Thursday evening prayer meeting. The people were stirred to pray, and one hundred remained for counsel. Nightly meetings continued for four months. McCheyne came home to a revived church. Revival spread to Perth, Aberdeen, and Newcastle.

Burns was in Canada from 1844 to 1846. He became the first missionary to China of the English Presbyterian Missionary Society from 1847 to 1868. J. Hudson Taylor was greatly influenced by this godly man who was called the "Man of the Book."

Wales. There were major revivals in Wales through the ministry of Christmas Evans, a Baptist, and John Elias, a Calvinistic Methodist. Christmas Evans (1766–1838), known as the "the Welsh Bunyan," was born on Christmas day (hence his name) in a cobbler's home.

When Evans lost his father at the age of nine, he was sent to live with James Lewis, a mean and drunken uncle who did little more than clothe and feed the boy. Christmas lived a wild life for seven years and had many miraculous escapes from death. A horse ran into a stable with a low door with him on its back. Another time he fell from a tree with an open knife in his hand.

When he left his uncle at the age of seventeen, he could not read. He soon learned to read and learned Latin in David Davies's grammar school. Davis was also his pastor.

He became a Christian in 1783 and lost his right eye in 1787 when he was beaten because of his Christian faith. He joined the Baptist Church at Aberdwar shortly after the beating and was ordained in 1789. He served two years at Lleyn in Caernarvonshire in Northern Wales, where his first sermons were borrowed from Beveridge and Rowland. He began to itinerate, speaking five times on Sunday and walking as far as twenty miles a day.

In 1791 he began his main ministry, which lasted until 1826, in the Isle of Anglesey. Here he learned Hebrew and Greek in order to preach better. About 1802 he had a special infilling of the Holy Spirit. Within two years he had ten preaching points and six hundred converts. Chapels were built for the crowds.

When the people rejected his advice about pastors, he was hurt at their ingratitude and went to Caerphilly. Here 240 were added to the church in one year. He moved to Cardiff in 1829 and Caernarvon in 1832.

His revivals were pastoral and based on biblical preaching. His advice to preachers was to lead a moral life, to read the Bible and pray, and to learn all they could, to teach evangelical doctrine, to watch their outward appearance in the pulpit, to avoid foolish gestures, and to preach clearly in love and from the heart. His sermons reflect vivid imaginative description in the preaching of Christ crucified. He prayed three times a day.

This six-foot, stout, black-haired man, often careless about his clothes, was idolized by the Welsh. He had a good preaching voice and was witty. On one occasion he received a large offering after saying that he hoped none of the sheep-stealers in the area would give.

John Elias (1774–1841), born in a weaver's home in Aberch, North Wales, was another famous Welsh revival preacher. His loving grandfather trained him in religion, and he could read the Bible at six years of age.

Daniel Rowland's sermon brought him under conviction and led him to salvation. In September 1793 he joined the Methodist Society at Hendre Howel. He was licensed in 1794, at the age of twenty, as an itinerant evangelist in Caernarvonshire. Some months of training in theology in 1796 with Evans Richards and his learning Greek and Hebrew through a lexicon helped to prepare him to preach.

He became pastor at Llanfechell and Llangefmi when he moved to Anglesey in 1799. He was always poor, and his wife opened a small millinery and drapery shop to supplement their income. He was one of the first group to be ordained in 1811 by Thomas Charles of Bala in what became the Welsh Calvinistic Church. It is claimed that his preaching started a revival in Caernarvonshire in which twenty-five hundred were saved.

He preached in Liverpool, Manchester, Bristol, and London as well as in Wales. His dramatic preaching served to draw many to Christ. It was said that there were about ten thousand at his funeral in Anglesey, so great was the love of the people for him. He ardently supported the London Missionary Society and the British and Foreign Bible Society. This humble man was to the Methodists of Anglesey what Christmas Evans was to the Baptists of the same area.

REVIVAL IN EUROPE

The Réveil *in Switzerland, France, and Holland.* Robert Haldane, in addition to being a generous patron of revival in Scotland, was used of God to bring revival to Switzerland, France, and, indirectly, to Holland. During the summer of 1816 he went to Geneva. He began studies on Romans three times a week from 6:00 to 8:00 P.M. in his home with about twenty-five theological students from the University of Geneva from February until June 1817. The students learned from Paul the authority of the Bible, human depravity, and the New Birth. Haldane would answer their questions with the question, "What does the Bible say?"

Henri A. César (1787–1864), converted in 1816, was one of these students. His preaching of salvation by faith alone cost him his pulpit.

Another hearer was François S. R. L. Gaussen (1790–1863). He was later a minister in the state church. In 1831 he organized the Evangelical Society of Geneva to promote sound doctrine in France and Switzerland. A theological seminary in Geneva was also set up. He wrote *Theopneustia,* an able exposition of biblical inerrancy.

John Henri Merle d'Aubigne (1794–1872) was also helped by Haldane. D'Aubigne wrote an excellent thirteen-volume history of the Protestant Reformation from the sources, which was published from 1835 to 1878. After a pastorate in Hamburg, he organized the Free Church of Geneva, taught in the Evangelical

Seminary, and edited the *Evangelical Gazette*. Other students who became pastors, scholars, and preachers were Frederic Monod, Henri Pyt, Ami Bost, Charles Rieu, and Christopher Burckhardt, who went to Aleppo.

Henri Dunant (1828–1910), who was saved in the *Réveil,* was born into a wealthy Genevan family. He helped to found the World Alliance of YMCAs in 1855 and to set up the first Red Cross in 1863 after he saw the carnage of the Battle of Solferino in 1859.

Robert Haldane left Henry Drummond to carry on his work in Geneva and went to Montauban, France. From 1817 to 1819 he held similar Bible studies to lay the foundation for the French *Réveil.*

Through Haldane's pupils, Malan and d'Aubigne, the *Réveil* was extended to Holland. The leaders were Holland's leading romantic poet, Willem Bilderdijk (1756–1831), Issak da Costa (1798–1860), a Portuguese Jew won to Christ by Bilderdijk in 1822, and Abraham Cappadose. They in turn won Groen von Prinster, a jurist, historian, and statesman. They organized the Christian Friends in Amsterdam, who met from 1845 to 1854 and who helped to keep Protestant orthodoxy and salvation by faith alive in Holland.

Some students at Utrecht in 1843 set up the *Sechor Dabar* ("Remember the Word"), which met once a week to study theology for three hours, to hear orations for one hour, and to have one hour of conversation when plenty of chocolate, tea, or coffee was drunk. Opposing students called them the "Chocolate Club" or "Prayer Club." Members of Sechor Dabar also taught working men and poor children to read.

John and Andrew Murray, who joined this club, organized Eltheto as a subsidary of this group to promote missions in twice monthly meetings. After he finished his theological studies in Holland, John became the promoter of revival in South Africa.

The Christian Reformed Church of Holland came out of the awakening of the *Réveil* and in 1854 set up its own theological school at Kampen. People from this group migrated to Iowa and Michigan. They are still strong exponents of Reformed theology. Such was the fruit of Robert Haldane's work on the continent.

The Erweckung *in Germany.* Wayne Detzler, in his 1974 unpublished thesis for the University of Manchester, amply demonstrated that an awakening, owing much to British and somewhat to American influences, occurred in Germany between 1813 and 1846. Berlin in the north and Württemberg in the south were the main centers. Missionaries, money, and literature were supplied to set up German counterparts to the Bible Society and Religious Tract Society. George Müller started an orphanage in Stuttgart, and Elizabeth Fry's visits helped to promote prison reform.

Johannes E. Gossner (1773–1858), ordained in 1796 as a Roman Catholic priest, was barred from preaching in Bavaria by the Jesuits. By 1815 he had completed a translation of the Greek New Testament into German. He was granted a chaplaincy in the German diplomatic corp in St. Petersburg, Russia, in 1820. He became pastor of the Bethlehem Church in Berlin in 1826, the year he became a Protestant, and he served there until 1846. In 1836 he founded the Gossner Mission, which sent out over 140 missionaries during his life, most of them to India. Men like this produced a revival minority in Protestantism.

Carl F. A. Steinkopf, aided by the English Bible Society, distributed Bibles. Robert Pinkerton, a Scot who founded several continental Bible societies, aided him. Three hundred thousand New Testaments were given to Prussian soldiers in 1848. The British and Foreign Bible Society gave nearly £177,000 to Bible distribution in Germany. The Baptists had thirty-one thousand members by 1884, partly as a result of this work.

Theodor Fliedner (1800–64) was born near Wiesbaden and trained in Geissen and Gottingen Universities. He began to preach in a small church near Kaiserswerth in 1823. When he visited Holland that year, he was impressed with the work of Mennonite deacons and deaconesses. A visit to England in 1824 to raise money for the social program of his church enabled him to visit Elizabeth Fry and raise over £700 for his work. He began prison work in 1825 and founded an association in 1826 to provide chaplains for prisons, to promote segregation of hardened criminals from first offenders, and to rehabilitate prisoners.

Fliedner had observed Thomas Chalmers's work in 1832 in St. John's Church, Glasgow. Under the influence of that work he founded an organization to train deaconesses to nurse the sick in 1836. A hospital to give the nurses training was organized. At his death more than six hundred were helping the poor, sick, and orphans. In 1851 Florence Nightingale spent some months in nurses' training in Kaiserswerth.

Another important figure, whose work will be discussed in a later chapter, was Johannes Wichern, who engaged in charitable work on behalf of orphans and prisoners.

Revival in Scandinavia. George Scott (1804-74) was sent as a Methodist chaplain to English laborers in Stockholm in 1830. His preaching drew large crowds, among which were Karl O. Rosenius and Anders Wiberg. He held services in Swedish, and a chapel was built to accommodate the large crowds. When the Lutheran state clergy forced him out, Rosenius continued this work, out of which developed the Free Church movement in Sweden.

Karl O. Rosenius (1816-68) was educated at Uppsala, became a lay preacher in the Lutheran state church, and led in a lay pietistic revival. His sermons and his magazine, *Pietisten,* had wide influence. The consequent Free Church was based on forgiveness of sin by faith apart from works. Two national groups emerged from the movement: the Evangelical National Institution of 1856 and the Swedish Mission Covenant of 1878. Immigrants from the Covenant group came to the United States and organized the Evangelical Mission Covenant Church in 1885.

Gisle Johnson (1822-94) taught church history at Christiana University in Oslo, Norway, from 1849 to 1894. He gave two-hour lectures in an Oslo church in 1849. His emphasis on the Bible was carried all over Norway by his students and led to an awakening which continued into the 1860s.

Nikolai F. S. Grundtvig (1783-1872) was born in Zealand, Denmark, and educated in arts and theology at the University of Copenhagen. From 1805 to 1821 he taught church history and wrote much fine poetry. He was ordained in 1811 and became chaplain at the Church of our Savior in Copenhagen in 1822. Between 1839 and 1872 he served as chaplain of a home for the aged. Folk high schools were organized by him. He also wrote over two hundred hymns. Denmark was saved from rationalism by this godly man's leadership in a revival of true religion in this area.

AWAKENING IN LATIN AMERICA

James Thomson (died ca. 1850) was a Scottish Baptist who was sent to Buenos Aires in Argentina in 1818 by the British and Foreign Bible Society and the English Foreign School Society. He used the monitorial system of Joseph Lancaster by which the more advanced students taught the less advanced to read with the New Testament as the text. He soon had five thousand in his schools. Invited by the authorities, he went to Chile in 1821, Peru in 1822 (where he was welcomed by José de San Martín), Ecuador in 1824, Colombia in 1825, and Mexico. When he returned home in 1826, he had won many to Christ. His was the earliest Protestant mission of any in Roman Catholic Latin America. There were only about thirteen thousand Protestants in Latin America in 1900, 3 million in 1949, and about 9 million in 1961, many of them Pentecostals.

REVIVAL IN THE PACIFIC

Titus Coan (1801-82), a cousin of Asahel Nettleton, carried revival to Hawaii. He was a farmer's son and was educated in a military school and Auburn Seminary as a Presbyterian. In the War of

1812 he served as a lieutenant. He taught school for some years, but after his conversion (about 1828) he taught in Auburn State Prison School, where he had two thousand converts. In 1833 and 1834 he was in Patagonia to assess the possibility of the American Board of Commissioners for Foreign Missions beginning missionary work there. In 1835 he went to Hilo, Hawaii, where and he and his wife opened boarding schools for boys and girls. He quickly learned Hawaiian. The revival that came was at its peak in 1837, when people often cried all night. On July 8, 1837, he baptized 1,705 and 2,400 took Communion. In 1839 and 1840, about 7,400 were taken into the church at Hilo and nearly 12,000 were baptized. He was influenced by Nettleton in all of this. He trained his converts to be self-supporting and self-propagating.

Revival came even earlier in Tonga. It began in July 1834 under the leadership of Isaiah Vovole and national pastors. In just a few days two thousand accepted Christ after Hobai (King George) was converted. He set up a Free Church with Methodist organization. In six years about nine thousand became Christians.

Fiji experienced revival under John Geddie (1815–72) in the 1840s. Geddie, a Scot brought to Nova Scotia from Scotland by his parents, was educated for the Presbyterian ministry. He was ordained and served churches in Prince Edward Island. He became a Presbyterian missionary and went to the island of Aneityum in the New Hebrides in 1848. In twenty years there he developed an alphabet and gave the former cannibals school texts, hymnals, and the Bible. Revival swept over two thousand into the church by 1854. Many became missionaries to other islands. It is said that there were no Christians there in 1848, but at his death in 1872 there were no pagans.

This description of revival from 1813 to 1846 surely merits consideration as a movement distinctly separate from the Second Awakening. Great numbers of ministers and missionaries led in revivals in different parts of the world. Reform resulted in America and England.

5. GLOBAL ANGLO-SAXON LAY PRAYER REVIVAL, 1857–1895

SLAVERY became a national problem during the 1840s and 1850s. The Missouri Compromise of 1850, the Fugitive Slave Law, the Kansas-Nebraska Act, abolitionist agitation, and the march of slavery in the South and West brought on the Civil War. Heavy Irish and German immigration in the same period introduced the continental Sunday into the country, which made Sunday—after morning service—like every other day in the week. The Panic of 1857, which reached a crisis on October 14, made people more aware of their spiritual need. Corruption during the Grant administration called for a stricter morality. Revival seemed like a necessity.

In contrast to earlier eras, the revival which started in 1857 had no great leader. It was a spontaneous, lay, prayer, ecumenical global movement, often led by businessmen. It had much favorable newspaper publicity. Laymen led brisk noonday prayer meetings. A typical meeting would involve a hymn, a prayer by the leader, the reading of a Scripture passage, the reading of prayer requests and the hearing of oral ones, and short prayers. The Keswick slogan "All in Christ" summarized the movement's ecumenicity. Papers at great length reported on numbers and results. Though American and Anglo-Saxon in its earlier stages, it soon became global. It spread from city to city and had an effect in colleges and universities, such as Baylor, Wake Forest, Emory, and Michigan. The first stirrings of this revival occurred in Canada. Estimates of 1 million each in the United States and Britain and multiplied thousands elsewhere in the world accepted Christ in a veritable Pentecost.

CANADA

Walter and Phoebe Palmer, revival leaders and exponents of perfectionist holiness, held camp meetings among Canadian Methodists in October 1857 in Hamilton, Ontario. Twenty-one were converted on the first day; one hundred responded one Sunday and more than three hundred were converted in all. Others had been renewed or saved in camp meetings that summer in Ontario and Quebec. (See pages 267–268 for more information on the Palmers.)

THE UNITED STATES

Lay Prayer Interdenominational Meetings. The officials of the old North Dutch Reformed Church at Fulton and Williams Streets in New York became concerned when their membership moved out to the suburbs. They engaged Jeremiah C. Lanphier (spelled Lamphier in some sources) as a lay missionary to reach the unchurched in that area. Born in Coxsachie, New York, in 1809, he had been in the mercantile business in that city for twenty years. He accepted Christ in the Broadway Tabernacle of Finney in 1842 and became a good singer, exhorter, and man of prayer.

Lanphier announced a prayer meeting for noon on September 23, 1857. After a half-hour the group gathered for prayer numbered three. The number grew to six on September 30 and to

GLOBAL ANGLO-SAXON
LAY PRAYER REVIVAL

CANADA
Hamilton,
Ontario
Palmers

BRITISH ISLES

SOUTH AFRICA
Murray
Worcester

UNITED STATES

England
Spurgeon
Pastoral revivalists

New York
Lanphier
Lay Prayer
  Ecumenical
  Revival

Ulster
Moore
McQuilkin

Wales
Jones
Morgan

Confederate Army

Planned, professional,
urban, mass revivalistic
evangelism outside the
church
North—Moody
South—Jones

1 8 5 7 – 1 8 9 5

twenty on October 17. The prayer meeting soon became a daily
event and was moved to John Street Methodist Church in February 1858. On March 17 it was held in Burton's Theater for the first
time. Within six months about one thousand were meeting for
prayer at noon in New York. There were ten thousand conversions in New York. The revival spread to Texas and the Ohio
Valley with nearly one hundred thousand converted by May 1858.

A young businessman, John C. Bliss, of the YMCA, began a
noonday prayer meeting on November 23, 1857, in the lecture

room of the Methodist Episcopal Union Church in Philadelphia. On February 3, 1858, it was moved to the larger Jayne's Hall. By March there were twenty-five hundred in that meeting and thirty-five hundred in other meeting places. A tent was purchased for $2,000 and opened for the prayer meeting on May 1, 1858.

A noonday prayer meeting was started in Boston during Finney's meetings in March. About two thousand men were meeting in Metropolitan Hall in Chicago on March 25, 1858. Dwight L. Moody attended all the prayer meetings and was much influenced spiritually; he led the YMCA noonday prayer meetings.

Two hundred ministers and laymen, mostly Presbyterian, met at Pittsburgh on December 1, 1858, for a three-day discussion of the need and means of revival. They appealed to the churches to have a call for renewal read in their pulpits on the first Sunday of the new year and to set aside the first Thursday for fasting and prayer for revival. A similar convention, held in Cincinnati in May 1858, became a prayer meeting for revival. Baptist pastors in New York state had a day of prayer for revival. The revival spread from the middle states to New England, to Texas, and to the Great Lakes. The Methodists and Baptists in the South gained a total of about 200,000 and 100,000 respectively in a three-year period. At Yale over 200 of the 447 students were converted, and in Amherst College nearly all the students accepted Christ in 1858. Half of Oberlin's students were won in prayer meetings. The revival helped to prepare the North spiritually for the crisis of the coming war.

Confederate Army Revival 1862-64. A major revival took place in the Confederate army from 1862 to 1864. Generals Robert E. Lee and Thomas J. "Stonewall" Jackson gave it their full approval. "Log chapels"—regimental churches—were set up for the converts.

Estimates of those won to Christ run from 45,000 to 150,000. In Virginia alone 15,000 to 50,000 were converted, so it is likely that an estimate of over 100,000 is a fairly accurate figure. Revival came through prayer, letters from home, tracts, Bibles, and six hundred godly chaplains and Christian officers. During the war 10,000 Bibles and 50,000 New Testaments, as well as 250,000 Scripture portions, were distributed to soldiers. The Thirty-seventh Alabama Regiment had Sunday meetings and prayer meetings during the week, and of the 1,000 men in the regiment about 250 made decisions to accept Christ. Over 100 responded to the invitation in a revival at Fredericksburg in the spring of 1863. The main revival was in the armies in Virginia, but during 1863 and 1864 the western armies wintering in Dalton, Georgia, experienced a revival in which thousands were converted. Interdenominational prayer meetings in Savannah, Georgia, in February 1862, preceded revival in the army. This awakening helped the South through the horrors and suffering of the war and provided many demobilized soldiers who could, as Christians, better work in the Reconstruction era.

Revivalistic Evangelists. From 1726 to 1846 pastoral or itinerant revivalists had worked in the churches. In the next era, however, professional revivalistic evangelists, using organized, mass, urban, ecumenical meetings outside the churches, engaged in revivalism. Finney had begun this transition in small cities, but it came into flower with Moody's meetings from 1873 to 1875 in England. Attention to the need of Christians to renew their first love occurred in the early part of the meetings, but the main thrust of the meetings was evangelistic. Moody, Sam Jones, and Edward P. Hammond, the leader of children's revival and evangelism, were examples. Spurgeon carried on the pattern of pastoral revival in England.

Edward P. Hammond (1831–1910), was born in Ellington, Connecticut, and raised in Vermont. At seventeen he was sent to school in Southington, where in church at Communion he thought of judgment. A lady in the home where he boarded gave him a copy of James's *Anxious Inquirer* to read. It so convicted him that he began to read the Bible and was converted in 1847. He

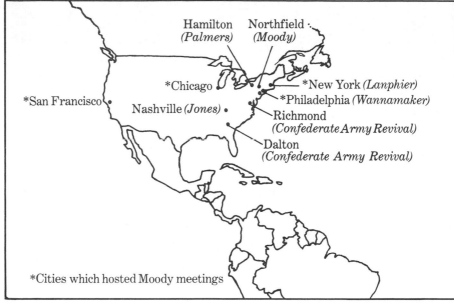

Hamilton   Northfield
(Palmers)   (Moody)

*Chicago
*San Francisco   *New York (Lanphier)
            Nashville (Jones)   *Philadelphia (Wannamaker)
                        Richmond
                        (Confederate Army Revival)
                        Dalton
                        (Confederate Army Revival)

*Cities which hosted Moody meetings

GLOBAL ANGLO-SAXON

received his education at Williams College and Union Theological Seminary in New York.

He wanted to go to Bulgaria as a missionary. In June 1859 he went to Britain and to the Continent, and he saw revival based on prayer and the Word in England, Switzerland, and France.

When he had only five dollars left, he was asked to preach in a church at Musselburgh, six miles from Edinburgh, where he was studying at the Free Church College. He held twenty-one weeks of protracted meetings there, and many were won, including many children. W. L. Alexander, visiting the church, went into the vestry to get his coat and was astonished at the depth and sincerity of the group of children there seeking Christ. Hammond gave children much attention in his meetings and became a children's evangelist. He held services for several weeks in Scotland with as many as ten thousand children in one meeting. In one year he had about seventeen hundred converts. The total of his con-

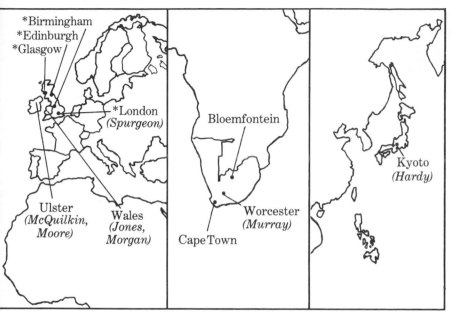

PRAYER   REVIVAL   1857-1895

verts in Canada was estimated to be as high as seven thousand.

When he returned to the United States in July 1861, he featured children's meetings. In Rochester, New York, in 1863 more than one thousand children were converted. His travels took him over eastern Canada and the eastern United States from 1861 to 1866. He preached ruin through sin and redemption through the cross of Christ.

Between 1866 and 1868 he worked in the British Isles, France, Italy, Egypt, and Palestine. There were five thousand children present at one meeting in Spurgeon's Tabernacle. His main desire was to win children to the faith.

Joseph Spiers (1837–1909), from North Wales, took his Sunday school class to Hammond's meetings in London in 1867. Spiers held his first children's meeting in Islington on June 2, 1867. By December of that year 265 children were attending those meetings. During the summer he held children's meetings on the beaches. Later he began to hold five- to ten-day missions for children in churches. Together with Samuel and James Tyler and Tom Bishop, he founded the Children's Special Service Mission on May 30, 1868. He quit his business near the end of that year to give full time to his mission. It has ministered to many children in Britain and her dominions.

Dwight L. Moody (1837–99) was the most prominent of the nineteenth-century mass urban revivalistic evangelists, all of whom owed much to the 1857 prayer revival.

Moody was born in Northfield, Massachusetts, the fifth of nine children of Betsy and Edwin Moody. His father was a lazy, genial brick mason who liked his whiskey. When he died in 1841, his creditor, Richard Colton, left the family impoverished, but Oliver Everett, the pastor of the Unitarian Congregational Church, helped them.

Moody grew up as a fun-loving boy who was fond of practical jokes and bargaining. He had an indifferent elementary education and had trouble with spelling all his life. When his uncles from Boston were with the family on Thanksgiving Day, Moody asked if he could go to Boston. He left home in March 1854 and got a job selling shoes for his Uncle Samuel on condition that he would attend E. N. Kirk's Mount Vernon Congregational Church. Edward Kimball, his Sunday school teacher, visited him at work on April 21, 1855, and persuaded him to accept Christ. The deacons delayed granting him church membership for a year until March 1856 because of his biblical ignorance.

He moved to Chicago in September of 1856 and soon got a job at thirty dollars a week in the Wiswall shoe store. He joined the Plymouth Congregational Church early in May 1857, and took part in the "great revival" of religion in Chicago in that year.

His interest in Sunday school drew him to the Wells Street Mission of the First Baptist Church, where he met Emma A. Revell, who became his wife. Told he could have a class if he recruited the boys, Moody showed up with eight ragamuffins from the street.

He was also a member of the young men's class of the First

Methodist Episcopal Church. Here he met John V. Farwell, a dry goods merchant, who gave him much money and supported his work. Farwell later served on the board of Moody Bible Institute from 1887 to 1908. Another friend and generous giver to his work was Cyrus McCormick, Jr., the son of the inventor of the mechanical reaper.

By 1858 Moody had a Sunday school in an abandoned railway car in the "Sands," a northside slum. He moved his school to an old saloon on Illinois and Dearborn Streets. Mayor Haines then allowed him free use of North Market Hall, but Moody and Farwell had to clear out the remains of the Saturday night dance before using it each Sunday. Lincoln visited the school and spoke in late November 1860. Sunday school attendance grew to fifteen hundred, and Moody built the Illinois Street Church for $24,000. This church, forerunner of the Moody Memorial Church, organized in December 1864 as a congregation.

Earlier in June 1860 a friend dying of consumption wanted Moody to go with him as he tried to win his class of girls to Christ. All of the girls accepted Christ within ten days. This so inspired Moody to winning people to Christ that he became known as "Crazy Moody."

In order to give full time to his Sunday schools, Moody quit his job with Buell, Hill, and Granger in June of 1860. He married Emma Revell on August 22, and she handled his money and wrote most of his letters from that time on.

When the Civil War began, he went to Camp Douglas, where there were more than nine thousand Confederate prisoners. There he held meetings and gave out literature. In the fall of 1861 he went with the Seventy-second Illinois Regiment to Kentucky. He served from then until 1865 as a delegate to the United States Christian Commission. He saw several battles and was under fire at Murfreesboro, Tennessee. He ministered to the physical needs of the men and held temperance and revival meetings.

Moody had left his unpaid job as librarian of the YMCA to do war work. When the YMCA wanted a building after the war, Farwell bought a lot for $3,000, and Moody raised nearly $200,000, with McCormick contributing $10,000, for the building which was named Farwell Hall. Moody served as president of the Chicago YMCA from 1866 to 1869 and held noonday prayer meetings and open-air services. When the hall burned in 1868, Moody raised money for a second building, which was later destroyed by the Great Fire of 1871.

When Emma's asthma grew worse in the spring of 1867, Moody was given the money to take Emma to England for four months. He also wanted to meet Spurgeon, Müller, and George Williams, the founder of the YMCA. While he was in London, he spoke at Exeter Hall and began a noonday prayer meeting in the London YMCA. He met Henry (Harry) Moorhouse (1840–80), who had been a wild drinker and gambler. A friend, Thomas Castle, won him to Christ with Romans 10:9-10 in 1861. Moorhouse began meetings in London and Wales where he would use textboards to draw crowds. In 1879 and 1880 he sold 120,000 Bibles and New Testaments. Moody casually said Moorhouse could preach for him if he came to Chicago.

Moorhouse came to the United States and spoke in Moody's church seven times on John 3:16 in February 1866. It was from Moorhouse that Moody learned to preach the love of God more than law, to study the Bible inductively by organizing all the passages, to build a theme, to give Bible readings, and to read the Bible publicly to the people who were asked to bring their Bibles to meetings. Moody usually had Bible readings in the afternoon in his meetings.

Moody met Ira D. Sankey (1840–1908) at an Indianapolis YMCA convention in the summer of 1870 and enlisted him as a song leader and soloist for his Chicago work. Sankey, born in Pennsylvania, became a Methodist choir director and Sunday school superintendent. After clerking in his father's bank, he served in the Civil War from 1861. For a time after the war he was a tax collector.

Sankey traveled with Moody for twenty-five years after 1870.

DWIGHT L. MOODY (1837-1899) preaching at the Hippodrome in 1876. Though his evangelistic work was based in Chicago, Moody traveled more than a million miles and preached to more than 100 million people. *(Courtesy of the Billy Graham Center Museum)*

From 50 million to 80 million copies of his *Gospel Hymns* and *Sacred Songs and Solos* were sold. Royalties were more than $1,250,000 by 1900. They were given to Moody Church, YMCAs, Moody Bible Institute, and the Northfield Schools. Sankey's songs, "The Ninety and Nine" and "Faith Is the Victory," became trademarks. Sankey pioneered as a revivalistic song leader, soloist, and composer of gospel songs.

About this time Sarah Cooke and Mrs. Hawxhurst told Moody that he needed the "power of the Spirit." In late 1871, after the Great Chicago Fire, he was in New York to raise money for his church and the YMCA; alone in a room near the end of that year, he was "baptized in the Holy Spirit." This, he felt, empowered him for his ministry. Wesley, Whitefield, Finney, and others had had similar experiences.

The Great Fire also taught Moody to give an invitation to go to the inquiry room at every meeting. In a meeting on October 8, 1871, before the fire, he had told the people to think about his message and accept Christ the following week. To his sorrow, many of those present died in the fire.

Exhausted with the raising of money for the YMCA and tabernacle seating 1,400, Moody went to London alone in the summer of 1872. Here he met an unusual man, Henry Varley (1835–1912) who taught him more about inductive Bible study and who told him that "the world has yet to see what God will do with a man fully consecrated to him." Moody determined to be that man. In 1851 Varley had gone to Australia; in 1855 he had set up a butcher shop which prospered. Not satisfied with spare-time Christian work, he sold his business in 1869 and devoted his time to meetings in Australia, South Africa, Canada, the British Isles, the Middle East, and the United States. Here he helped Moody in his Chicago meetings during the World's Fair in 1893.

During this same visit to England, Moody spoke at the Arundel Square Church at the invitation of Pastor Lassy. To his surprise, many people stood at his invitation to accept Christ. When he repeated it, scores went to the inquiry room and in ten days four hundred united with the church. He found later that a bedfast invalid named Marianne Adlard had prayed for revival in the church. This impressed him with the power of prayer in revival.

William Pennefather, founder of what became Mildmay Conference in 1856, with two other men asked Moody to hold meetings in England. Moody and Sankey arrived in Liverpool in June 1873. The two went to York and started a noonday prayer meeting in the YMCA. Several hundred were converted. After three weeks they went in July to Sunderland, where Moorhouse joined them for a "disappointing" five weeks. Real revival came at Newcastle upon Tyne, where Sankey had his first songbook printed. Between 1873 and 1875 the book brought in $35,000 in royalties.

They went to Edinburgh in November 1873 and stayed with the famous theologian, William Blaikie. During the seven weeks of meetings, Moody met Henry Drummond (1851-97). Drummond was impressed as he saw Moody raise a large sum of money for a mission in one day of door-to-door visitation. Drummond worked during the rest of Moody's time in Britain in young men's meetings. About three thousand were converted in Edinburgh and three thousand in Glasgow in the Moody meetings.

Moody stayed with Andrew Bonar in Glasgow during a meeting from February to May 1874. Three thousand Sunday school teachers were present at one meeting. Sankey first used the poem, "The Ninety and Nine," written by Elizabeth Clephane in 1868, in Edinburgh. Revival in Scotland was also exported to Belfast and to Dublin, where he ministered from September to November of 1874.

Moody again held meetings in Manchester, Sheffield, and Birmingham. In Liverpool he first used a portable tabernacle, built for his meetings at a cost of $17,000. From March 9 to July 12, 1875, he was in Islington, London, at the Agricultural Hall, which seated 21,300. Lord Shaftesbury and Prime Minister Gladstone were in some of those meetings. Moody held afternoon Bible readings for Christians and spoke to the wealthy and titled at meetings in Queen's Opera House. C. T. Studd's father, Edward, was converted there in one of 285 meetings with a total attendance of about 1.5 million. Royalties from Sankey's songbook were given to the London Committee and to the completion of Moody's church. The interdenominational emphasis, the use of laymen, and meetings in halls outside of churches impressed the British.

Home at Northfield, to his delight, his mother and brother, Samuel, rose for prayer at a meeting in the Northfield Church. He bought a twelve-acre homestead there with Edward Studd's gift of £500. This became his home.

With his system to revive Christians and save sinners worked out in the period from 1873 to 1875, Moody began to preach in the large cities in the United States. In each city advance agents enlisted Christians to pray, organized house-to-house visitation, and set up a large central meeting place with an adequate inquiry room. After 1878 he would divide a city into sections and minister in each section for a week during his eight to ten weeks there. This method was first tried in Baltimore in October 1878 to give him time to study and prepare fresh sermons. Sankey would sing a solo and lead the hymns for half an hour, then Moody would preach. He was informal and used Scripture with illustrations. Like Hammond, he had special meetings for children.

His first American meeting was in Brooklyn in the fall of 1875. He held meetings from November 21, 1875, to January 16, 1876, in Philadelphia in a freight shed. The shed, renovated for him by John Wanamaker, held over ten thousand people.

John Wanamaker (1838–1922) opened the retail store which made him wealthy in 1861. He promoted Sunday school at Bethany Presbyterian Church, which in fifty years became the world's largest Sunday school. Wanamaker was also the first secretary of the Philadelphia YMCA, serving from 1857 to 1861. Between 1889 and 1893 he was postmaster general of the United States. He continued to back Moody financially even after this meeting. Sad to say, he had a moral lapse which gave Moody much concern in 1899 and may have contributed to Moody's death in that year.

From Philadelphia, where 86,900 attended his meetings with 17,000 "inquirers," Moody went to New York, where 5,000 made decisions in the spring of 1876. Next he went to Chicago for meetings from October 1876 to January 1877, with 6,000 decisions. He then went to Boston where he met Henry Durant, the founder of Wellesley College, who helped Moody financially in founding the Northfield Schools. In 1878 he went to Baltimore, where he spent a week in each section of the city during the eight- to ten-week meeting. This enabled him to have more time for Bible study to keep his sermons fresh. From October 1878 to May 1879 he spoke 270 times.

Moody again visited the British Isles from 1881 to 1884. In Scotland he left behind many converts, new YMCAs, and mission halls financed by offerings from his meetings. He was in London for eight months in 1883 and 1884 in metal tabernacles set up at eleven different sites. Wilfred Grenfell, later a medical missionary in Labrador, was converted as a result of those meetings. Moody's meetings with students at Cambridge were initially disturbed by rowdy students in November 1882, but by the last night two hundred had responded to the invitation. Partly as a result of this meeting, the famous Cambridge Seven (C. T. Studd and six others) went as missionaries to China in February 1885. Moody also had a successful meeting at Oxford.

Moody held his first Northfield conference for pastors and Christian workers in September 1879. In August 1886 he held a conference for 250 students from 100 colleges and universities. At this meeting 100 volunteered as missionaries. In 1888 the Student Volunteer Mission was formally organized to evangelize "the world in this generation." By 1930 this organization had recruited over 20,000 for the mission field.

Like most of the great leaders of revival, Moody became increasingly interested in education. Northfield School was opened for girls in November 1879. Mt. Hermon School for boys was opened in 1881 and named by Hiram Camp, a clockmaker from New Haven whose gift of $25,000 made the school possible. These schools eventually became large secondary private schools. Moody lived at Northfield from May to September each year and held meetings from October to April.

In 1870 he met Emma Dryer, principal of the Illinois State Normal School for Women. In a conversation with her in 1873 he urged her to set up Bible classes for women in Chicago. Between 1883 and 1889 she conducted the May Institute, a short-term Bible school with notable teachers. Through her urging, Moody gave his "gap-men" talk in which he said that laymen trained in the Bible could do city mission work and would occupy a position between the clergy and laity. The Chicago Evangelization Society was formed on February 5, 1887, and on February 12 chartered by the state. Moody raised $250,000 for a building of which Farwell gave $100,000 and McCormick $25,000. The school, now known as Moody Bible Institute, opened in September 26, 1889, with R. A. Torrey as superintendent. It was called the Bible Institute for Home and Foreign Missions until March 1900, when it was given its present name. Nearly 39,000 had graduated by 1966, with over 4,600 alumni serving as missionaries.

In 1891 to 1892 he worked in Britain for the last time. He also took a vacation trip to France, Italy, Egypt, and Palestine in 1892. On the way back to New York in the *Spree* the drive shaft broke and the ship drifted in danger of foundering until the *Huron* took it in tow to Queenston, Ireland, one thousand miles away. During the days of drifting Moody had no fear of death. He comforted those on board by speaking on Psalm 91 and 107:20-23.

Back home he took advantage of the 1893 World's Fair to use his distinct plan to evangelize in several areas of Chicago with the aid of several ministers who ministered in each of the district churches from May 28 to October 31. Nearly 2 million people were in the audiences. He set up the Colportage Association in 1894 to make inexpensive Christian books available. His last meeting was in Kansas City in November 1899. Serious heart trouble struck, and he was home until his death.

He was not excessively emotional as he proclaimed the love of

God to meet the need of man. His theological principles were that man was ruined by the Fall, that he inherited total depravity and committed actual sins, and that man could be redeemed by Christ who was our penal substitute and be regenerated by the Holy Spirit to experience the New Birth.

Because he was irenic and ecumenical, Moody did not engage in polemics. In fact, some were disturbed because he allowed Henry Drummond, an evolutionist, and George Adam Smith, a biblical critic, to minister in the Northfield Conferences.

This five-foot-six, grey-eyed, very stocky layman (he weighed 280 pounds in later years), was very outspoken but was humble enough to apologize if he hurt anyone. At Northfield he indulged his love of farming with ponies, goats, an orchard, and a large garden. But his main interests were revival and evangelism, educational institutions, and societies. He had spoken to multiplied millions in his meetings and 750,000 decisions were recorded. Under God he was able to accomplish much.

Benjamin F. Mills (1857-1916) was born in New Jersey and educated at Lake Forest College, where he became a close friend of J. Wilbur Chapman. Ordained as a Congregational minister in 1878, he held successful pastorates in Vermont, Minnesota, and New York until 1886. For ten years after 1886 he won thousands in services he held in all parts of the United States.

He used his "District Combination Plan" in a meeting in Cleveland in 1891. Cooperative evangelists held meetings in churches in the several districts into which the city was divided, with Mills speaking in a large central hall. He claimed seven thousand made decisions on decision cards which he used in Cleveland. In twelve years he claimed 5 million heard him and two hundred thousand signed cards. He would also have days for prayer in his meetings. After the Cleveland meeting, he used the "District Combination Plan" for several years.

Mills turned to the social gospel in 1899, left his ministry, and even served as pastor of a Unitarian Church in Oakland, California, from 1899 to 1903. But in 1915 he renounced Unitarianism, was received into the Chicago Presbytery, and held smaller meetings.

"The Moody of the South," Samuel Porter Jones (1847–1906), was born in Alabama into a Methodist family of preachers. Four uncles and a grandfather were ministers, but his father was a lawyer and businessman. The family moved to Cartersville, Georgia, where he was educated in an academy. Sherman's Civil War march broke up the family for a time.

Plagued by ulcers, Jones quit school and started drinking to ease the pain. He was admitted to the Georgia Bar in 1869, but his drinking ruined his law practice, and in 1872 his wife left him. He held jobs as a teacher, fireman in a mill, and finally as a drayman. When his dying father asked him to meet him in heaven, he said he would. He accepted Christ and experienced a call to preach.

Jones's first sermon, based on Romans 1:16 and delivered in his grandfather's New Hope Church near Cartersville, won four to Christ. He was admitted to the North Carolina (Methodist) Conference as an itinerant preacher on the poorest Van Wert circuit in March 1872. In three years, giving increased 1200 percent and membership increased at a rate of two hundred a year. He was ordained and elected as an elder in 1876. During the next five years two thousand members were added on other circuits. He also served as an agent for the North Georgia Orphans' Home in Decatur and from 1880 to 1892 raised $20,000 to pay off its debt.

From 1884 to 1895 he held large urban meetings. Most of these were in the South, but he was also involved in large meetings in the West and Midwest. His first union meeting was in 1884 in Memphis, where there were one thousand decisions for Christ.

At a meeting in March 1885 in the Tulip Street Methodist Church in Nashville, 150 made decisions for Christ in a month. Though Jones's grammar was poor, and he attacked church members' sins, he was still able to reach the upper-middle class. He moved to a tent seating three thousand in May 1885, a practice which he kept up until 1892, and soon ten thousand were added to the churches in Nashville.

After meetings in Chicago (three thousand decisions), Boston, and other cities, he returned to Nashville in the fall of 1888. Thomas G. Ryman, president of a riverboat company, was converted in one of the meetings. Ryman developed the idea of a permanent tabernacle instead of a tent for the meetings, and the Union Gospel Tabernacle was built between 1889 and 1892. Eighteen series of meetings were held in it. It later became the "Grand Ole Opry House" of radio and television and is still known as the Ryman Auditorium.

Motivated by the Bible as his authority and by a love for souls, Jones sought to awaken church members to their first love before preaching to sinners. In his practical personal talks in the vernacular, he never ranted or yelled. While he had a special section for blacks, he did at least admit them to his meetings. He is reputed to have had five hundred thousand converts out of a total of 25 million people in his meetings, most of which were in Nashville.

Jones opposed liquor, gambling, and evolution in his meetings. His major thrust for reform until his death was opposing liquor interests, partly because of its ruinous effects on his own life.

Roman Catholic Revivalism. Clarence Walworth, a lawyer who was converted in Rochester in 1842, became a Roman Catholic priest and mission speaker. He told Finney in England that he wanted to do in the Roman Catholic Church what Finney had done in his protracted meetings for Protestants.

Jay P. Dolan in *Catholic Revival* (Notre Dame: University of Notre Dame, 1978) makes a case for revivalism in the Roman Catholic Church but is vague on his definition of conversion. He claims that the Roman Catholic Church helped to shape the "piety of the people" through parish missions. Meetings were held in barns, houses, churches, and courthouses, sometimes for up to four weeks, but usually for one to two weeks. Many sobbed and cried out in these meetings in which the missioners sought to bring people under conviction to confess sin and to commit themselves to Christ. The Jesuit Father Francis Weninger held 170 of these meetings in the Midwest, and Joseph Wessel held 1,000 during his ministry. The missions began in the 1850s and reached a peak in the 1890s.

The Catholic missioners advocated a stern moral code and were willing to preach the dangers of hell. They opposed drink and immorality. Catholic revivals may have differed from Protestant revivals by more stress on sacramental revivalism, and, in some cases, conversion to the church instead of to Christ.

The later equivalent to the movement since 1967 is the charismatic awakening in the Roman Catholic Church.

REVIVAL IN GREAT BRITAIN

Presbyterians in Ulster. While Lanphier was holding his prayer meetings in New York in September 1857, another group was meeting for prayer in Ulster. Mrs. Colville, a Baptist missionary from Newcastle upon Tyne, went to Ballymena to visit from house to house and do personal work. In November 1856 she visited a Miss Brown. There she met James McQuilkin, a linen warehouse worker who raised fighting cocks. McQuilkin asked her if she was a Calvinist. She replied, "You have never known the Lord Jesus Christ," and spoke of his need of the New Birth. He was converted a little later in Antrim under the preaching of William Campbell, a Methodist. John H. Moore, the minister in McQuilkin's hometown in Connor parish for twenty-two years, told him to "do something more for God," such as reading the Bible to others. Inspired to action by Bible reading and Müller's life, McQuilkin asked the others whom he had won to Christ—John Wallace, Jeremiah Meneeley, and Robert Carlisle—to meet with him for prayer and Bible study in September 1857. They met in the Old School House near Kells, prayed for revival, and conducted a Sunday school at Tannybrake. The prayer meeting grew to about fifty.

News of the New York meetings reached Ulster, and Moore

told his people of these meetings. The 1858 assembly of the Irish Presbyterian Church sent William Gibson and William McClure to the United States to observe and report on these prayer meetings. When they reported later, the assembly sent out a pastoral letter urging prayer for revival.

Revival began with the conversion of a young man in Connor in December 1857. More than sixteen were saved by May 1858. Prayer meetings were held each night. Six of the nine saloons were soon closed and the remaining three sold less liquor than before the revival.

Revival spread to Ahoghill in mid-March 1858, after prayer meetings and the testimony of one of the Connor converts, Samuel Campbell. The church proved to be too small, and three thousand stood in the street in the rain to hear Meneeley speak. People fell to their knees in the mud.

Testimony in Belfast touched off revival there in May and on June 19, 1859, an open-air prayer meeting of twenty-five thousand was held in the Botanic Gardens until 3:30 A.M. The crowd broke into groups of five hundred to one thousand to pray. Ten thousand were won in Belfast.

J. H. Moore held open-air meetings in Ballymena near Ahoghill in June 1858, and by 1859 there were over 300 converts and 2,000 in prayer meetings. In June 1859, Connor converts spoke in Coleraine and won an additional 150 converts. This lay prayer revival, peaking in 1859, won 100,000 in Ulster.

Chacteristics of the revival included prayer, Bible reading, lay witnessing and preaching, singing of great hymns (such as "Just As I Am" and "All Hail the Power"), and ecumenicity. Methodists and Anglicans united with Presbyterians. Deep conviction of sin with prostrations, loss of speech or sight, and trances or visions often preceded conversion. Counseling sessions and inquiry rooms were used by ministers to care for the converts. Many witnesses testified to the large number of young people who were converted.

Revival in Wales in the Welsh Calvinistic Methodist Church.
Trevecca students had experienced revival in the winter of
1857–58. News of Lanphier's prayer meetings in New York
reached Wales in 1858. Prayer meetings for revival multiplied and
in the two years of 1859 and 1860 over 100,000 accepted Christ.
This was about one-tenth of the population.

Humphrey R. Jones (1832–95) was born near Aberystwyth.
While under conviction for seventeen months, he began preaching
in Wales, and twelve were saved in one place and eight in another.
He was converted and followed his parents to America in 1854. He
was ordained in the Methodist Episcopal Church and preached to
the Welsh in the United States. His itinerant preaching of revival
in 1857 and 1858 was done mostly in Wisconsin. Twenty-one were
saved in his first meeting at Cambria. He returned to Cardiganshire, Wales, in the summer of 1858 to hold prayer and revival
meetings.

David Morgan (1814–88), a Welsh carpenter, was converted in
1836 and began to preach in 1841. The Welsh Calvinistic Methodist Church ordained him in May 1857. After two preaching tours
in North Wales, he was called to Ysbytty Ystwyth in March 1858.
On September 30, 1858, he heard Humphrey Jones, who by that
time had about 440 converts in seven places. Morgan talked with
Jones and prayed with him on October 2, 1858. Both were filled by
spiritual power about 4:00 A.M. in an enduement of the Holy
Spirit. Morgan announced nightly prayer meetings at his church,
and the two preachers had 200 converts in a population of 1,000
within a few weeks. One Saturday night, when the two were on
their way home, they obtained permission from the landlords of
three bars, the Tremble, Mason's Arches, and Black Lion, to pray.
All the patrons left.

In Aberystwyth in December 1858, Humphrey Jones, worn out
with preaching and prayer meetings, said that only the Bible and
prayer were to be used in the Queen Street Wesley Chapel, and
that the Holy Spirit would come on a certain night. When the
Spirit did not come, Jones retired in shame to years of seclusion

until he returned to Chilton, Wisconsin, in 1871.

David Morgan spoke in Llwyn in February 1858, and had two hundred decisions. He itinerated extensively in 1859 and 1860 and by the end of 1859 revival spread all over Cardiganshire and then all over Wales and Anglesey. In one town 400 were added to the church. Nearly 110,000 (of whom 80 percent were nonconformists) were converted in all of Wales. Jones was the spark and Morgan the flame of the revival. Morgan talked individually to converts, set up catechumenal meetings for instruction, and promoted prayer for revival. Twenty thousand attended one open-air prayer meeting at Llangleitho. Unlike the Ulster awakening, which was led by laymen, the Welsh awakening was led by clergymen.

Revival in Scotland. Newspaper reports of the American lay prayer revival and accounts of the Ulster and Welsh awakenings led people to pray for revival in Scotland. Reginald Radcliffe, an English evangelist, came to Aberdeen in November 1858, and a five-month revival began with earnest prayer and biblical preaching. Edward P. Hammond had meetings, especially with children, in Annan. The revival spread all over northern Scotland. A revival in Glasgow led to awakening all over southern Scotland through daily prayer meetings.

Revivalistic Evangelists in England. The revival reached England in the late summer of 1859. The Palmers and Finney were in England at this time. Prayer meetings here too were the key to revival which brought over four hundred thousand into the churches, but leading preachers of revival also were active in renewal.

Brownlow North (1810–75), born into a Scottish noble family, was a graduate of Magdalen College, Oxford. Converted in 1854, he was led by the Duchess of Gordon into the ministry. He ministered ably all over the British Isles.

Reginald Weaver (1827–96), an ungodly, immoral boxer, had a praying mother. He was converted in 1857, left the coal mines, and began itinerant work as a Primitive Methodist preacher.

Henry Moorhouse, who helped Moody, was saved through Weaver's ministry.

Duncan Matheson (1824–69), a stonemason, was won to Christ in 1846 and was given £00 by the Duchess of Gordon to do mission work. Between 1854 and 1857 he ministered to soldiers in the Crimea. After the war he traveled in Wales from his home in Aberdeen.

Charles Haddon Spurgeon (1834–92), now known to history as the "Prince of Preachers," experienced years of perpetual revival in his Metropolitan Tabernacle. Born in Essex, he was tutored spiritually by his grandfather, James Spurgeon, with whom he lived from 1835 to 1840. He later became an assistant in a school. He came under conviction and went to a Primitive Methodist Chapel in Colchester on January 6, 1850. A local preacher spoke to a sparse audience on Isaiah 45:22, pointed to Spurgeon, and said, "Young man, look to Jesus Christ." Spurgeon accepted Christ and was persuaded by the Baptist principal of his school to be baptized by immersion.

Spurgeon was elected pastor of Waterbeach Church near Cambridge some time later. After some years there he was called to New Park Street Chapel in London in February 1854. The congregation grew so large that in February 1855 he moved to Exeter Hall. When that proved to be too small, he moved to Royal Gardens Surrey Music Hall in October 1856. On October 19, 1856, someone yelled "Fire!" in the hall, and the crowd of twelve thousand panicked. Seven were killed and twenty injured. In sorrow Spurgeon moved to the Crystal Palace in December 1857, and later to the Agricultural Hall at Islington.

His congregation built the Metropolitan Tabernacle, seating about six thousand and costing £31,000. It opened in 1861 and Spurgeon baptized about fifteen thousand in it. He knew most of the five thousand members by name.

In addition to his duties as pastor, Spurgeon started the Pastors' College in a home in the mid-fifties. A total of 1,045 ministers had been trained in it by 1903. It continues today as Spurgeon's College. The Stockwell Orphanage, set up on the family cottage plan, was another of his works. It had five hundred children in 1867.

The Metropolitan Tabernacle Colporteurs was founded by Spurgeon. Between 1873 and 1878 his colporteurs sold £8,276 worth of religious literature. *The Sword and Trowel* carried his sermons for years. They were finally combined in *The Metropolitan Pulpit* (49 volumes, 1856-1904). His *Treasury of David* (7 volumes, 1870-75) was a masterly devotional outline and exposition of each of the Psalms. His *Morning and Evening* was a popular compilation of his devotional writings.

Spurgeon, an evangelical Calvinist who loved the writings of the seventeenth-century Puritans, was a master of preaching. His clear voice, his sense of humor, and his mastery of the English language were allied with a grasp of Scripture. The result was some of the noblest preaching of any age. Throughout his years in the pastorate he looked upon revival as a "reawakening of religious fervor" brought about by the Holy Spirit. His ministry exemplified this.

Hay Aitken (1841-1927), an Anglican, was born in Liverpool and educated at Wadham College, Oxford, which granted him an M.A. in 1857. He began religious work at the age of seventeen in Scotland and worked with William Pennefather at the Mildmay Conference for five years. Between 1875 and 1900 he conducted many missions in England, the United States, and Canada. He preached about 22,000 sermons. Many found renewal and salvation through his missions.

This revival, which began in Ulster in 1857, brought an estimated 1 million to Christ, with 100,000 in Wales, 300,000 in Scotland, and 400,000 in England. This million amounted to about 3 or 4 percent of the population. As in America, the key was prayer by the laity. The Salvation Army, Keswick conventions, and many reform organizations were a result of these meetings.

AFRICA

The most noted revival in Africa came in Worcester, South Africa, under Andrew Murray (1828–1917) in 1860. His Scottish father had gone to minister in South Africa.

Andrew, who was born in Graaff Reinet, was sent with his older brother, John, to Scotland in 1838 for their education. He went to grammar school and learned Latin in the era of James Burns's revivals in Kilsyth and Dundee. He even carried Burns's Bible and cloak to church. Murray finally earned his M.A. at Marischal College, Edinburgh. He and his brother studied theology at Utrecht for three years.

He was converted because of *Réveil* influences. The brothers became members of the *Sechor Dabar* ("Remember the Word") group in 1843. They were mainly responsible for founding Eltheto, a missionary society meeting bimonthly. Andrew criticized lectures in theology at Utrecht as being such that one could not get anything from them. Student morals were also deplorable. The boys graduated in 1848, and on May 9, Andrew was ordained.

They were back at Cape Town by November 1848. Andrew was sent to Bloemfontein in 1849 and served English and Dutch settlers. He did much itinerant preaching to isolated farmers and administered baptism and Communion.

He returned to England early in 1854 to plead with the British government not to give up control of the Transvaal. While there he spoke in London, Scotland, and the Netherlands. Back home in Africa by 1855, he helped set up Grey College at Bloemfontein and became its rector.

Near the end of 1859 Murray moved to Worcester where he ministered from 1860 until 1864. A conference of 374 ministers was called in Worcester in April 1860 to consider missions, revival, and education. Andrew's prayer in the conference was so powerful that many thought that it signaled the beginning of the Worcester revival.

The revival began in September with sixty young people in a prayer meeting. A young Fingo girl's earnest prayer was followed by all the people praying. Murray could not stop them when he tried. Many were revived and saved. The conference and this event led to prayer meetings and consequent revival in the Dutch Reformed churches.

From 1864 to 1871 Murray was senior pastor of churches in Cape Town with five thousand adherents and three thousand communicants. From there he went to Wellington, where he served from 1871 to 1906.

In 1874 he opened a ladies' Huguenot Seminary at Wellington, modeled after that in Mount Holyoke in the United States. He raised £2,300 for it. A Mission Training Institute was set up by him in the fall of 1871 at Wellington. About 145 missionaries were trained in it for the Dutch Reformed Church. When he went to the United States in 1871 to find teachers for his Huguenot Seminary, he saw revival under Moody's labor.

By 1876 he had experienced the Keswick type of sanctification and opened up a South African Keswick, which he led from 1889 to 1917. He was speaker at the Keswick in England in 1895.

Trouble with his throat from 1879 to 1882 drove him to Europe for medical help. This experience led him to practice prayer for healing of himself and others by faith.

His first English book, *Abide in Christ,* was published in 1882 and sold over forty thousand copies in four years. During six periods as leader of the synod he fought liberalism in the Dutch churches. He urged missions to the African people. Between 1858 and 1895 he wrote many books to help Transvaal farmers in areas where there were no churches.

Between 1879 and 1891 he held meetings in all parts of South Africa. These meetings revived the churches and brought in the unconverted. He cooperated in meetings with Henry Varley, Gypsy Smith (the 1906 Peace Mission), and F. B. Meyer when they visited South Africa.

Murray went to Europe, Britain, and the United States in 1895. He was a featured speaker at Exeter Hall, the Mildmay Conference, and Keswick. Moody had him speak to four hundred at the

Northfield Conference. His contributions to revival and the deeper life affected South Africa and the entire English-speaking world.

Madagascar, off the coast of southern Africa, also experienced revival in this era. Radama, the ruler, desiring education for his people, permitted David Jones to open a palace school in 1819 and David Griffith another in 1820. Unfortunately, they ignored local customs. When Radama died in 1828, Queen Ranavalona persecuted the church, and between 1835 and 1861 hundreds were cruelly executed. The queen's sons Ramonga and Rakatsehen secretly became Christians. When the queen died in 1861, they readmitted missionaries of the London Missionary Society. A student revival from 1887 to 1893 grew out of prayer meetings and spread through the island from 1893 to 1895.

ASIA

Mention should be made of the relation of revival to education in Japan. In 1871 Captain Jones opened Kunamoto School—with studies in western civilization and the Bible as well as mathematics, geography, and physics. Nearly all the senior class accepted Christ in classes in his home. In January 1876, thirty-five men pledged themselves in a declaration drawn up on Mount Hanaoka to preach the gospel in Japan, even at the cost of their lives. They became known as the Kunamoto Band.

Neesima (Shimeta) Hardy (1843–90), who came to the United States in a ship owned by Alphaeus Hardy, was befriended by Hardy and took his name. Hardy educated him at Phillips Academy, Amherst College, and Andover Seminary. Neesima traveled in Europe with a Japanese embassy in 1872 and 1873 to study education. He was ordained in 1874 in Mt. Vernon Church in Boston.

When he went back to Japan, he baptized twenty-seven in 1880 and four hundred in 1881. He founded Doshisha University at Kyoto in 1875. It was the center of an 1885 revival in which two hundred students were converted and spread the revival all over Japan. Neesima believed that individual reform by conversion must precede social reform.

Indonesia, under Dutch rule in the nineteenth century, enjoyed revivals led by Dutch missionaries. The Batak Church in Sumatra became self-supporting, self-propagating, and self-governing under the leadership of Ludwig I. Nommensen (1834–1918). He was trained in the Rhine Mission School and went to Sumatra in 1826. After some of the chiefs were converted, a peoples' revival with lay witness developed until by 1911 the church grew to over 100,000. The Bible was related to the Batak culture by the indigenous church.

Most of the revivals described in this chapter came about because laymen prayed.

6. GLOBAL AWAKENING, 1900-1945

WHEN revival in the twentieth century is discussed, most people think of the Welsh revival under Evan Roberts. Actually, the Pentecostal revival which began in 1900 should have the priority. This movement became worldwide. Other revivals occurred later in Asia and Africa.

THE UNITED STATES

The Pentecostal Awakening, 1901. This movement was evangelical in upholding the Reformation doctrines of biblical authority, depravity, salvation by faith, the priesthood of believers, and belief in the premillennial Second Coming of Christ. Divine healing, and a separate baptism of the Holy Spirit—with speaking in tongues as the evidence of the baptism—set them apart doctrinally. Some were influenced by the Calvinistic Princeton theology, but more were Arminian. Their church polity was congregational. Many of the leaders came out of the holiness churches.

Through storefront churches they reached the farmers and workers. Itinerant evangelists carried the message throughout

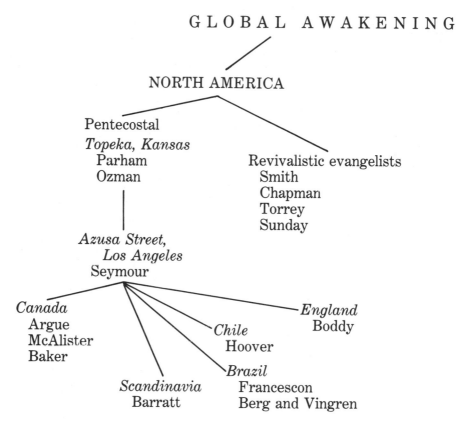

the country. Noisy meetings, money-seeking leaders, and adherents with professions of faith but low morals tended to discredit the movement in its early stages.

In 1960 about 10 million people held Pentecostal views throughout the world. There were 2.3 million in the United States, 700,000 in Chile, and over 800,000 in Brazil.

The earliest manifestations of this awakening can be traced to Charles F. Parham (1873-1929), who was born in Muscatine, Iowa. He was a sickly boy and spent much time reading the Bible. His conversion came at the age of thirteen under Mr. Lippard of the Congregational Church. While he was at Southwestern College in Winfield, Kansas, he held services at different churches.

He was ordained at the age of nineteen in the Methodist Episcopal Church and called to Eudora, Kansas, for two years. He

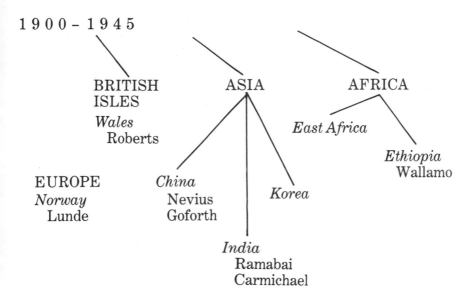

then moved from Eudora to Linwood. From 1894 to 1899 he was a nondenominational evangelist. He also opened a healing home in Topeka, Kansas, and visited Dowie in Zion, Illinois, and A. B. Simpson at Nyack. Both of these men practiced divine healing.

In October 1900 he opened a Bible school in an old mansion called "Stone's Folly" in Topeka, Kansas. The Bible was the only text, continuous prayer was maintained in the tower, and the students took services on the weekends.

When Parham went away for a three-day trip late in 1900, he asked the students to study the biblical evidence for the baptism of the Holy Spirit. All agreed that it was speaking in tongues. On January 1, 1901, at 11:00 A.M. Agnes Ozman, later Mrs. N. O. LaBerge, asked them to lay hands on her. She spoke in tongues and was unable to speak English for three days. Parham and twelve others also had the same experience later.

When the building was sold, Parham moved his school to Kansas City. He then went on to El Dorado where Mrs. Mary A. Arthur's eyes were healed. He then moved in 1903 to the Arthur home in Galena, Kansas, where he held meetings.

Walter Oyler of Orchard, Texas, who spoke in tongues in Galena, asked Parham to preach in Orchard. He did so and went on to Houston, Texas, in 1905. His followers claimed that twenty-five thousand were brought under revival influence in the winter of 1905–06.

He opened a Bible school in Houston in December 1905. W. J. Seymour (d. 1923), a one-eyed black man, attended and later carried this message to Los Angeles.

Parham continued to preach all over the United States, mostly in the South and Southwest. Between 1927 and 1929 he traveled in Italy, Greece, Egypt, and Palestine. At the time of his death he was credited with 200,000 conversions.

Neeley Terry, a black woman from a Nazarene church in Los Angeles, spoke in tongues at Houston and invited Seymour to Los Angeles. He went to her church as an associate pastor, working with Julia Hutchins, who had begun the church as a Nazarene mission. When she locked Seymour out of the church for his views on Acts 2:4, Richard and Ruth Asberry invited him to their home. On April 9, 1906, seven people spoke in tongues. The group had secured an old frame Methodist church building on Azusa Street by April 19, 1906. Frank Bartleman, a newspaperman present in the early period, said Seymour sat behind two shoe boxes and kept his head in the top one in prayer.

When word of the Azusa Street meetings spread, people came from great distances. William H. Durham, pastor of the North Avenue Mission in Chicago, visited Azusa Street and spoke in tongues on March 2, 1907. He carried the message back to Chicago. It was in his church that Eudorus N. Bell, a later leader in the Assemblies of God, and A. H. Argue, a real estate dealer from Winnipeg, each spoke in tongues. Bell became a leader in the organization of the Assemblies of God in April 1914 at Hot Springs, Arkansas.

R. E. McAlister, a holiness preacher, also spoke in tongues. The Pentecostal Assemblies of Canada was organized in 1919 on foundations laid by McAlister in Ottawa, Ontario, C. E. Baker in Montreal, Quebec, and A. H. Argue in Winnipeg, Manitoba. J. Eustace Purdie (1800–1977), an Anglican minister in Saskatoon, became head of the Assemblies' Bible school. Through his students, the Canadian movement had a more Calvinistic tone.

Aimee Semple McPherson (1890–1944), who was born in Ontario, created a strong Pentecostal organization. She was converted in meetings held by the Hebdens in Los Angeles and became a missionary to Hong Kong in 1910. She returned to the United States when her first husband died in 1911. From 1918 to 1923 she crisscrossed the United States several times in revival meetings. She organized her International Church of the Foursquare Gospel and incorporated it in 1927. (The major points of the "foursquare gospel" were Christ as Savior and Healer, baptism of the Holy Spirit, speaking in tongues, and the Second Coming.) Angelus Temple, dedicated in 1923, was the center of the movement. On February 6, 1924, she broadcast her first radio message over KFSG, thus becoming the first Pentecostal revivalist to use the electronic media on a wide scale.

Soon the Pentecostal movement spread beyond North America. Thomas B. Barratt (1862–1940) was taken from Cornwall to Norway by his parents. A good musician, he studied under the composer Edvard Grieg. He opened the Methodist Central City Mission in 1902 and went to the United States the same year to raise funds for it. He spoke in tongues in a prayer meeting in New York in mid-November 1906. His work in Norway grew, and in 1916 he left the Methodists and founded the Filadelfia Church which soon had over two thousand members.

Lewi Pethrus of Sweden read of the Oslo revival in newspapers. When he went to Oslo in 1907, he spoke in tongues. He founded the Filadelfia Church in Stockholm which numbered over six

GLOBAL AWAKENING

thousand members after World War II. By 1962 there were 115,000 Pentecostal adherents in sixty churches in Sweden.

Barratt went to Denmark; there the conversion of Anna Larsen, a famous actress, publicized his work. He also visited Finland in 1911, and a work sprung up there in 1912. Jonathan Paul (1853–1931) of Germany visited Oslo and in March 1907 spoke in tongues. He became the pioneer of the German Pentecostal movement.

Alexander A. Boddy of All Saints' Church in Sunderland visited Barratt's church in Oslo in March 1907 and spoke in tongues. He carried the Pentecostal message back to his church where he had "waiting" meetings, called "tarrying" meetings in the United States and Canada. A convention at Sunderland spread the message all over England.

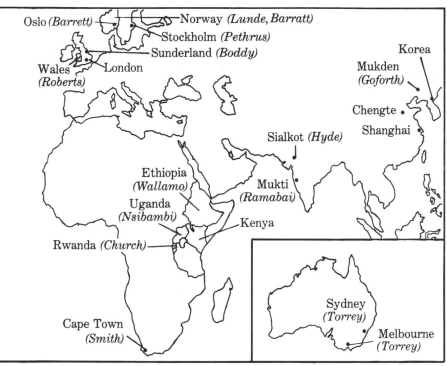

Oslo *(Barrett)* ——— Norway *(Lunde, Barratt)*
——— Stockholm *(Pethrus)*
——— Sunderland *(Boddy)*
Korea
Wales ——— London
(Roberts)
Mukden
(Goforth)
Chengte •
Sialkot *(Hyde)*
Shanghai •
Ethiopia
(Wallamo)
Mukti
(Ramabai)
Uganda
(Nsibambi)
Kenya
Rwanda *(Church)* ———
Cape Town
(Smith)
Sydney
(Torrey)
Melbourne
(Torrey)

1900 – 1945

George Jeffreys, who was saved in the Welsh revival of 1904, founded the Elim Pentecostal Churches in 1918. His churches spread from Wales to Scotland and Ireland. His brother Stephen worked with him for a time in the Elim group and started their work in Wales before he joined the English Assemblies of God. Faith healings helped to publicize the Elim churches, and Bible schools provided workers.

Pandita Ramabai of Mukti, India, held daily prayer meetings in 1905 in her orphans' and widows' home. Many of the girls spoke in tongues. Minnie Abrams, her helper from Chicago, sent a pamphlet describing the movement to Mrs. W. C. Hoover, her former Bible school classmate then in Chile, and it helped to start a similar church there. (Ramabai's role in Asian revival is discussed in more detail on pages 198–199.)

A. G. Gaus and Nettie Moonau, who had spoken in tongues in the Azusa Street Mission, spread the message to China in the summer and fall of 1908. This occurred in a Christian and Missionary Alliance School.

Willis G. Hoover (1858–1936), a Methodist missionary in Chile from 1893, wrote to T. B. Barratt to find out more about the work of the Holy Spirit. His wife heard of the tongues-speaking in India through Minnie Abrams. People had begun to speak in tongues in Hoover's Methodist church in Valparaiso by 1909. He and 4,000 others left the Methodist Church in April 1909, and founded the Methodist Pentecostal Church of Chile. Pentecostals in Chile soon numbered 500,000, more than 8 percent of the population.

Early in 1910 Louis Francescon, an Italian who had spoken in tongues in Durham's church, went to Sao Paulo in Brazil where there were well over a million Italians. By 1978 his followers numbered over 500,000 and in 1961 about 620,000. The Assemblies of God of Brazil now claim to have about 3.8 million adult members.

David Berg and Gunnar Vingren felt called to Pará, Brazil. They had to get an atlas from the library to locate the state. They went to Pará in 1910 and formed the Brazilian Assemblies of God. In 1982 there were about 6 million baptized followers.

The first world Pentecostal Conference was held in Zurich, Switzerland, in 1947. Conferences have been held every three years since then to coordinate and inspire work throughout the world.

Initially, Pentecostalism appealed mainly to blue-collar workers. David duPlessis, a South African Pentecostal, has helped to carry the Pentecostal position into ecumenical circles and the mainline churches, and today there are Pentecostals from all classes of society.

Revivalistic Evangelists. Though J. Wilbur Chapman and Gypsy Smith began their work before 1900, they made their greatest contribution after 1900. R. A. Torrey and Billy Sunday were a major part of revival in this century.

Rodney (Gypsy) Smith (1860–1947) was born in a gypsy tent in England. His father, Cornelius, and his two brothers wanted to be Christians. A landlady in a beer shop gave them a copy of *Pilgrim's Progress*, which a bystander read to them. When Cornelius went to a Primitive Methodist chapel at Cambridge, Henry Gunn's sermon convicted him. Through a dream of Christ and help in Henry Varley's Latimer Road Mission Hall, Cornelius and Gypsy's brother Bartholomew were converted. Thirteen other gypsies were saved the next morning. Later their brother Woodstock was converted. William Booth encouraged the brothers in the ministry.

Rodney was converted in a Primitive Methodist chapel in Cambridge in November 1876 and soon learned to read and write. When William Booth heard him sing and pray in a meeting in June 1877, he asked him to become an evangelist in the Salvation Army. He became a captain and was sent to Hull. He soon had large crowds in a former icehouse and five hundred in a prayer meeting before the Sunday services. In December 1881 he went to Hanley, where he held meetings in a former circus building and in the open air. He was successful again. Over five thousand were in his last open-air meeting. Booth peremptorily dismissed him in 1882 for accepting a gold watch, which the people had given him because of their love for him.

The Gospel Army gave Smith £300 a year to hold meetings from 1883 to 1886. Back at Hanley his crowds were more than four thousand. G. Campbell Morgan's support, Matthew Henry's *Commentary*, and Finney's *Lectures on Revival* helped him. From 1886 to 1889 he held missions in churches until his throat troubled him so that he had to rest nine months.

B. F. Byrom, a cotton manufacturer, guaranteed Smith against financial loss if he would go to the United States. In January 1889 he held meetings in Brooklyn for a Methodist Episcopal church;

over four hundred were won. One Sunday, Ira Sankey took him for a drive. Smith reminded Sankey that Sankey had put his hand on his head as a gypsy boy and said, "The Lord make a preacher of you, my boy." Smith was impressed with the American emphasis on prayer in meetings in Trenton, Philadelphia, and Cincinnati.

After his return to England he made his home in Manchester for twelve years and served as the National Council of Free Churches' evangelist. He was in America for the second time in 1891 and spoke at the Ocean Grove Camp Meeting of the Methodists. Back in Edinburgh in 1892 he had 150 converts.

When B. F. Byrom bought him an around-the-world ticket in 1894, he went to Australia, where he had many conversions in meetings in Melbourne and Sydney. He went home by way of the United States. By 1936 he had visited the United States twenty-seven times.

Smith's South African trip in 1904, after the Boer War, was called a "Peace Mission." When he issued an invitation in Cape Town and Johannesburg, 8,000 responded in each city. There were over 16,000 converts in the crowds totalling 300,000 in South Africa.

After his 1906 meeting in Portland, Maine, he used decision cards and personal workers in his inquiry room after the altar call. During World War I he ministered to the soldiers at the front line under the auspices of the YMCA. He continued to conduct revival meetings until shortly before his death.

J. Wilbur Chapman (1859–1918) helped to bring revival to Presbyterians in the United States. Chapman was born in Richmond, Indiana, and drove a milk wagon as an eleven-year-old. Through the efforts of Mrs. C. C. Binkley, his Sunday school teacher and the wife of a state senator, he was saved in September 1876 and joined the Presbyterian church. In 1879 he graduated from Lake Forest College, where B. F. Mills was his classmate and friend, and in 1882 he graduated from Lane Seminary. Moody helped him to have assurance of his salvation in 1877 in a meeting in which he used John 5:24.

Ordained in 1881, Chapman served a two-point pastorate in the corner of Ohio and Indiana with much success. Through Mills he became pastor of a Dutch Reformed church in Schuylerville, New York, from 1883 to 1885. When he went to First Dutch Reformed Church in Albany, he made use of gospel songs and an inquiry room in that staid church.

Through the counsel of F. B. Meyer and Moody, Chapman yielded to an infilling of the Holy Spirit in 1886, when he visited Northfield. In 1895 he organized and became director of the Winona Lake Conference for fourteen years and made his home there from 1902 to 1916. He also organized conferences at Montreat, North Carolina, and Stonybrook, Long Island.

In 1890 he was called to Wanamaker's Bethany Church in Philadelphia and was pastor there from 1890 to 1892 and from 1896 to 1899. In a month-long meeting there, 440 were added to the church, and the people in the prayer meeting numbered 4,000. In 1891 he worked with B. Fay Mills in Simultaneous Evangelistic Campaigns in Cleveland and Cincinnati. The cities were divided into districts, with several preachers speaking in different sections of the city and the main evangelist in a large central hall. He also worked with Moody at the 1893 World's Fair meetings.

Between 1892 and 1895 he served as an evangelist. After his second pastorate in Bethany he served at Fourth Presbyterian Church in New York City from 1899 to 1902; 650 were added to the church. He was one of those who helped to develop the Fourteen Articles of the Niagara Conference.

Chapman supervised more than fifty evangelists when he was appointed corresponding secretary of the General Assembly Committee on Evangelism of the Presbyterian Church in the fall of 1901. He later became its general secretary.

Between 1908 and 1918 Charles M. Alexander helped him as a song leader in major urban meetings. John H. Converse of the Baldwin Locomotive Works supported him in the Simultaneous Evangelistic Campaigns. His Simultaneous Campaign in Philadelphia in March and April of 1908 brought 8,000 converts into the churches. His most successful meetings of this type were in Boston in January and February of 1909. There were 7,000 decisions with 720,000 attending the meetings with 30 speakers and 1,000 personal workers. He went back to the centralized meeting in 1909.

Thousands were converted in Chapman's 1909 tour to the Far East and Australia. Two thousand made decisions in Swansea, Wales, in 1911. Another 2,000 were saved in Auckland, New Zealand, in a second tour to Australia in 1912–13.

Chapman usually gave an altar call and spoke to and shook hands with the converts before they went to the inquiry room where personal workers awaited. When he was fifty-three, he had preached about 50,000 sermons to 60 million people. Billy Sunday was his advance man from 1893 to 1895 and began his work with sermons loaned to him by Chapman.

R. A. Torrey (1856–1928) was a reckless, strong, sports- and horse-loving but bashful boy who became a revival leader, educator, pastor, and author. He was born in Hoboken, New Jersey, to a banker who won and lost two fortunes. He received his education at Yale University, where he was converted in 1874, and in its divinity school. Here he met Moody, who, after speaking in chapel, was asked by the men to tell him how to do personal work.

Between 1872 and 1878, when he received ordination, he served as pastor of the Garrettsville Congregational Church. Here he sponsored a union revival which increased the church membership in several churches. For a year he studied in Leipzig and Erlangen Universities. Here he learned to take the Bible by faith and not worry about critical problems.

From 1883 to 1889 he served a Congregational church in Minneapolis and become superintendent of a city mission in 1886. Here he experienced an infilling of the Holy Spirit which cured his shyness; he learned to live by faith and "pray through."

In 1889 Moody called Torrey to be superintendent of the Bible Institute in Chicago, a position he held until 1908. He also served as pastor of the Chicago Avenue Church, now Moody Church, from 1893 to 1905. Here two thousand were added to the church in eight years and as many as two thousand attended his Saturday class on the International Sunday School Lessons.

In January 1898, at the end of a week of prayer at Moody Church, Torrey, teachers, and managers of the institute began to pray each Saturday evening at the institute for revival. This continued for three years. Soon four hundred were praying each Saturday evening. A smaller group remained after the conclusion of the main meeting and often continued until 2:00 A.M. Torrey was impressed in one meeting to ask God to use him to lead a world revival.

Shortly after that, two men from Australia, Doctor Warren and G. P. Barber, whose son was a student at Moody, arrived in Chicago from Britain, where they had gone to search for an able evangelist to go to Australia. They felt led to ask Torrey to go to Australia with his song leader, Charles M. Alexander (1867–1920). From 1902 to 1905 Alexander worked with Torrey as an excellent personal worker as well as song leader.

On his way to Australia, Torrey stopped in Japan, where 131 students accepted Christ. Mrs. Warren had organized 2,100 prayer circles for the simultaneous mission in Melbourne. She told of this at Keswick in England in July 1902. About 30,000 persons in prayer circles prayed over several years for Torrey's meetings. Alexander popularized the theme song of the meetings, the "Glory Song," in Melbourne. It became the trademark for that and later meetings. Over 8,600 responded to the invitation in Melbourne. In Bendigo, Robert Harkness joined them as a pianist. About 20,000 were converted in Australasia in three months.

On his return trip, Torrey addressed 400 missionaries at their decennial conference in India. In the British Isles for three years, he had over 70,000 decisions. He preached the power of the blood of the atonement to save, the power of prayer, and the power of the Holy Spirit. A tabernacle to seat 12,500 was built for him in

Liverpool at a cost of $15,000. Ten thousand were saved in two series of meetings there. Alexander met and married Helen Cadbury of the cocoa-making family in July 1904. Torrey held 202 meetings in London with about 1,115,000 in attendance, of whom 17,000 were saved. His instructions to converts were to keep looking to Jesus on the cross, confess him, put away sin, surrender to God, study the Bible fifteen minutes a day, keep on praying, and witness. He also held children's meetings on Saturday afternoons with about 12,000 present each time and a total of 1,300 decisions.

He worked in American cities from 1906 to 1911. Oswald Smith of the People's Church was one of the 4,500 converts in his meeting in Toronto. He also helped to establish the Montrose Summer Bible Conference in the Blue Ridge Mountains of Pennsylvania, where he had 2,500 at the first meeting.

In 1908 he resigned from Moody and became superintendent of the newly founded Bible Institute of Los Angeles (Biola). In 1915 he also assumed the pastorate of the Church of the Open Door. While in these positions he took two trips to the Far East in 1919 and 1921. He resigned from both positions in 1924 and led revival meetings until he died. He wrote nearly forty books, as well as many pamphlets.

The learned Torrey differed from the slangy, untrained Billy Sunday in personality and mode of speech. Yet the two men shared the common goal of reviving the church and winning the unsaved.

William A. ("Billy") Sunday (1862–1935), so named at the desire of his father, a Civil War soldier, was born in a log cabin on a farm in Ames, Iowa. The father died; the mother remarried and had two more sons. The boys moved to their grandfather Martin Corey's farm when the mother remarried.

Billy was a sickly boy who could hardly walk until he was three, but a man named Avery cured him with herbs. In 1874 he and his brother were sent to orphan homes, first in Glenwood and then in Davenport, Iowa, where discipline was Christian but strict. They left the home in 1876 to work on Corey's farm, but Billy quarreled with his grandfather.

He moved to Nevada, Iowa, and worked first as a hotel errand boy and later as a stable boy for John Scott, who sent him to high school for four years. He built up his speedy running by running alongside the race horses he was exercising. The Marshalltown fire brigade baseball team needed a fast base runner and gave Billy a job at a funeral home.

A. C. Anson, manager of the Chicago White Sox (Cubs), vacationed at his aunt's home in Marshalltown. At her request Anson gave Billy a tryout in Chicago. He ran barefooted against Fred Pfeffer, the fastest runner on the team, and won. He played as a professional from 1883 to 1891. In 1890 he stole 96 bases in 100 games, a better record than that of Ty Cobb who stole 98 bases in 150 games. Billy could circle the bases in fourteen seconds.

One Sunday in 1886 he was invited by Harry Monroe into the Pacific Garden Mission where "Mother" Clark counseled him and led him to Christ. He went to Jefferson Park Presbyterian Church where he met and in 1885 married Helen A. Thompson. He played for teams in Pittsburgh and Philadelphia, but he refused to play on Sunday. In 1887 and 1888 he coached the Northwestern University baseball team and took courses in rhetoric.

He was released from his contract with Philadelphia at $500.00 a month in 1891 and became assistant secretary at the Chicago YMCA at $83.33 a month. Here he busied himself from 1891 to 1893 in conducting street meetings, distributing tracts in bars, speaking at the YMCA, and leading prayer meetings.

J. Wilbur Chapman engaged him as an advance agent for his meetings from 1893 to 1895, and Billy learned the technique of small city evangelism. When Chapman returned to Bethany Church, Billy was asked to preach in a meeting at Garner, Iowa, in January 1895. He used sermons Chapman loaned to him, and 268 people were saved. He couldn't stay a second week because he had no more sermons. He had people raise hands, shake hands with him, sign decision cards, and take a pamphlet entitled "What It Means to Be a Christian."

Sunday was ordained by Chicago Presbytery in 1903, even though he displayed ignorance of many theological questions. J. Wilbur Chapman preached his ordination sermon.

Sunday used a tent for his meetings from 1898 till October 1908, when a snowstorm in Salida, Colorado, destroyed it. From then on, beginning in Perry, Iowa, tabernacles were erected for his meetings. (After each crusade, the tabernacle would be dismantled and the materials sold for scrap.) Sunday used sawdust on the board floors to deaden sound.

Until 1906, most of Sunday's meetings were in small towns of 10,000 to 20,000 people, with half the meetings in towns of less than 2,500 people. As his fame increased, he preached in larger towns and to larger crowds. In September 1907, *American Magazine* gave him national publicity for his Fairfield, Iowa, meeting. His first big meeting was in Spokane, Washington, with an attendance of 100,000 and more than 5,600 decisions. Up to 1907 he had about 100,000 converts, 75,000 of whom joined churches.

The Philadelphia meeting from January to March 1915 was probably his best meeting. There were nearly 42,000 converts.

He went to New York for ten weeks in the spring of 1917 because of a petition of 55,000 people from 500 churches. The huge tabernacle erected for his meeting held 20,000 people. Nearly 80,000 met for prayer in 6,313 home prayer meetings, and 6,000 sang in three separate choirs. Attendance was 1,443,000 and there were 87,000 decisions. He gave his love offering of more than $120,000 to the Red Cross, YWCA, and YMCA. This was the peak meeting of his career.

In Boston he had 700 homes for prayer meetings, with about 80,000 praying. Grace Saxe led Bible studies for businessmen and women during the meetings.

His staff had grown to thirty-three by 1918. Homer Rodeheaver became his song leader. E. Honeywell served as an advance man

BILLY SUNDAY (1862-1935), flamboyant American evangelist who reached thousands with his superbly organized campaigns and sensational preaching. Here, in a sermon against drunkenness, he imitates "John, the drunkard, marching up to the butcher shop." *(Courtesy of the Billy Graham Center Museum)*

and Fred Siebert oversaw the tabernacles. Advance preparations involved building a tabernacle, organizing prayer meetings for revival, training and rehearsing choirs, and house-to-house visitation. His team usually lived in private homes during the meetings. Services were held on Sundays at 10:00 A.M., 3:00 P.M., and 7:00 P.M. with cooperating churches giving up their services. The upper-class was reached in special Thursday morning meetings.

Sunday tried to stir the church during the first week of meetings. He normally stayed eight to ten weeks. His period of greatest power and usefulness was from 1908 to 1918.

Sunday had more than 593,000 shake his hand in 300 meetings. He received about $1,400,000 in love offerings but gave much away. (He had always tithed the income from his meetings.) His estate was only $50,000 when probated.

This five-foot, ten-inch man, who never weighed more than 160 pounds, prayed much in informal conversational tones and read much. He was shy socially but an extrovert in the pulpit. Like Moody, he proclaimed a gospel of ruin, redemption, and regeneration. He would use the same sermon as often as one hundred times. His sermon against liquor, titled "Booze," was probably his favorite, and it often led to enforcement of laws against liquor and local option. He was dramatic and slangy; he used short sentences and good illustrations. He intensely attacked sin rather than individuals. He often shed his coat, vest, and collar during a sermon to give himself freedom for gestures and actions. A final heart attack killed him while he was preaching in Mishawaka, Indiana, in 1935. God honored the generous expenditure of his energies by using him to build the church and win many to Christ.

THE WELSH REVIVAL

The revival in Wales from September 1904 to June 1905 is associated with Evan Roberts in the popular mind, but others played important parts in it. Rosina Davies, who held meetings from 1882 to 1942, was saved through the Salvation Army. Her fine singing and preaching were first used in her meetings to awaken Christians to help with later soul-winning. She had 250 converts in meetings in 1905 in many Welsh towns.

Jessie Penn-Lewis, converted in 1882, led Bible classes in Richmond, Surrey. She set up a Welsh Keswick in 1903.

Seth Joshua (1859–?) became a Christian in 1872 and was ordained by the Welsh Presbyterian Church. By 1904 he was an evangelist for that group and also held Bible conferences for believers to interest them in a deeper life. He was used of God in the first stages of the awakening which began in Cardiganshire.

Joseph Jenkins began pastoral work in New Quay in Cardinganshire in South Wales in 1892 and directed his efforts to stopping spiritual decline. In February 1904, he had a Keswick type meeting; Florrie Evans, a shy girl, said in a Sunday meeting, "I love the Lord Jesus Christ with all my heart." Several young people were stirred and sought salvation.

Seth Joshua went to New Quay in September 1904, and many were renewed and saved in his meeting. He spoke in the Newcastle Emlyn preparatory school where Evan Roberts heard him. On September 27, at a conference at Blaenannerch, fifteen converts from New Quay testified.

Evan J. Roberts (1878–1951) was a miner's son at Loughor where he attended the Calvinistic Methodist Church called Moriah Church. He went into the mines at the age of twelve, but in 1902 began to do the work of a blacksmith. He felt a call to preach and went to the academy at Newcastle Emlyn in September 1904 to prepare for ministerial training at Trevecca College.

During the spring of 1904 he had been repeatedly awakened from 1:00 to 5:00 A.M. by a sense of God's presence and communion with him, after which he would return to sleep. At a Thursday meeting near the end of September 1904, Seth Joshua prayed, "Lord, bend us"; Evan Roberts prayed, "Lord, bend me," and had a deep sense of God's grace and the need to preach. He told Sidney Evans that God would give them 100,000 souls in Wales.

He never returned to the academy, but drew out his savings of

£200 and went home to Loughor, eight miles from Swansea, to hold young people's meetings at Moriah Church. Sam Jenkins, Sidney Evans, and a group of young women from New Quay, who became known as the "Singing Sisters," accompanied him. On Monday, October 31, 1904, he held his first meeting; three were converted. Six were saved on Tuesday. On Wednesday he gave his famous "Four Points" sermon in a meeting at Mount Pisgah near Loughor. The people were admonished to put away unconfessed sin, to give up doubtful habits, to obey the Spirit promptly, and to confess Christ publicly.

The revival at Loughor was followed by one in November at Aberdare when Seth Joshua was preaching at Ebenezer Chapel. About six hundred were converted by the end of October, and the revival spread from South to North Wales. *The Western Mail,* a South Wales newspaper, provided publicity, and visitors from England, France, Germany, Russia, and other countries came to observe the revival.

After three weeks of rest in February 1905 (he had been working sixteen hours or more each day), Roberts went to preach to the Welsh at Liverpool, England, and 750 were won. He then traveled in North Wales for two months. By the end of 1905, 100,000 were converted. The Calvinistic Methodist Church gained 24,000, the Wesleyans 4,000, the Congregationalists 26,500, and the remainder went to Anglican and Baptist churches. Revival spread to England and Cornwall, and news of it went around the world.

Roberts desired to "bend the church" to "save the world." However, he permitted emotional excesses and neglected the preaching of the Word. By the late fall of 1905 his influence had waned. Early in 1906, in a rundown state of health, he went to the Penn-Lewis home in Leicestershire for several months. His later ministry was mainly intercessory prayer from 1907 to 1932. He moved to Cardiff in 1930.

The Welsh revival of 1904 and 1905 received much more publicity than that of 1859. Prayer, praise in ecstatic singing, and testimony of lay converts with much emotion was emphasized. Roberts was an exhorter rather than expositor, and he neglected preaching and teaching the Bible. In the 1859 revival the ministers had preached the Word and discipled the converts in doctrine and life. The 1904 awakening was more subjective and often mystical in its expression of God's love, loyalty to Christ and the Cross, the need for the Holy Spirit, and a love for souls.

It did, however, have practical results in the short run. Confession of sin brought restitution of property and money. Gambling and the consumption of liquor dropped in many places. Swearing in the mines ended; the pit ponies even had to learn to respond to a new vocabulary of gentle words to replace the cursing of former days.

Revival spread to Methodist churches in Ulster. There were thirteen hundred inquirers in Newtonards. In Belfast, Seth Joshua spoke on the Welsh revival to the Irish Presbyterian ministers and elders of the Presbyterian General Assembly. When news of the Welsh awakening reached Cambuslang, Glasgow, and Edinburgh, revival resulted there. Joseph Kemp, pastor of Charlotte Chapel in Edinburgh, soon had one thousand inquirers when he told of what he had seen in the Welsh revival. Revival had come to the Welsh in western England through Evan Roberts's visit to Liverpool in 1905.

REVIVAL IN EUROPE

The most significant European revival in this era took place in Norway under Gustave A. Lunde (1877–?), who was a native of southern Norway. He became a sailor at the age of eighteen and for a time was a customs officer in New York. He received Christ in a Salvation Army meeting in Chicago and felt called to preach to Norwegians in the Dakotas. After a brief ministry to sailors in New York, he went back to Norway in 1901. He traveled all over Norway, preaching to crowds of up to five thousand. Prayer was an important element in this revival which energized both the free and state churches. Revival spread in 1905 into Denmark, where it centered in the Lutheran Inner Mission until 1908.

REVIVAL IN ASIA

India, China, and Korea were blessed with notable revivals a few years after the Welsh awakenings. Pandita Ramabai and John Hyde were leaders in India, Nevius and Goforth in China, and Hardie and Nevius in Korea.

India. Pandita S. Ramabai (1858–1922) was a daughter of a learned but poverty-stricken Braham in southern India. He educated her in the Indian classical scriptures. She could recite eighteen thousand verses from the Puranas at age twelve and was the only woman in India to be named *Pandita* (mistress of learning) by Bengali scholars.

During famine about 1874 her parents starved to death. She married a lawyer in 1880, but in nineteen months he died, leaving her with a baby girl named Manorama. Ramabai went to England in 1883 to get an English education. She taught Sanskrit in Cheltenham College for three years. The sisters of a Church of England order at Wantage won her to Christianity, and on September 9, 1883, she was baptized.

In 1886 she was in the United States for three years to raise money for a nonsectarian school in Bombay for the high-caste Hindu girls, especially child widows. While in the United States she became a friend of Frances Willard, the temperance reformer.

She went back to Bombay in 1889 and opened a widows' home, but in a year she moved it to Poona where she soon had forty child widows from the ages of fifteen to twenty-five. Instruction in Christianity was given to about half who elected it. The Brahmans tried to take over and exclude Christian teaching. When they removed twenty-five widows, she moved to Mukti. She also got a hundred-acre fruit farm at Khedgaon, forty miles south of Poona, and set up a school to teach girls how to be self-supporting. Her more formal Christianity became more real through a deep spiritual experience about this time.

She began to rescue temple prostitutes as well as child widows, and by 1897 she had 300 girls. Ten years earlier she had enlisted Minnie F. Abrams as her assistant. At one time she had as many as 2,000 girls.

Ramabai formed a prayer circle of 70 early in 1905 when news of the Welsh revival reached her. Soon more than 250 were meeting twice daily for prayer. Revival started on June 30, 1905, and in a two-month period 1,200 were saved.

Revival came to Dohnavour on October 22, 1905, where an Irish woman, Amy Carmichael, was speaking in the church. She was stopped by a lad who began to pray and broke down. For four hours the school boys cried and asked forgiveness of one another. The revival spread to the older people through proclaiming the Word and prayer.

An assembly of the Assamese Presbyterian Church heard of the Welsh revival late in 1904, and all sensed an unusual experience of the presence of God. Many children were saved in March 1905. In a few months 8,000 people were added to the church in Khasia.

John Hyde (1865–1912), called "Praying Hyde" later, was born in Illinois and educated at Carthage College and McCormick Seminary. He and twenty-five of his classmates felt called to be missionaries. A classmate at Carthage organized a Presbyterian association to support him in India.

Hyde went to India in October 1902, and experienced an infilling of the Holy Spirit upon arrival. Because he put Bible study first, he was slow in learning the native language. For nearly twenty years he was a village missionary-evangelist. He also taught English Bible for some years in a boys' school in Ludhiana. He also prayed at noon and from 4:00 to 5:00 P.M.

Revival occurred at a girls' school in Sialkot and spread to the seminary. Hyde helped to organize the Punjab Prayer Union in 1904. Hyde and Turner Patterson prayed for thirty days and nights before the missionary conference at Sialkot in late 1904, and missionaries and nationals were convicted, made confession, and were renewed or converted. During the 1905 conference, Hyde, the principal speaker on John 15:26-27, prayed so much that he rarely slept. He later spent "days of [village] visitation and nights of prayer."

Beginning in 1908, he asked God to let him win one soul a day, and four hundred were saved in that year. He asked for two a day in 1909, and eight hundred responded. In 1910 he asked for four a day.

In March 1911 he went home by way of England after nineteen years in India. His preaching, prayer, and life of victory won many to Christ and energized the missionaries and the national church.

Sadhu Sundar Singh (1888-1929?), a Sikh born in a high-caste family in North Punjab, India, at first hated Christianity and burned a New Testament given to him by an American missionary. Later he read Matthew 11:28 and had a vision of Christ which led to his conversion. His family drove him out and tried to poison him.

The Presbyterian Mission at Ludhiana took him in, and he was baptized in September 1905 at Simla. He adopted the saffron robe of a *sadhu* holy man and became a Christian *sadhu*. In annual tours for twenty years he witnessed to Christ in Afghanistan, India, Tibet, Nepal, Burma, Ceylon, Singapore, China and Japan. In 1919 his father was converted. Singh disappeared on a trip to Tibet in 1929, and nothing more was heard of him.

China. Revival at Shanghai in 1925 was led by Mr. and Mrs. Henry Woods, missionaries of the Southern Presbyterian Church. Mrs. Woods had missionaries meet in her home for prayer for worldwide revival on New Year's Day of 1924. A continuing committee and a world prayer movement was born that Mrs. Woods called Worldwide Revival Prayer Movement. A convention was held in July 1926, in the Union Church at Shanghai, and soon the church was too small for the crowds. Revival continued from July to September. Dora Yu and Leland Wang experienced renewal in these meetings, and fifty were set apart for evangelism.

Northern China experienced indigeneous revival in 1936 and 1937. It was under the leadership of Marie Monsen of the Norwegian Lutheran Mission. She had been held by pirates for thirty-three days and after her release began an earnest prayer life and counseling of women.

When Miss Monsen spoke at Chefoo in northeast China, both missionaries and nationals in a theological school later were brought under conviction, confessed sin, and were renewed. In the fall of 1929 at Shantung, where some women had been praying since 1925, a major revival came in schools, seminaries, and churches that affected both leaders and members.

Manchuria was visited in a revival led by Jonathan Goforth (1859-1936), formerly an Ontario farm boy. Lachlan Cameron's preaching in a Presbyterian church led him to accept Christ at the age of eighteen. When he read the memoirs of Robert Murray McCheyne, he decided to enter the ministry. He decided to become a missionary through hearing G. L. Mackay of Formosa. He was educated at Knox College in Toronto. While a student, he worked in the William Street Mission in the slums for two years.

After graduation in 1885 he spent four years as a missionary of the Toronto Mission Union. Both here and in a multipoint field in Muskoka, many were saved. In 1886, Knox students raised money to send him and his wife, Rosalind, an artist whom he had married in 1885, to China.

He was ordained in 1887, went to China the following year, and soon learned the language at Chefoo. He met Nevius at Honan and visited Korea to observe the revival there in 1907. Reading the books of Finney and Edwards on revival increased his desire to see one begin.

In early 1908 he was the speaker at Mukden, Manchuria, where an elder's confession precipitated revival after a sermon on Zechariah 3:4. Over eight hundred were convicted, confessed sin, and made restitution. In the same year the church in Chengte was revived. The Presbyterians had thirteen hundred baptisms in five years. Goforth characterized this awakening as the "mightiest." The revival spread to other cities in Manchuria.

Goforth went home to Canada from 1910 to 1911 and served as a delegate to the World Missionary Conference in 1910 at Edinburgh. He also spoke at Spurgeon's Tabernacle.

Back in China he won General Feng to Christ and became his close friend. On one occasion at Kiksungham 969 men were baptized and 4,600 took Communion.

Goforth, in all his preaching in the period of revival which he led, emphasized Bible reading, obedience to the Word, God's holiness, sin's destructive force, man's helplessness, the need of prayer, and Christ's ability to save.

John L. Nevius (1829–93), a Presbyterian missionary of Dutch descent, attended Union College from 1845 to 1848. While he was in Georgia in 1849, he was converted and joined the Presbyterian church. He attended Princeton Seminary from 1850 to 1853. He married Nell Coan in 1853 and went to Ningpo in China to study the language in 1854.

After years of service in China, in 1890 he was asked by missionaries in Korea to tell them of the principles he had developed for missionary work. He had published those principles in 1885 under the title "Planting and Development of Missionary Churches" in the *Chinese Recorder.* They had been reprinted in book form by the Presbyterian church in Shanghai.

These principles, which were followed in China and Korea, were intended to produce indigenous, self-supporting, self-propagating, and self-governing churches. These three principles had been advanced earlier by Henry Venn, son of John Venn, and Rufus Anderson. The laity was to be trained by life and word to witness. Nevius advocated unpaid national workers itinerating with the missionary. Bible class teaching, Sunday observance, and scriptural discipline were to be the tasks of the elders under a simple church government. The churches were to be of native architecture, not American.

Korea. The Korean church has been one of the fastest-growing churches in the world, with Christians now numbering about 25 percent of the population. This was in part because of the extensive application of Nevius's principles and extensive itineration by early Presbyterian missionaries. Perennial revival in the Korean church was another reason.

A pioneer Presbyterian missionary, Horace G. Underwood (1859–1916), had read Nevius's principles in the *Chinese Recorder* and was responsible for his two-week visit to Korea on his way back to China in 1890. In 1903 two women missionaries of the Methodist Episcopal Church in Wonsan were led to pray for revival among the missionaries. Their influence led to a conference for prayer and Bible study in which a Korean confessed letting his wife die of neglect. Fredrik Franson also gave a week of Bible study and prayer in Wonsan.

A 1903 summer missionary conference on prayer, led by R. A. Hardie, resulted in the revival of seven missionaries, and thousands of people were added to the church in 1904. In August 1906 Hardie led a conference in Pyongyang in studying 1 John and praying for revival. In that September, Howard R. Johnston told the story of the Welsh and Indian revivals. The annual Bible training meeting for Bible study was held at Pyongyang in January 1907, with fifteen hundred men and women present. On Monday January 14, after a short sermon by Graham Lee, the people began to weep, confess sin, ask for forgiveness, and make restitution. This meeting lasted until 2:00 A.M., but the same phenomena continued for several days. The Presbyterian Korean Church grew quickly, with about fifty-nine thousand additions to the church between 1906 and 1910. Jonathan Goforth also visited Korea in 1910 and told of the Mukden revival in China.

The Korean church has always been a praying, Bible-believing church which earnestly studies the Bible, prays, gives, and witnesses. This deep stirring of the Spirit is all the more remarkable when one remembers the Asian ideal of not "losing face." ("Losing face" is necessary when there is confession and restitution.) South Korea's churches are the largest in the world. The army is about 15 percent Christian. Earlier revival laid the foundation for all of this.

AFRICAN REVIVALS, 1900–1945

Notable regional revivals between World War I and World War II occurred in the Anglican Church in East Africa and in the Wallamo tribe in Ethiopia. The first came through a lay medical missionary and the second was an indigenous revival.

East Africa. The Church Missionary Society first sent Alexander M. Mackay (1849–90), a Scot who had studied engineering in Germany, to Uganda in 1876. He preached, translated, and printed books for the tribes, but his main work was building a 230-mile wagon road from Sadani on the coast to Mpwapwa in the interior to make it easier for missionaries to reach the interior.

George L. Pilkington (1865–97), a first-class linguistic classical scholar who graduated from Pembroke College, Cambridge, translated the Scriptures by 1896 into Luganda, the main native language of Uganda. He was used in bringing revival in 1893 and 1894 that resulted in an increase in the Ugandan church from 3,429 to over 50,000 by 1896. He was killed in border fighting.

The Imperial British East Africa Company, which had political rule as well as engaging in trade, decided to leave Uganda in 1890 as governing Uganda was costing too much. The missionaries wanted the company to remain in East Africa. Bishop Alfred Tucker, bishop of the church in Uganda, was on furlough when he met William Mackinnon, a director of the company. Mackinnon called on Tucker's host in the Highlands of Scotland. He told Tucker that Uganda was costing the company £40,000 a year but that they would remain for another year if the mission would raise £15,000. Mackinnon gave £10,000 and raised £5,000 from his friends. In one mission meeting £8,000 was raised and in two weeks £16,000 was in hand. This enabled the company to remain, stop Arab slave trading, keep the Germans out of Uganda, and protect the missionary work. The British government then made Uganda a protectorate because public opinion for it was given time to force the government to act.

The 1893 revival was followed by another in 1906 that enabled the church to grow to about 100,000. Coldness soon set in in the national church until revival came through the laity in the late 1930s. Many thousand of Abakolole or "Bakoloe" (saved ones) were added to the church in Rwanda, Uganda, Kenya, and South Africa.

Algernon C. Stanley Smith, son of one of the "Cambridge Seven" who went to China, and Leonard Sharp finished medical training in 1914. Both wanted to be medical missionaries in Uganda. Sharp went to Mengo Hospital in Kampala, Uganda; Stanley Smith, who had joined the British Army, was posted there by the army in 1915. The two became interested in Rwanda because of the Duke of Mecklenberg's book, *In the Heart of Africa*. They toured Rwanda in 1916.

The two doctors went to Kabale in Kigesi district in the Ankole province of southwest Uganda near Rwanda in February 1921. In two years they had a 125-bed hospital. There were more than three hundred churches in the area, but the Christians were superficial, consumed alcohol, and were often immoral.

The doctors were able to open a work in Gahini, Rwanda, by 1925, and in 1926 the Church Missionary Society formed the Rwanda General and Medical Mission under its aegis. The doctrinal basis was "Bible, Protestantism, and Keswick lines."

John ("Joe") Church was a medical doctor who had been healed of tuberculosis when he had promised God he would be a missionary if God healed him. He went to Uganda in December 1927 with support from the Cambridge Intercollegiate Christian Union. He had been under strong Keswick influence in England.

Church went with several volunteer medical staff personnel and about twenty evangelists to start a hospital at Gahini in June, 1928. They helped the tribal people through a severe famine in 1928 and 1929. Church started Bible studies based on the Scofield Bible with Africans and Europeans in June 1929. Blasio Kigosi came under the gospel near the end of 1929. Harold Guillebad had translated the New Testament into the Rwanda dialect by 1930.

When Church went for a visit to Kampala in September 1929, he met Simeoni Nsibambi. Both men felt the need of a deeper spiritual life. In late September they spent two days praying for the infilling of the Holy Spirit and studying the Scofield Bible references on the Holy Spirit and the victorious life. They "surrendered all to Jesus" and experienced an infilling.

The revival began with these two men. Nsibambi gave up his work in the public health service to preach and help Yosiya Kinuka, unhappy with his hospital work, to have the same experience. Through a prayer meeting in Gahini, Rwanda had revival by 1931. The missionaries felt a burden to pray in a convention in September 1931 in Gahini. In the Gahini Christmas convention in December 1933, with the Africans as the main teachers, December 27 was marked by the intense Bible teaching, conviction, crying, and confession, both of missionaries and nationals. William Nagenda experienced deeper spiritual life in these meetings. By 1935 the revival had spread to Burundi.

Blasio Kigosi (1909–36), a brother of Nsibambi, as head of the Evangelists' Training School at Gahini, faced a strike by students, and six out of seventy left in April 1935. Conscious of his weakness, Blasio took a week off and experienced an infilling of the Holy Spirit. Through him and Yosiya Kinuka revival spread in the Kigesi district around Kabale. Joe Church and a team made up of Blasio Kigosi and his brother, Simeoni Nsibambi, were invited to the town of Kigesi from September 22–30, 1935. Later Yosiya Kinuka joined the team. Church's Bible readings and Nsibambi's sermon on sin and holiness awakened believers. Revival spread over the province of Ankole in Uganda in January 1936. Blasio died the same month.

Joe Church, at the request of the authorities, spoke at the Bishop Tucker Theological College in Uganda in June 1936. Soon forty students were converted and carried the revival through Uganda. Missions by Church and Nsibambi continued through 1937. In February, fifty were saved and the church renewed at one station. Deep conviction, confession of sin, love for others, team witness, joy, and singing marked all the meetings. Soon Burundi, Tanganyika, and Kenya experienced revival under the Bible-centered, Christ-centered teaching of those two men and prayer. This revival was mainly confined to the Anglican Church in the countries of East Africa from about 1930 to 1950. Through Joe Church the work in the southern Sudan and the Congo was revived. A team went to Pretoria and Cape Town, South Africa. Through William Nagenda and Yosiya Kinuka it influenced England in 1947.

Revival generally came through missions by teams of lay believers and three-day regional and national conventions of up to four thousand, mainly in the Anglican Church, but a feeling of superiority to other Christians and excessive emotionalism sometimes hindered the work. The teams emphasized Bible reading and prayer. Revival continued in the 1940s and 1950s. In Kenya the revival helped to give the church spiritual stability through the Mau Mau uprising and helped the church in Uganda endure the cruelties of the Idi Amin regime.

Ethiopia. When Christian missionaries were forced to leave Ethiopia in April 1937 because of the Italian invasion, they left a church of forty-eight members led by Dana Maja, a chief who was aided by Diasa, Buru, Wandero, Wilder, and Boleti, a woman. This group of converts was the result of nine years of work. The church suffered severe persecution during the Italian regime, but when missionaries were permitted to return in 1942, they found a greatly enlarged church. By July 1945 about fifteen thousand believers were organized into many local churches following New Testament principles. Revival in this Wallamo tribe has continued and spread into other areas of Ethiopia in spite of persecution under the Marxist-oriented regime.

God indeed blessed the church all over the globe from 1900 to 1945. The Pentecostal movement, the Welsh revival, and great revivalistic evangelists and missionaries carried revival worldwide.

7. REGIONAL REVIVALS 1945–

SOME think that revival since 1945 is merely a revival of religion or the "faith in faith" of former President Eisenhower. While there has been no global revival such as that of 1857 to 1895, there have been regional movements. Billy Graham has carried revivalistic evangelism to every major country and city in the world in his crusades. Much more revival is happening than people generally think.

THE UNITED STATES

The United States has experienced several movements of revival since 1945. Both the awakening of 1950 at Wheaton College and that of 1970 at Asbury College were similar to the awakening at Yale in 1802. The Jesus movement brought many of the social dropouts of the 1960s back in touch with the church. Denominational charismatics certainly stirred the mainline denominations to think of the work of the Holy Spirit. Electronic evangelists, such as Jerry Falwell, and healing evangelists, such as William M. Branham and Oral Roberts, have brought renewal of many believers' "first love" and consequent witnessing which has won many to Christ.

College Awakenings. Such awakenings began on a small scale in 1905 at Asbury College. The college experienced a revival in which E. Stanley Jones, later a missionary to India, was converted. In the same year McInville (now Linfield) College had an awakening for which the great church historian Kenneth Scott Latourette, then a student, was partly responsible.

When a gospel team from Wheaton College visited the University of Toronto in the fall of 1935, they became leaders of prayer meetings for revival on the campus. Don Hillis and Robert Evans, later leaders of missionary societies in Asia and Europe, were among the student leaders.

Robert C. McQuilkin, president of Columbia Bible College in South Carolina, was invited for the midwinter special services at Wheaton in early 1936. After the first meeting he was forced to spend the rest of the week in the infirmary because of influenza. The president of the college, J. Oliver Buswell, was in Chicago on trial by the Presbytery of Chicago for his support of an independent Presbyterian foreign missions board.

Dr. Harold Laird, who was helping Dr. Buswell in the trial, and Dr. Walter Wilson filled in for Dr. McQuilkin for a few days. After Dr. Wilson's sermon on Thursday morning the song leader, Homer Hammontree, read an anonymous note from a student stating that he was a Christian and loved the Lord but wanted to experience a personal revival. Don Hillis, a senior, rose to say that he had written the note and that he had not allowed God to control his life fully. He asked why they could not have a revival then. This started a meeting of prayer and confession on the part of many of the one thousand students. Dr. Laird spoke that evening, and the meeting continued into the night. Chapel was prolonged on Friday, and there was an all-day prayer meeting on Saturday.

Both faculty and students made confessions and righted wrongs. Twenty-five seniors became missionaries, among them

REGIONAL REVIVALS 1945—

CANADA
Saskatchewan
  McLeod
  Sutera

BRITISH ISLES
Scottish
Hebrides

ASIA

Taiwan
Mountain
Tribes

Timor

UNITED STATES

Colleges
Wheaton
Asbury

Jesus People
California

Denominational
Charismatics
Bennett

Revivalistic
evangelists
  Fuller
  Maier
  Graham
  Palau

Samuel Moffet of Korea. Carl F. H. Henry, later the first editor of *Christianity Today* and a prominent evangelical theologian, was also touched by the revival.

Some of the renewed students became leaders in the Student Foreign Mission Fellowship at the Keswick conference on June 28, 1936. When a constitution was adopted in 1938, Kenneth Hood, later a missionary in Central America, was the first full-time secretary. In 1941 there were more than twenty-six hundred members and thirty-six college chapters. In 1945 the group merged with Inter-Varsity Christian Fellowship.

Wheaton was again visited by revival in 1943. Harold P. Warren, pastor of the North Shore Baptist Church, led the special services from February 7 to 14, with Al Smith as song leader. Unusual spiritual concern marked the day of prayer on Tuesday. Confession as the basis of forgiveness was Warren's subject in the Thursday morning chapel service. The captain of the cross-country team rose to confess that he had ignored college policy and led his team in a Sunday race. Other students confessed pride, criticism, cheating, and other sins. Lunch and dinner were ignored as confession continued until the evening meeting. The same pattern prevailed on Friday.

Billy Graham, a student at Wheaton at the time, was greatly influenced toward the ministry by this revival. When a female student told her roommate in the hospital of the revival, she became a Christian. When her letter, telling her mother of her decision, was read by the pastor of their church in Washington, D.C., sixty responded to the invitation. Forty seniors became missionaries. Two other students who were influenced were Torrey Johnson and Robert Cook, who helped found Youth for Christ.

When Dr. J. Edwin Orr spoke on revival in April 1949 at Bethel College in Minneapolis, there was revival. Private and public sin was confessed. The revival spread to St. Paul Bible Institute.

Wheaton College experienced another major revival in 1950 as student leaders felt a special urge to pray for revival during the fall semester. Torrey Johnson was the speaker at the special services of Wheaton Academy, which was related to the college. An awakening came among the Academy's students and their parents.

Edwin Johnson of Seattle was the speaker for the February 1950 special services at Wheaton College, and George Beverly Shea was the song leader. Johnson, whose heart had been stirred by a local revival in his Mission Covenant Church in Seattle, spoke on 2 Chronicles 20:12 on the Sunday evening.

A student asked the president, V. Raymond Edman, if he could tell the students of how his sins had been forgiven and how victory in his life had come. He did this at about 7:15 P.M. in the eve-

ning meeting on Wednesday, February 8. Other students quickly
followed him. Students continued to give testimony all through
Wednesday evening, Wednesday night, all day Thursday and
through Thursday night.

News of the revival reached Chicago, and reporters from the
newspapers and *Life* magazine came to campus. Papers in Miami,
Seattle, Los Angeles, and New York gave the revival front-page
coverage. North Park College, Northern Baptist Seminary,
Houghton College, Asbury College, and other colleges and Bible
institutes had similar movements of renewal in their student
bodies and faculties. The one at Asbury involved 118 hours of confession, testimony, and song in late February 1950.

A remarkable revival occurred at Asbury College again in 1970.
Instead of preaching at the 10:00 A.M. chapel on Tuesday,
February 3, the dean gave his testimony and then gave the
students opportunity to testify. The next day, February 4, after
an all-night prayer meeting, students also began to testify in the
Asbury Seminary chapel. Confession, testimonies, prayer, and
singing continued in the college chapel for 185 hours.

Visitors came from as far away as California, Florida, and
Canada. In the next few months about two thousand teams went
out from the college on weekends to churches, 130 other colleges,
and seminaries. When a team of Asbury students went to Azusa
Pacific, 150 of the 800 students and faculty were influenced by the
revival. In many places people were freed from drugs and alcohol.
Family problems were resolved. One team went to the South
Meridian Church of God in Anderson, Indiana, where meetings
ran from February 12 to April 12 for fifty nights, with a total attendance of 75,000 in this revival. Prayer and the preaching of the
Word were prominent in all of these areas touched by the Asbury
revival.

The Jesus Movement of the Sixties in California. Haight
Ashbury in San Francisco, Sunset Strip in Hollywood, Peachtree
Street in Atlanta, and Greenwich Village in New York became

the haunts of dropouts from fourteen to twenty-four years of age from middle-class homes in the 1960s. About 35 percent of them were Jewish. These "hippies" with long hair and strange dress provided the converts of the Jesus people which surfaced in the late 1960s, first in California and then in Seattle.

The young people of the movement were antihistorical, anticultural, anti-intellectual, and experience-oriented. There was no question of the genuineness of their conversions or their devotion to the Bible. They generally had a "last days" complex with a premillennial conception of Christ's Second Coming. Many of them were charismatic and spoke in tongues and practiced divine healing. Their music was usually accompanied with guitars and ran the gamut from rock music with atonal rhythms to nineteenth-century folk music. Some groups practiced communal living. They were Fundamentalists theologically and hippies socially.

There is no doubt this revival, beginning about 1967, was genuine. Those who had sought reality in subjective experiences in drugs or Buddhist meditation now found it in Christ. Diversity was a hallmark of this group, which Don Wilkerson of Teen Challenge estimated to number about 300,000 at its peak.

Hollywood Presbyterian Church opened the Salt Company under the leadership of Don Williams to reach the dropouts on Sunset Strip. Ted Wise, a sailmaker, and his wife Elizabeth, both of whom had been on drugs in Haight Ashbury, were converted in 1966. With the help of some friends they opened the Living Room late in 1967 in Haight Ashbury to meet and to talk with drug users of the street about Jesus and the Bible. They contacted over 30,000 in the two years the Living Room was open.

When they rented a house in Novato, four couples moved in with them to this House of Acts. They then rented two other houses in Costa Mesa and one in Santa Ana called the House of Miracles. Hundreds stayed with them and many accepted Christ as their Savior.

The Christian Foundation at Saugus was set up in 1966 by

Susan and Tony Alamo, who were Pentecostal in background. Calvary Chapel was built in 1969 in Costa Mesa under Chuck Smith. The Full Gospel Bethel Tabernacle in Redondo Beach under Breck Stevens and the Christian World Liberation Front all welcomed these young people.

Duane Pedersen also converted about one thousand of the street people and is credited with coining the name "Jesus People." Pedersen published his *Hollywood Free Press* in 1969 and by 1971 claimed a circulation of over 425,000. *Right On* was first issued in July 1969, by the Christian World Liberation Front sponsored by evangelical churches. These papers served to pull diverse groups together.

David Berg's communal Children of God was the most extreme of these groups. Berg had been an Arizona pastor who worked among Indians for a time. He also directed a coffeehouse called "The Light Club" for Teen Challenge in Huntington Beach.

Berg formed a communal group of fifty, which he moved to Tucson because he believed California would be destroyed by an earthquake. By 1971 Berg had 2000 to 3000 followers in about 40 colonies. Scripture memorization and witnessing by pairs was emphasized. They often held vigils dressed in red sackcloth and with ashes on their foreheads. Berg attempted to break up identification of converts with their own families by lack of privacy and control by "elders" under his leadership. Later he only communicated to his flock by letters. His practices became increasingly bizarre, as attested to by his daughter's autobiography. Berg serves as an example of a man whose originally valid ministry became subverted by unchristian elements.

Arthur Blessit, who was born in Mississippi, became a Baptist minister and went to Hollywood in 1965 to set up "His Place" and do sidewalk evangelism, but he was harassed by the police. His trademark was carrying a cross.

The Jesus People formed a counterculture which indicted the churches by their sincerity. But they needed doctrinal teaching and the experience of adult Christians to temper their sometimes unwise zeal. Many churches did begin to help them between 1966 and 1970. The movement rescued many from drugs and immorality and turned them to Christ.

The Denominational Charismatics or Neo-Pentecostals. If the Jesus movement brought revival to many of the drug-using street people, the charismatic movement brought revival to many middle-class affluent people in the mainline denominations. The trademark of the group was speaking in tongues.

This charismatic revival was promoted by Demos Shakarian (b. 1913), who owned the Reliance Dairy in Downey, California. He was a friend and disciple of Charles S. Price and Oral Roberts, healing evangelists. He shared the idea of a charismatic businessmen's fellowship with Oral Roberts in 1950, and Roberts favored it. His first meeting in the Clifton Cafeteria of twenty-one Pentecostal businessmen in 1951 featured Roberts as the speaker. They later incorporated as the Full Gospel Business Men's Fellowship International in 1953. They soon had 100,000 members in 600 chapters. *Voice* magazine, started in 1953, had a circulation of 250,000 by the early seventies. They had 300,000 members and over a $1 million budget by 1972. They sought to reach businessmen for salvation and the charismatic experience through the sharing of testimonies at banquets.

They cooperated with the mainline denominational charismatic movement, which first appeared among Episcopalians. Dennis Bennett was born in London and earned his B.A. at San Jose State College and his B.D. from the Chicago Theological Seminary in 1949. He became an Episcopalian and became rector of St. Mark's Episcopal Church in Van Nuys, California. He had a group of seventy tongues-speaking people in his church by April of 1960. He had to leave the church and go to a rundown church, St. Luke's in Seattle. Jean Stone, a member of his church in Van Nuys, had a charismatic experience and started a paper which circulated widely among classical and charismatic Pentecostals. It was estimated in 1981 that there were about 21 million classical and charismatic Pentecostal believers in the world. Many millions of these charismatics were in the mainline churches.

By 1963 this movement had spread among Lutherans through Larry Christensen, a Lutheran with a charismatic experience. Harold Bredesen in the Reformed Church and Howard Ervin among the Baptists were leaders in promoting the charismatic experience in their respective denominations.

The Roman Catholic Church was also affected by this emphasis. In August 1966, four faculty members at Duquesne University in Pittsburgh read David Wilkerson's *The Cross and the Switchblade*. Ralph Keifer, Patrick Bourgeois, and Kevin and Dorothy Ranaghan first spoke in tongues in January 1967, and were responsible for introducing tongues-speaking at Notre Dame University in March 1967. By June 1970 there were ninety charismatics in Notre Dame. A large charismatic Roman Catholic convention at Notre Dame in 1973 drew about 25,000 from twenty-five nations, and one in Rome in 1974 drew about 30,000.

This charismatic revival of the 1960s differed from that of the classical Pentecostals early in the century. The revival of the 1960s appealed to the middle class in denominational churches; the classic Pentecostal revival had appealed to blue-collar workers in storefront meeting places. The classic Pentecostals embraced evangelical doctrines, whereas the charismatics stressed experience rather than doctrine. The Pentecostals developed their own denominations; the charismatics remained in their denominations. Both reached many people for God and brought renewal to the churches.

Revivalistic Evangelists. As pastoral revivalistic evangelists sought to rouse the church to renewal and witness in the past, so leaders in revival have done the same in the period since World War II. The latter, however, have had the advantage of radio and television to reach a wider audience both at home and abroad.

Pioneers in broadcasting the gospel over the air were evangelist Paul Rader and Aimee Semple McPherson. Charles Fuller and

Walter A. Maier devoted themselves full-time to the work of revival over the radio.

Paul Rader (1879–1938) was pastor of Chicago's Moody Memorial Church from 1914 to 1921. He began serving as pastor of the Chicago Gospel Tabernacle in 1922 and also began his famous radio broadcasts that year. Known as an evangelist to the Jazz Age, Rader was one of the first pastors to effectively reach a wide audience with his message via radio.

Aimee Semple McPherson and her International Church of the Foursquare Gospel have been discussed earlier. McPherson began her radio broadcasts in 1924.

Charles E. Fuller (1887–1968), a six-foot, ruddy-faced man who was initially timid and shy, was among the first to see the potential of the radio for revival. He was born in Los Angeles. At Pomona College he majored in chemistry and was president of his class in 1910, his senior year. His wife Grace was trained in a school of expression which served her well in later radio work with her husband.

After graduation, Fuller worked for his father, managing a gold dredging work on the American River in 1910 and 1911. He became a fertilizer salesman and an orange grower until January 1913, when a killing frost ruined him financially. He then managed an orange packing plant and moved to Placentia.

Fuller joined the Presbyterian church in 1914 and served in various offices. Interest in Paul Rader as a former athlete drew him to a meeting at the Church of the Open Door in Los Angeles where Rader was speaking. He was convicted and converted while driving home that day, July 30, 1916. His Bible class at the Presbyterian church grew, but he felt called to expository evangelistic preaching.

He resigned from the packing plant and studied at Biola. R. A. Torrey and William Evans had much spiritual influence upon him.

When his Bible class at the Presbyterian church grew to 175, he had to move it from the church. The class became the nucleus of Calvary Baptist Church, founded in 1925 with Fuller, who was ordained in May of that year, as its pastor.

In November 1926 he joined the field department of Biola as a Bible conference leader and evangelist. He became a trustee of the school in 1927 and chairman of its board in 1929.

Fuller realized the value of radio for the gospel on February 11, 1929, when he spoke over the radio during meetings in Cadle Tabernacle in Indiana. Station KREG carried his evening service from 1929 to 1933. He later added a program called the "Happy Hour." He resigned from the Biola board in 1932 to give more time to radio messages and set up a "Radio Bible Class" to replace the broadcasting of his services. The next year he resigned from the pastorate of Calvary Church and organized a Gospel Broadcasting Association on May 8, 1933. His broadcast, later called the "Old-fashioned Revival Hour," was first heard on the air in the spring of 1934. It became a national broadcast in 1937 and international in 1941. The song "Heavenly Sunshine" became its trademark.

In 1943 he founded the Fuller Evangelistic Foundation. In 1948 the foundation set up a department of field evangelists with sixteen teams that held 180 meetings in the United States and Canada. The foundation also founded Fuller Theological Seminary, which opened its doors in September 1947 with Harold Ockenga as president, and Carl F. H. Henry, Wilbur Smith, Everett Harrison, and Harold Lindsell as faculty, and about fifty students.

Fuller was a pioneer in full-time radio preaching. He also held large rallies all over the United States.

Walter A. Maier (1893–1950) was born in Boston and trained for the ministry at Boston University and Concordia Theological Seminary. He worked with German war prisoners from his ordination in 1917 until 1919. He became executive secretary of the young people's Walther League of the Lutheran Church. He served as professor of Old Testament at Concordia from 1922 to 1924. He became the popular and helpful speaker on the "Lutheran Hour" at its beginning and served in that capacity in

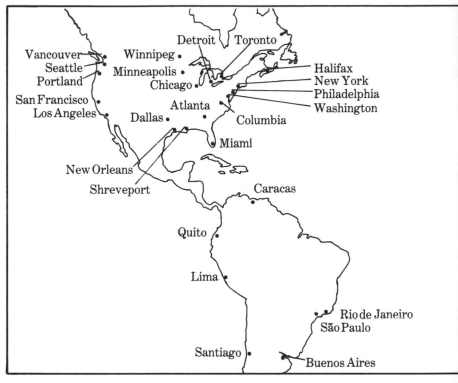

Vancouver
Seattle
Portland
San Francisco
Los Angeles

Winnipeg •
Minneapolis •
Chicago •

Detroit   Toronto

Dallas •

Atlanta
•

Halifax
New York
Philadelphia
Washington

Columbia

•   Miami

New Orleans
Shreveport

Caracas
•

Quito
•

Lima
•

Santiago
•

Rio de Janeiro
São Paulo

Buenos Aires

MAJOR BILLY

1930 and 1931 and from 1935 to 1946. His evangelical and evangelistic radio messages were heard all over the world.

Billy Graham (b. 1918) has preached a message of renewal to Christians and salvation for the unconverted. By 1985 he had addressed over 100 million people in crusades and other meetings and had nearly 2 million go forward for counseling. He had conducted about 250 crusades by 1978. This man, more in Moody's pattern, has spoken to more people than any other man in history.

William Franklin Graham was born on a dairy farm in Charlotte, North Carolina. Milking cows morning and evening was one of his arduous chores, but he still had time to indulge his passion for baseball. At the age of ten he proudly shook hands

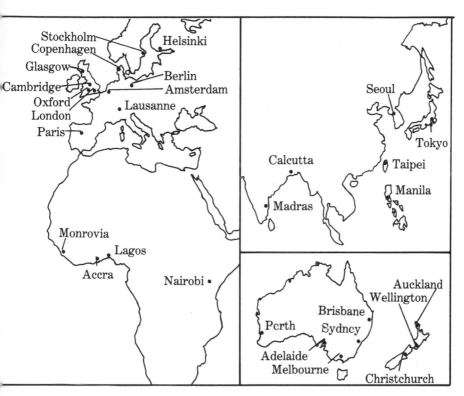

GRAHAM CRUSADES

with Babe Ruth. The family attended the Associate Reformed Presbyterian Church.

Mordecai Ham (1877–1961) was born in Kentucky and farmed and engaged in business until 1900 when he became a Baptist revivalist. He was invited to preach in Charlotte from September to November of 1934, and Billy Graham was converted in his meetings. Graham and Grady Wilson were invited and counseled by J. D. Prevatte, a clothing merchant. In all, 6,400 decisions were made. Ham claimed he had won over 300,000 to Christ during his ministry. He also preached prohibition strongly and fought liberalism and the teaching of evolution.

Graham enrolled at Bob Jones University in the fall of 1936, but after a semester transferred to a small Bible institute, now Trinity College, at Tampa, Florida, where he studied from 1937 to 1940. He started preaching at a Baptist church near Palatka, Florida, at the urging of the dean, John Minder, who then had him preach to his young people at the Tampa Gospel Tabernacle. Disappointment in a love affair and moral lapses of Christians he had admired only strengthened Graham's call to preach. In March 1938 he felt that call strongly and was desirous to "win souls." He was ordained in 1939 as a Southern Baptist minister and graduated in 1940.

Wheaton College's president Raymond Edman's mother, his brother Elner, and Paul Fischer were in Florida in 1940, and Graham caddied for them on a golf course near the Bible institute. Fischer promised to pay his board and room and Elner a year's tuition if he went to Wheaton College. He met his future wife, Ruth Bell, daughter of a medical missionary in China, shortly after his arrival at Wheaton in 1940. He kept busy with a major in anthropology, a small hauling business, and, from July 1941, the pastorate of the Gospel Tabernacle, of which Dr. Edman had previously been the pastor.

Robert VanKampen persuaded him to go to the First Baptist Church of Western Springs, Illinois, as pastor from 1943 to 1945. He organized dinner meetings for men at the Spinning Wheel Restaurant at which the men would hear the gospel with as many as three hundred men in attendance. In October 1943 he took over the program "Songs in the Night," with George Beverly Shea as soloist, from Torrey Johnson. On May 20, 1944, he spoke to a Youth for Christ meeting in Orchestra Hall, Chicago, at Torrey Johnson's request, and forty-two of the twenty-eight hundred in attendance responded to his gospel invitation.

Mumps prevented him from completing a commission as a chaplain during World War II. Instead he became a full-time organizer and evangelist for Youth for Christ at Torrey Johnson's invitation. He served in that capacity from 1945 to 1947. In 1945 he flew 200,000 miles to meetings in forty-seven states and spoke to crowds as large as 16,000 at Detroit. Cliff Barrows joined him as song leader in 1945.

Torrey Johnson asked Graham, Stratton Shufelt, and Charles Templeton to go to England in early 1946. Stephen Olford helped Graham to know the fullness of the Holy Spirit at one meeting in Wales. Between October 1946 and March 1947 they held 360 meetings in twenty-seven towns during a second trip to England.

William B. Riley persuaded him to become president of Northwestern Schools with over seven hundred students. He served in this capacity and also as an evangelist from 1947 to 1952.

Between September 25 and November 20, 1949, he gained national prominence when for eight weeks he held meetings in a tent in Los Angeles. Acting on orders from William R. Hearst, the Hearst newspapers gave him good publicity and brought him national prominence. There were 4,600 weekly prayer meetings held for the crusade. Those who accepted Christ in the Los Angeles meetings included Stuart Hamblen, a radio cowboy singer; Jim Vaus, an electronics expert working with the gambler Mickey Cohen; and Louis Zamperini, an Olympic track star. About 350,000 attended the meetings during the eight weeks, and there were about 3,000 first-time decisions.

He went on to Boston in January 1950 to meetings at the Park Street Church. The size of the crowds forced him to move to the 13,000-seat Boston Gardens. Of the 105,000 at the meetings, 3,000 made decisions.

The meeting in May 1950 in Columbia, South Carolina, was the first which he called a "crusade" at the suggestion of Willis Haymaker. Here, through Bernard Baruch, he met Henry Luce, the son of missionaries in China and publisher of *Time*, *Life*, and *Fortune*. Luce gave Graham much coverage in his magazines from then on.

During most of July and August 1950, the team was in Portland, Oregon. Over 500,000 attended the meetings with 9,000 inquirers. The first film of a crusade was made by Dick Ross of Great Commission Films; the film was titled *Mid-Century Crusade*. When

Graham was asked to go on the radio on a national hookup, he asked God to provide him $25,000 if he was to do so. The exact amount came in, and he began his radio broadcast from Atlanta on November 5, 1950. The broadcast was named "The Hour of Decision," the name suggested by his wife, Ruth. It was aired on about 750 stations in the U.S.A. and abroad in 1984, with a listening audience estimated at 20 million.

He returned to England in March 1954 and held a crusade in the Harringay Arena in London. The last meeting was held in the large Wimbledon Stadium, and 2,000 made decisions. There were 38,000 decisions from a total attendance of over 2 million in the crusade. Operation Andrew, which involved bringing unsaved friends to the meetings, was begun in meetings in Scotland in 1955. They had an overall attendance of about 2,650,000, with over 52,000 decisions.

The major crusade of 1957 was conducted in New York City at Madison Square Garden from May 15 to September 1. Total attendance was about 2.4 million with over 61,000 decisions.

During the San Francisco crusade in 1958 a school of evangelism for ministers and theological students was suggested by Lowell Berry. The first school in Chicago in 1962 and later schools were largely financed by Lowell Berry. One school in Seoul drew 9,000.

Crusades were conducted in the major cities of Australia and New Zealand from February to May of 1959. The crowds numbered about 3,250,000, with about 150,000 decisions. During most of 1960 the team conducted meetings in Africa with about 40,000 decisions. Graham used closed-circuit television for the first time in meetings in England in June 1967. The meetings were telecast to twenty-five other cities in an all-Britain crusade. The same procedure was adopted at Dortmund in April 1970, when the EURO-70 crusade featured closed-circuit television in thirty-six centers in ten countries of Europe. In a meeting in Seoul, Korea, over 1 million heard Graham in one open-air meeting on June 3, 1973. He has also had meetings in such Com-

BILLY GRAHAM (b. 1918), who has preached to more people than any evangelist in history, at home in Montreat, North Carolina. *(Photo by Russ Busby, BGEA)*

munist countries as Hungary (1977), Poland (1978), and the Soviet Union (1982).

More than 100 million people have heard Graham speak in person at crusades, public meetings, or meetings in universities.

Crusade preparations are elaborate. Prayer groups are organized, and worldwide appeal is made for all Christians to pray for coming meetings. More than four thousand prayer meetings enlisting thousands engaged in prayer for the Tokyo Crusade. The training of several thousand counselors takes place before each crusade. Many Christians experience renewal or obtain assurance of salvation in those sessions. Choirs of several thousand are enrolled and trained. Since 1958, schools of evangelism in crusades have drawn as many as five thousand in each crusade to help ministers and theological students in revival and evangelism. Begun in 1981, telephone counseling centers had received nearly 208,000 calls with 96,000 decisions by 1984. Prime-time telecasts of crusades were seen on 275 stations in 1983.

Graham has maintained a humble spirit in all of this work and gives God the glory for all his success. His integrity is demonstrated by his paying his team members fixed salaries and channeling money through the Billy Graham Evangelistic Association.

He also developed additional agencies to help people. His column, "My Answer," begun in 1952 to answer problems, was carried in 200 papers by 1975. *Christianity Today*, with the financial backing of J. Howard Pew of Sun Oil and Graham's father-in-law, Nelson Bell, as executive editor, came into being in 1954. Carl F. H. Henry became its first editor, and publication began in October 1956. Ministers and laity alike have benefited from its articles on theology and religious news coverage. It is now a major religious periodical. *Decision* magazine with Sherwood Wirt as editor was founded in 1960 to give news of the crusades and to promote renewal and evangelism. By 1984 it had reached more than 2 million homes.

Graham's first book, *Peace With God*, published in 1953, sold about 1,250,000 copies. The first edition of *How to Be Born Again* sold 800,000 copies, the largest ever of a first edition. *World Aflame* is a useful and practical summary of evangelical theology. *Approaching Hoofbeats*, based on the first part of Revelation, has sold over 500,000 copies since it was published in October 1983.

As a spokesman for evangelical theology and practice, Graham has been careful to maintain a consistent evangelical position. However, for the most part he has refused to respond to critics of the theological right (who have often felt that Graham has compromised with theological liberals) and of the left (who have accused him of having no social message). This policy was suggested to him years ago by V. Raymond Edman, a close friend and member of his board. The policy has served Graham well, keeping him out of theological controversies and allowing him to reach a broad audience through his crusades and books.

He has supplemented the printed page with audiovisual techniques, beginning with the Portland Crusade. Films such as *The Hiding Place*, (the story of Corrie ten Boom's life) have reached millions and resulted in thousands of decisions. Approximately 130 films had been produced and distributed by 1984 by his Worldwide Films organization.

His organization has also sponsored and supported large conferences to promote revival and evangelism. The World Congress on Evangelism in Berlin was sponsored by the Graham organization and *Christianity Today* under the direction of Stanley Mooneyham in October 1966. About 1,200 were present to pray together and discuss the relevance, urgency, nature, and problems of world evangelism. A similar conference of Asians, led by Asians, convened in Singapore in 1968.

The Lausanne Conference, directed by Don Hoke and Paul Little in July 1974, drew over 2,400 people from 150 countries. A third of the people attending were from Third World churches. The Lausanne Covenant asserted loyalty to the inspired Scriptures as the infallible rule of faith and practice. It also stated that social concern and action—as well as the primary duty of evangelism—were integral parts of the gospel.

An itinerant evangelists' conference in Amsterdam from July 12 to 21, 1983, gathered over 3,800 evangelists from 133 nations around the world for inspiration and instruction. About 1,200 others attended. Books, tape recorders, and clothes were given to poorer evangelists. The Amsterdam Affirmation set doctrinal, spiritual, and personal goals for such workers. A day of witnessing in Amsterdam by those in the conference won many to Christ. All testified to the inspiration of the conference.

The Billy Graham Center at Wheaton College hosts the college's graduate departments, which train people in theology, Bible, church history, missions, Christian education, and communications. The Graham Center also has an instructive museum of evangelism from Whitefield to Graham. The archives hold thousands of original documents pertaining to revival, and the library houses what is probably the world's best collection on revival and evangelism. The Institute of Evangelism conducts short schools of evangelism for pastors in this country and those of the Third World who are brought to the meetings.

Billy Graham, now over sixty-five, has been used for good by God as few men have. His work has been done in humble dependence upon God and for his glory. It has been supplemented by the work of other revivalistic evangelists, such as Luis Palau, whom God has used in South America, the United States, and Britain.

Graham, like Fuller and Maier, has made extensive use of the electronic media. Missionaries have also made extensive use of radio to promote revival and evangelism. Station HCJB in Quito, Ecuador, ELWA in Africa, and the Far East Broadcasting Company developed programs in the 1950s. There are now at least fifteen major stations in the world devoting their efforts to reaching the unreached masses of the world.

Other revivalistic evangelists now operate from their churches in the U.S. Rex Humbard has used television since 1953 to augment his outreach. His Cathedral of Tomorrow in Akron, Ohio, was especially designed for television. His program had reached eighteen countries on 650 stations by 1980. Robert Schuller has televised the services from his Crystal Cathedral on the "Hour of Power" since 1970. He has supplemented his television ministry with many popular books.

Jerry Falwell operates from the Thomas Road Baptist Church in Lynchburg, Virginia, the center of his numerous activities. This church has about seventeen thousand members. Liberty University enrolls several thousand students and his "Old-Time Gospel Hour" goes out over approximately three thousand television stations in the United States and seventy abroad. The Moral Majority, which he founded in 1970, had grown to about 400,000, including 72,000 ministers, by 1980. In late August of 1980 he sponsored a National Affairs briefing of 12,000 ministers, before whom Ronald Reagan appeared. In January 1986 the Moral Majority became part of Liberty Federation, Falwell's organization created to fight communism around the world and back a strong national defense in the U. S.

Others who have used radio and television made divine healing a major part of their ministry. William Branham was prominent in the period from about 1945 to 1960. But Oral Roberts, who first used television in 1954 in his meetings, became the most prominent healer. He has built an empire in Oklahoma, including Oral Roberts University and other enterprises. Kathryn Kuhlman had a preaching and healing ministry over radio and television from Pittsburgh in the 1960s and 1970s.

Pat Robertson, the son of a former U.S. senator, set up the Christian Broadcasting Network (CBN). CBN maintains a university, and Robertson's "700 Club" is viewed on 130 television stations and some cable systems. Jim Bakker, formerly an associate of Robertson, organized his "PTL" ("Praise the Lord") telecast, broadcast from Charlotte, North Carolina, as a talk show.

These broadcasters and others have received criticism because of the large sums of money they raise and because of their alleged failure to sufficiently encourage their followers to work with local churches. While some of these men do at times seem to stress the raising of money over ministry, their telecasts have won many to Christ, including many people who are not reached by local churches. With a total of sixty-six religious programs, these men reached an estimated audience of 20 million in 1980, according to Arbitron figures.

CANADA

A remarkable revival occurred in the province of Saskatchewan in 1971. Wilbert McLeod (b. 1918), a potash miner, was converted by reading a book. He became a pastor of Ebenezer Baptist Church in Saskatoon in 1963 and prayed earnestly for revival for two years before it came.

Ralph and Lou Sutera (b. 1932), twins of Italian extraction and graduates of Bob Jones University, came to McLeod's church for their sixty-sixth meeting in October 1971. On October 13 many became convicted and made confessions of sin. Even some of the fifteen counselors admitted sin. As the size of the crowds increased, they moved the meetings from smaller to larger churches until they finally filled the 2,000-seat Civic Auditorium. "Afterglow" services, which followed the regular meetings, lasted until 3:00 A.M. McLeod called for a minister's conference, which ran from 10:00 A.M. one day until 5:00 P.M. the next day. Love, honesty which involved restitution, and healings marked the seven weeks of meetings by the Suteras in Saskatoon. Most of the converts were young people.

A team went to Winnipeg, Manitoba, in the latter part of November. McLeod spoke in the 1,600-seat Elim Chapel for seventeen days. Lay teams went out to witness. Many, especially German Baptists, were helped by the meetings. McLeod also spoke of the renewal in the Central Baptist Seminary in Toronto, but Saskatchewan and Manitoba were most affected by the revival.

EUROPE

Walter Sawatsky points out the growth of evangelicals by revival in Russia since World War I in his *Soviet Evangelicals Since World War II* (Scottdale, Pa.: Herald Press, 1981). English colporteurs of the British and Foreign Bible Society sold Bibles early in the nineteenth century and by 1819 had organized a Russian Bible Society which operated for several years.

From 1917 to 1924 evangelicals increased from about 150,000 to 750,000. The Baptists in the Ukraine were the largest of these groups, with 1,000 Baptist churches compared to 200 evangelical churches. Baptists, Mennonites, and Pentecostals in the state-registered churches were not so heavily persecuted as those not conforming and registering.

These churches were made up only of regenerated persons holding to a Bible-centered theology, the ordinances of baptism and the Lord's Supper, and democratic congregational government. The worst efforts of Communist dictators in Russia, Cuba, and China cannot suppress the church, which continues to grow.

Sawatsky estimates that church attendance in Russia since 1945 is 400 percent higher than it is in Britain and that perhaps 20 percent of the population is born-again in spite of campaigns by Stalin, Khrushchev, and their successors to eliminate Christianity.

ASIA

After World War II revival among the mountain tribes of Taiwan created a strong church in that part of the island. Estimates of the number of Christians in China in house churches run from 25 to 50 million during the period of Communist rule from 1949 to the present.

Parts of Indonesia experienced a great revival in 1965 and 1966. The threatened takeover by Communist generals in October 1965, was averted, and an estimated 300,000 to 500,000 Communists were massacred by Muslims who cooperated with Suharto. Revival occurred on the island of Timor in the midst of this unrest.

Between 1960 and 1971 church membership there increased from 97,000 to about 312,000. Not enough pastors were available to staff churches emerging from the witness of lay teams.

Nias, an island off northwest Sumatra, experienced revival from 1916 to 1922. As a result of that revival, the church grew from about 20,000 in 1915 to 110,000 by 1967. Even more remarkable was the Timor revival of 1965 and 1966. A Christian school teacher, J. A. Ratuwalu, was called to preach in April 1961 and was recognized by the church as an evangelist and healer. He held a healing meeting in the Soe church in October 1964. The pastor, Daniel, in the early part of 1965, preached the Word faithfully. Ditmar Scheunemann was in Timor in July 1965 with a team of students from the Batu Bible Institute. In their meeting in Soe, Henni Tunli, an Indonesian of twenty-five who had been reared in a Dutch pastor's home, felt called to go to the Bible school. Her testimony in the Soe church at a farewell meeting led to an 8:00 to 12:00 P.M. meeting in which over one hundred young people were renewed or saved. Teams of young people went all over the island. Team Number 36 reputedly won about 30,000 to Christ.

Between 1966 and 1969 the Evangelical Church of Soe added well over 1,000 baptized members to its membership of 3,000. In all, there were about 80,000 converted in Soe. The church in Timor, which numbered about 375,000 in 1964, grew to 650,000 by 1967. Of the professing Christians, 65 to 80 percent also experienced renewal. The revival was mainly in the south of the island around Soe.

In 1966, Pak Elias (b. 1928), a schoolmaster converted in 1957, was leader of a team which went to Rote, an island south of Timor. Over 1,000 were converted. He organized the converts into prayer groups. The use of lay teams, love of the Bible, and obedience to the Holy Spirit led to revival of Christians, conversions, and some miracles of healing, prophecy, and visions. Public confession of sin by members brought forgiveness, cleansing, and witnessing.

The Christian and Missionary Alliance Church in Vietnam was

revived in 1971. Missionaries at Nha Trang experienced revival that awakened both missionaries and nationals in May and those at the Bible institute in December. Between December 1971 and April 1972, eighty churches in the south gained 9,300 members, and about 150 healings took place. Prayer meetings replaced siestas.

SOME REFLECTIONS ON REVIVAL

Some generalizations seem apparent from this consideration of revivals since 1726. Revivals have begun in Anglo-Saxon Great Britain or her colonies and dominions. They have been carried to Germany and Scandinavia. As an exception, Pietism in Germany d.d develop as the earliest revival in the Great Awakening. Out of it developed the Moravian Church in the early seventeenth century.

Revivals originated for the most part in what might be termed the north Atlantic basin and civilization. Germany, Scandinavia, and the British Isles are on the eastern edge and the United States and Canada on the western edge geographically. Thus revival has been intercolonial, international, and global, especially in the era from 1857 to 1895.

Renewal has for the most part been a middle-class movement. The revival under Hauge in Norway was an exception, appealing to the farmers and laborers. The work of the Clapham Sect in England shows that revival has occurred among the upper class.

Revival has been almost exclusively a Protestant movement in the modern era. The Roman Catholic Church has had missions and missioners who promoted revival, but it has not been as widespread as Protestant revival.

With the exception of the Wesleys, who were Arminians, revival was predominantly Calvinistic theologically until the days of Finney. The Calvinists emphasized the supernatural activity of the Holy Spirit in revival rather than the means of revival. According to Calvinists, the sovereign God was active in the promotion of revival, and man's role in bringing about revival was relatively small. Although he admitted this, Finney stressed man's free will and consequently viewed revival more as a natural historic phenomenon which would naturally follow the use of the right techniques. It was not necessary for people to wait for God to act; renewal could be "worked up" by appropriate use of the right methods. The Calvinistic revivalists did use human means, such as prayer, preaching, and counseling the convicted, because that would help the elect (those whom God had chosen to save) to come to salvation. Thus, until the Civil War, with the work of Finney as an exception, revivals were thought to be for the most part the act of the Holy Spirit by the will of a sovereign God. With prayer and preaching as means, they resulted in deep conviction and final acceptance of God's grace and the new birth in God's own time.

Early revivals usually came in local congregations under local or itinerant pastors who counseled those convicted. Moody and others organized large-scale meetings that involved more people than any church building could hold.

Beginning with Finney, who was a transitional figure and a forerunner of urban evangelism, revival, especially after 1865, was usually professional in that the revivalist devoted all of his time to organized mass meetings in large urban areas. Finney was a forerunner of this type of meeting, with work in smaller cities in New York and the east coast. Most of his meetings were still held in churches at the invitation of local pastors. The following diagram will illustrate the difference:

Before 1865	*After 1865*
Calvinistic	Moderately Calvinistic or Arminian
Bound will	Free will
Man passive	Man dynamic
Stress on sovereignty of God and Holy Spirit	Stress on human means ("New Measures")

| Natural depravity and original sin | More stress on actual sin of the individual |
| Await God's revival | Revival more "worked up" by human agents |

Finney and his later successors (Moody, Jones, and others) in the early days of a meeting addressed themselves to professing Christians in order to revive them to Christian witness and work. They held that man must be more active in revival and exert his will to choose Christ.

The laity played an important part in revival in all of these eras. Howel Harris, H. N. Hauge, and Dwight L. Moody were laymen. John Wesley, Theodor Frelinghuysen, and Hauge used lay preachers to help carry on their work. The laity in the Clapham Sect in England sponsored many voluntary missionary, Bible, and reforming societies. Wilberforce and Buxton carried on anti-slavery activity as laymen. Their helpers, Sharp, Macaulay, and Clarkson were laymen. Shaftesbury belonged to the laity. Hannah Ball, Hannah More, and Robert Raikes, famous in Sunday school work, were lay people.

Many laymen in commerce and politics supported both spiritual and reform activities. In England, John and Henry Thornton and Robert Arthington spent their money lavishly for reform and missions. Arthur and Lewis Tappan, Thomas G. Ryman, John Wanamaker, and Robert Converse supported the "Benevolence Empire" that was behind the interlocking directorate of the voluntary societies in the United States.

Until recently the role of women in revival has been neglected. Women who were touched by revival became leaders both in revival and reform. Hannah Ball of High Wycombe founded what was the first Sunday school in 1769. Hannah More later organized several Sunday schools in the Cheddar area near Bristol.

Peggy Dow sacrificially stayed at home, praying for Lorenzo while he held meetings. Indeed, after he proposed marriage he was absent for several months on a preaching tour in the South, and the day after their marriage he left her to go on a long tour of the Southwest. Wives of circuit riders had to look after their homes and children while their husbands were riding circuits for several months at a time.

Lydia Finney, whose prayers helped to win Charles Finney to Christ, supported his work with infant schools, mother meetings, and prayer meetings. His second wife, Elizabeth, organized women's prayer meetings to support Finney's work both in the United States and in England on their two tours (1849–51 and 1858–60). During the second trip she began to preach to women with great effect in separate meetings.

Phoebe Palmer led "Tuesday meetings" for years in her home to promote holiness. She was instrumental in founding the Five-Points Mission in New York, the forerunner of the settlement house. After her experience of "entire sanctification" in 1837, she began preaching. In their 1857–60 tour of England she claimed 17,300 individuals were converted or "sanctified."

Moody had Francis Willard hold meetings for women during his Boston meeting. Grace Saxe conducted women's Bible studies for Billy Sunday.

Most revival leaders from Wesley to Graham had an experience in which they felt that the Holy Spirit had given them power to preach. Zinzendorf and his Moravians had such an experience. The Wesleys received such an enduement of power early one morning in a meeting with the Moravians. Finney had a similar experience in the woods and Moody had one in New York. Billy Graham had an infilling in England early in his career. This points up the role of the Holy Spirit in enduing these men with power for their special work.

Revivals have brought an ecumenism in which denominational loyalties were largely ignored. This was true of revival associated with Whitefield, especially in the thirteen colonies. Camp meetings in the west linked Methodists and Presbyterians in soul-saving. The prayer revival of 1857 was especially marked by inter-denominational cooperation. Billy Graham's meetings have attracted a wide spectrum of denominations in cooperative effort.

Prayer has preceded and followed religious awakening. Freling-huysen arranged for prayer meetings led by laity in his Dutch Reformed churches in New Jersey. Before the Second Awakening, Carey and other Baptist leaders in Great Britain started a concert of prayer for revival in the 1780s in the British Isles, and Isaac Backus organized a Concert of Prayer in 1795. The Second Awakening in Britain and the United States followed this wave of prayer. The revival of 1857, beginning in New York, was almost exclusively a lay revival based on prayer in various countries. Moody, Torrey, and Graham enlisted thousands in numerous small prayer meetings and attributed what success they had to prayer. Revival has always followed sincere prayer on the part of the church.

The spontaneity of revival speaks of the sovereign work of the Holy Spirit. Lanphier's prayer meetings in New York had their counterpart in Ulster in McQuilkin's prayer meetings, both of which brought revival at the same time in two lands. Revival in Wheaton College in 1950 seemed a spontaneous movement of the Spirit.

Revival, since the days of Hezekiah when revival moved him and the people to oppose Sennacherib of Assyria, has helped to prepare God's people to bravely face opposing forces in a crisis. The lay prayer revival of 1857 and 1859 fortified the North spiritually to withstand the stress of the Civil War. The Confederate army revival of 1862 to 1864 helped the South in defeat by providing a core of about 100,000 Christians, renewed or converted in the Army, to face the stresses of reconstruction. Revival after 1900 prepared people for the agonies of World War I, and the Korean revival provided spiritual resources when the Japanese took over.

Contrary to William Sweet's view, revival has not disappeared but has continued in many areas of the world. God grant that it may increase until it is again global.

PART TWO *The Fruits of Revival*

8. CHURCH GROWTH AT HOME AND ABROAD

REVIVAL resulted in increased witnessing on the part of Christians as they felt the pressure of Christ's mandate (the Great Commission) in Matthew 28:18-20 and were assured of his power and presence with them in fulfilling it. Under the influence of the Holy Spirit they realized that they were to be witnesses to Christ and work from "Jerusalem . . . to the uttermost part of the earth" (Acts 1:8). The witness was abroad as well as at home, for modern foreign missions came out of revival. The diagram on page 000 shows the impact of revival on the witness, walk, and work of Christians in chapters eight to ten.

REVIVALISTIC EXPANSION AT HOME

The First Amendment to the Constitution of the United States decreed a separation of church and state that barred any established state church or civil interference with the practice of religion. Thus, if people were to be brought into the church, it had to be by voluntary means. The state church grows by natural birth as children are baptized and confirmed. This was true in England, Germany, and Scandinavia, though there was toleration for dissenters. Thus evangelism was important in these lands as well as the United States if the masses were to be brought into the church. Only a church activated by revival would seek to win the masses to Christ and bring them into the church. Consequently, the laity became more important in church affairs and lay witness.

When professing Christians were quickened by revivals, large numbers were added to the church after the manner of Acts 2:47 and 5:14, and new churches were formed. Pastoral revivalists and later revivalistic evangelists inspired and led the church in this endeavor to fulfill the mandate in Acts 1:8 to be witnesses to the "uttermost part of the earth."

The Great Awakening in New England added 25,000 to 50,000 (in a population of about 340,000) to the churches, and 150 new Congregational churches were formed. Methodists alone in England numbered over 70,000 by the time John Wesley died. Thousands more were saved in the Welsh, Scottish, and English Calvinistic groups.

During the Second Awakening, thousands came into the church through the camp meetings, activity of godly pastors and itinerant pastor-evangelists, and college revivals. Pastors won their fifties and hundreds in revivals in about 150 New England churches around 1800. Through the activities of the Episcopalian pastor Devereux Jarratt in Virginia and Methodist preachers here and elsewhere, the Methodists grew rapidly and numbered 120,000 by 1800. Between 1800 and 1802 the Baptists multiplied from 5,000 to nearly 14,000 in Kentucky alone and the Methodists from about 3,000 to over 10,000. This was a growth rate of about 300 percent.

Thousands were added to the church in the period from 1813 to 1846 as a result of Methodist camp meetings, revivalistic pastors, and evangelists. In England the Primitive Methodists increased from their beginning in 1808 to over 7,800 members in 1820 and to about 110,000 by 1852. According to one scholarly estimate, about 200,000 were added to evangelical churches in the United States between 1826 and 1832. The Congregationalist Nettleton is credited with about 25,000 converts, the Baptist Jacob Knapp claimed about 100,000 converts, and the Presbyterian Daniel Baker had about 20,000 converts in the South. Finney won about 500,000 during his evangelistic career.

During the lay prayer meeting revival, which began in 1857, over 1 million came into the churches in the United States and the same number was added to the churches in Great Britain. Sam Jones in the South is credited with 500,000 converts and Moody with 750,000 in this era.

Large numbers of persons became church members between 1900 and 1945. R. A. Torrey saw about 100,000 come to Christ in his meeting. Billy Sunday had 593,000 sign cards in his meetings. In 1904 and 1905 Evan Roberts was given the 100,000 he felt God had promised him in Wales. About 300,000 were added to the church in England. Thousands were converted in Korea during the great revivals of 1904 to 1907. By the end of this era classic Pentecostalism had gained millions of born-again believers, especially in the United States and Chile. Brazil alone had about 1 million members. An indigenous tribal church among the Wallamo grew from 48 in 1937 to 15,000 in 1945, most of the time without missionaries. It is estimated that China currently has more than 25 million believers.

From 1945 to March 1984, Billy Graham alone has recorded about 1,928,201 decisions for Christ in his crusades. One might add to this about 200,000 converted in the Indonesian revival in Timor from 1965 to 1966. Charismatics in the mainline denominations were thought to number about 11 million by 1980. Classical Pentecostals were estimated to number over 10,000,000 in 1980. Many parachurch agencies are also active in winning people to Christ, particularly the young people.

Multiplied millions have been added to the church during the era of Protestant revival. How many more millions of professing Christians have been won back to their first love, witnessing, and service? The Lord is still adding to his church those whom he calls (Acts 2:47). Eternity alone will give the true tally of those who were won in revival.

MISSIONARY EXPANSION

Kenneth Scott Latourette terms the period from 1815 to 1914 "The Great Century" of missions in his seven-volume history of missions. He devotes the last three volumes of the set to describing missionary expansion. But the missionary enterprise began long before 1815. There is a close connection between revivals and missions dating from the Moravians of the eighteenth century. The first Protestant missionaries were Lutheran pietists. King Frederick IV of Denmark sent two men from Halle to India in 1706. They were Bartholomew Ziegenbalg and Heinrich Plutschau whose work has already been discussed (see pages 34–35).

Missionaries to the American Indians. In the New World, missionaries came with the Spanish and Portuguese explorers. The priests and friars who accompanied the gold-seeking *conquistadores* were genuinely concerned for the spiritual welfare of the natives of the lands newly claimed for Spain and Portugal. The French in Canada also carried on missionary work with the Indians.

In the territories that later became the United States, godly men were also concerned with the souls of the native peoples. The Indian princess Pocahontas, who married Englishman John Rolfe, was converted under Alexander Whitaker, an Anglican minister in Virginia. The visit of Pocahontas to England aroused the Church of England's interest in missions.

By 1652 Thomas Mayhew had established an Indian church at Martha's Vineyard, Massachusetts. By 1664 there were more than two hundred "praying Indians" in that church.

John Eliot (1604–90), a Puritan Anglican minister, got in trouble with Archbishop Laud, moved to Boston in 1632, and became teacher of the Roxbury church until his death. He began to work among the Algonquin Indians. By 1663 he had translated the Bible into their language and set up Indian Christian villages. By 1674 there were over 3,000 Indians in these villages with 1,100 under Eliot and 2,000 under the Mayhews. The villagers were dispersed by the tragedy of King Philip's War in 1675 and 1676.

David Zeisberger (1721-1808), a Moravian, studied the Mohawk language and preached to Indians in New York, Massachusetts, Pennsylvania, Ohio, Michigan, and Canada from 1745 to 1808. He formed the Delaware Indians into Christian villages in 1745.

John Sergeant (1710-49), a tutor at Yale in 1734, was ordained in 1735 and sent by the Society for the Propagation of the Gospel as a missionary to the Housatonic Indians at Stockbridge, Massachusetts. He baptized 182 of them and accepted about 60 as church members. Later Brainerd's converts from Kaunameek joined them. Sergeant's home was later occupied by Jonathan Edwards, who also acted as a missionary to the Indians at Stockbridge.

David Brainerd (1718-47), born on a farm in Haddam, Connecticut, was converted on July 12, 1738. He went to Yale in 1739 in the midst of the revival. After hearing Ebenezer Pemberton speak on missions and Christ's love, he resolved "to be wholly the Lord's, to be forever devoted to his service." When his comment that a tutor, Chauncy Whittelsy, had "no more grace than a chair," was reported to the college authorities, he was expelled in his junior year in 1742. (Old Side Presbyterians—those who opposed the new revivalism—were often criticized for their lack of warm, heartfelt religion.) The New Side Presbyterians then founded the College of New Jersey (now Princeton University) to train their men.

In 1742 Brainerd studied theology under Jedediah Mills, was licensed by the Congregationalists, and was sent by the Scottish Society for the Propagation of the Gospel (SPG) to Stockbridge with Sergeant to learn the Indian language. From 1743 to 1744 he preached to Indians at Kaunameek near Albany and operated a school for Indian children. After his Indians moved to Stockbridge, he ministered to the Delawares in eastern Pennsylvania from June 1744, when he was ordained by the Presbyterians, to 1745. In that same year he went to Crossweeksung where a revival came among the Indians from July to November of 1745. Forty-three adults and forty-two children were converted.

In late May 1746 his health broke under tuberculosis, melancholy, and lack of care of his body. He went to Edwards's home where his fianceé, Jerusha, nursed him until he died in 1747. His *Journal*, edited by Jonathan Edwards, had a great influence on Henry Martyn, William Carey, Thomas Coke, and Samuel Marsden.

His brother, John Brainerd (1720–81), educated at Yale and ordained in 1748, carried on David's work after his death. John was elected a trustee of the College of New Jersey in 1784. Between 1762 and 1777 he worked with Indians at Brothertown, New Jersey, and served pastorates.

Eleazar Wheelock (1711–79) was born in Windham, Connecticut, and educated at Yale. In 1735 he became pastor of a Congregational church in Lebanon, Connecticut, where, during the revival of that year in his church, he spoke 465 times. Joshua Moor (More) gave him two acres of land and a house in which he opened Moor's Indian Charity School with two pupils in 1754.

Of the twenty pupils in 1762, Joseph Brant was notable. Brant, who was in England in 1755 and 1756, was sent to Moor's School about 1761 by William Johnston at the request of Samuel Kirkland. He was an important Indian chief in Canada later.

Wheelock's first pupil was Samson Occom (1723–92). Occom was converted about 1740 by the fiery James Davenport. The SPG provided £60 a year for his support while he was in the school. When his poor eyesight ended his schooling, he went to Montauk, Long Island, where he served as a teacher, preacher, and judge from 1749 to 1761. The Presbyterians ordained him and he ministered to the Oneidas between 1761 and 1764.

He made a trip to England in 1766 and 1767 with Nathaniel Whitaker to raise money for Wheelock's school. He was a guest of

Whitefield, who presented him to the Earl of Dartmouth. He spoke in Whitefield's tabernacle and was presented to George III, who gave him £200. Crowds numbering up to three thousand gathered to hear him in Scotland, where he raised £2,529, and Ireland. English people gave him £9,500. On January 26, 1767, a board was set up to handle the money which totalled £12,000. Dartmouth was president and John Thornton treasurer of the board. Most of the credit for raising the money should go to Occom, who spoke over four hundred times. Lady Huntingdon influenced him very much. He went to Mohegan on his return to America in 1768. The church there had a great revival. He was in Brothertown, New Jersey, from 1789 until his death.

Wheelock used the money raised by Occom to move his school to Hanover, New Hampshire, in 1770. New Hampshire gave him a charter and forty thousand acres of land as an endowment. He accepted both colonists and Indians, and forty ministers had graduated from the school by 1800. It later became known as Dartmouth College, named after its main patron, the Earl of Dartmouth.

Samuel Kirkland (1741–1808) also devoted his life to Indian work. He studied at Wheelock's school in 1760, where he learned Mohawk from Joseph Brant, at Yale, and at the College of New Jersey. His main work was with the Iroquois Indians. From 1764 to 1766 he ministered to the Senecas and from 1766 to 1808 was with the Oneidas except for a three-year period from 1776 to 1779 when he was a chaplain in the Revolutionary War. He was responsible for the founding of Hamilton and Oneida Academy in 1793; it became Hamilton College in 1810.

Great Britain and Her Missionaries. The London Society for Propagating the Gospel Among the Jews was founded in 1809 to reach the Jews with the gospel. The German J. G. Frey had come to England to work with Jews, and sympathetic Evangelicals heeded his call for an organization. For a time George Müller received training from this society.

Before missionaries were officially admitted to India in 1813, William Carey (1761–1834) began work in Danish territory in India. Carey was born in Northamptonshire and became a cobbler. While repairing shoes, he educated himself and learned Latin, Dutch, French, Greek, and Hebrew. John Warr, a fellow apprentice, led him to Christ and he was baptized by immersion in 1783. He married and became the village schoolmaster, shoemaker, and Baptist preacher at Moulton in 1785 and was ordained in 1787.

Carey organized a prayer meeting for revival and missions in 1784. He pressed the need of missions upon the Baptists and on May 12, 1792, published "An Enquiry into the Obligation of Christians to Use Means for the Conversion of the Heathen." His sermon on Isaiah 54:2 to Baptist preachers at Nottingham had these divisions: "Expect great things from God" and "Attempt great things for God."

Carey volunteered to go to India, in spite of the reluctance of his wife, who later died there of a mental disease. Although he reached India in 1793, he had to go to Danish Serampore because of opposition from the British East India Company. He took a secular position as superintendent of an indigo factory to earn his living. During his lifetime he gave £4,000 to his society.

Joshua Marshman (1768–1837) and William Ward (1769–1820), a printer, joined him in India. In 1801 Carey became a tutor in Bengali and Sanskrit at Fort William College, the government college at Calcutta. In 1818 he founded Serampore College as a Christian institution. All this time he also worked as an ardent evangelist and also as a gardener, introducing many new plants to India. He had translated the whole Bible into Sanskrit by 1818 and by 1809 into Bengali. In 1829, because he showed that the practices were not in the Hindu scriptures, Carey influenced the governor to ban *sati* (the practice of burning widows on their husbands' funeral pyres) and infanticide.

When his first wife died in 1807, he married Charlotte Rumohr, a Danish countess, in 1808. She gave her lovely house to the mission. Carey's work laid foundations for Protestant work in India.

Evangelicals in England sent Claudius Buchanan and later Henry Martyn as chaplains of the British East India Company. Claudius Buchanan (1766–1815) was born in Cambuslang, the center of revival in 1739 and 1839. He received his education at Glasgow University and Queen's College, Cambridge, where he came under the influence of Charles Simeon.

After his ordination in 1796, Buchanan went to India as a chaplain of the trading company and was vice-principal of Fort William College from 1799 to 1807. Buchanan translated the Bible into Hindustani and Persian. The first Anglican bishopric in India in 1818 owed much to his efforts.

Henry Martyn (1781–1812) was another company chaplain-missionary. He was born at Truro, Cornwall, in a miner's home. His friend, Kempthorne, won him to Christ. He graduated from St. John's College, Cambridge, where he won all the prizes for proficiency in classical languages. In 1802 he became a fellow at his college and in that same year joined the Church Missionary Society. He was Charles Simeon's curate for some years.

After his ordination in 1805, when Charles Grant offered him a chaplaincy in India and Simeon urged him to take it, Martyn went to Calcutta. Brainerd's life and journals and Carey's work helped him to develop a passionate missionary heart. On the way to India, Martyn served as chaplain to troops on 150 ships sent to capture Cape Town from the Dutch. He saw its capture.

In 1806 he arrived at Calcutta and in 1809 was sent to Cawnpore. His Hindustani New Testament was ready for the press in 1810. In January 1811 he went with his Arabic and Persian translations to Persia to polish his work. He worked from 1811 to 1812 in Shiraz on his Persian New Testament. Ague and tuberculosis killed him at Tokat in Turkey in 1812. By 1816 his Persian and Arabic translations of the New Testament were published. Both he and Buchanan were products of the evangelical awakening in the church.

Early missionaries to India and South Africa had to cope with opposition from trading companies and the colonial government, which looked upon them as a nuisance and disturber of the peace (since they tried to change the religion of the nationals). This attitude was changed when the charter of the British East India Company was renewed in 1813. Control of immigration to India was taken from the company and given to a board of control. The company was required to permit missionaries to enter India, set aside money for education of the nationals, and allow the establishment of an Anglican bishopric. These changes came as a result of the work of William Wilberforce and others. They pressured Parliament to pass this changed charter by public meetings, pamphlets, and letters to the *Times* of London. They presented 837 petitions with over 500,000 names supporting these changes in the charter. Missionaries could now go to India, and Christianity was recognized as a legal religion in India.

Alexander Duff (1806–78) entered India under the new charter. When Simeon toured Scotland with James Haldane in 1796, he helped Stewart, the minister at Moulin, to preach Christ crucified. Duff's godly father was a member of the Moulin church and trained his son in the faith. While Alexander was at St. Andrews University, he initiated Sunday schools and a college students' missionary organization. He was ordained in 1829 and became the first missionary of the Kirk of Scotland.

He lost nearly all of his 800-volume library when he was shipwrecked near Cape Town on his way to India. He arrived in Calcutta in May 1830 after a second wreck. With Carey's blessing he set about his plans for education. In his school for nationals the Bible was to be read and taught as the core of the English language curriculum in order to evangelize Hindus through education. Aided by Raja R. Ray, he opened the school in July 1830 with five pupils. By 1832 four students had become Christians. He returned home from 1835 to 1837 and spoke to the Kirk's General Assembly on the need for missions. When the assembly distributed 200,000 copies of his speech, his talk set "Scotland on fire" for missions.

In 1843 the Free Church, and Duff, came out of the Kirk

because of revival and the problem of patronage. By that year he had twelve converts in India. Between 1850 and 1855 he traveled in Scotland and the United States to promote missions. He was honored by being allowed to speak to the House of Representatives in the United States and by his election as moderator of the Free Church in Scotland in 1851.

Duff was again in India from 1855 to 1863 and served as head of the college which he had founded after leaving the Kirk. When he finally returned to Scotland, he was made superintendent of Free Church foreign missions and took the chair of missions in the Free Church theological school from 1864 to 1878. Revival was the factor behind his work.

We must now consider the founding of the major missionary societies and their most important missionaries. The Baptist Missionary Society, founded in 1792, was the first in the field with Carey as its first missionary.

The interdenominational London Missionary Society was founded in 1795. In July 1794, John Ryland of Baptist College, Bristol, shared a letter with David Bogue, a Presbyterian pastor of the Congregational church at Gosport and spiritual advisor to the Haldanes, and with Mr. Stephen of Bristol. The three men joined with Mr. Hey to pray about how they might awaken people to interest in missions. Bogue published a paper pleading for missions in the September 1794 issue of the *Evangelical Magazine*. In November of the same year, Thomas Haweis published a review of Melville Horne's book, *Letters on Missions*, and wrote that he had an offer of £100 from one individual and £500 from a minister (himself) to help organize a society and send out six missionaries to the South Sea Islands.

John Eyre, editor of the magazine, and Matthew Wilkes began a bimonthly meeting at the Castle and Falcon Inn, Aldersgate Street, to pray for missions and to plan how they might set up a society. A larger meeting of ministers met on February 17, 1795, and thirty-four signed a document pledging to work for the founding of a society. The society came into being at a meeting on

September 21, 1795, and the next day the two hundred ministers named the society and drew up a constitution. On Wednesday, September 22, they nominated twenty-five directors. On Thursday they found seven people who were ready to go to the South Seas as missionaries. On Friday they elected the directors and a treasurer. They drew up their "fundamental principles of missions" on May 9 to complete the work.

The society bought the *Duff*, and in August 1796 the first group of missionaries was taken to Tahiti. A second contingent arrived in 1798. But by 1800 only seven of the original thirty continued in the work. Twenty had left the work and three had been killed. Of the remaining seven John Williams was the most important. Johannes Vanderkemp was sent to Cape Town in 1797. Work was also started in India, China, and the West Indies. By 1807 the society had 170 European and English missionaries, nearly 500 native helpers, and 131 national churches.

The Moravian George Schmidt (1709–85) opened the first work at the Cape in 1736 to help the Hottentots but was ordered out by the Dutch colonial government in 1743.

Johannes T. Vanderkemp (1747–1811) was the son of a Lutheran minister in Rotterdam. After completing his education at the University of Leyden he served as a dissolute Dutch army officer for sixteen years. He then took medical training as a doctor in the University of Edinburgh. He accepted Christ and joined the London Missionary Society (LMS) as a missionary after the accidental drowning of his wife and daughter in 1791. He was ordained by the Presbyterian Church of Scotland in 1797 and went to South Africa in 1799. He set up a mission at Bethelsdorp among the Hottentots. His marriage to a seventeen-year-old Madagascar slave and the disinclination of the Hottentots under him to work as slave laborers angered the Dutch farmers who opposed his work.

Robert Moffat (1795–1883) was more successful. He was a Scottish gardener who went to South Africa in 1817. While in the back country north of Cape Town he won Afrikaner, a notorious native outlaw, to Christ and took him to Cape Town in 1819, much to the joy and wonder of the authorities, who forgave the outlaw. Moffat settled at Kuruman in Bechuanaland and by 1857 had given the people a Bible in Sechuana, their own dialect.

Robert Morrison (1782–1834), another translator in China, was born in Morpeth, Northumbria, and became the first Protestant missionary to China. He was trained under David Bogue from 1803 to 1805 at Hoxton Academy (now Highbury College) near London. He was ordained and sailed via New York as an LMS missionary. The hostility of English traders at Canton forced him to go to Portuguese Macao in the summer of 1808. The British East India Company appointed him to be a Chinese interpreter at £500 a year. His first convert, Tsae A. Foo, was baptized on July 16, 1814, and by 1817 his Mandarin Chinese New Testament was printed. By 1819 the whole Bible was in Mandarin. In 1823 the company published his Anglo-Chinese dictionary at a cost of £10,000. He and a later colleague, William Milne (1785–1822), organized an Anglo-Chinese college at Malacca. Thus he opened the door to missions in China.

John Philip (1775–1851) was another notable LMS leader in South Africa. Born into a Scottish weaver's family, he was influenced by revival to enter the ministry. He trained for it for two years at Hoxton Academy. Between 1803 and 1819 he was a pastor of a large Congregational church in Aberdeen. His powerful body, his keen piercing eyes, and his oratorical skill won friends and converts. In 1817 George Burder, secretary of the LMS, asked him to superintend the work of the society in South Africa.

Philip began his work in Africa in 1822. He fought for legal equality of Hottentot and white and for native land rights. He later proposed treaty states in which native chiefs would rule under tribal law but leave foreign relations to a British resident who might help missionaries and keep whites from exploiting the blacks. The South African government was forced by English public opinion—and Ordinance Fifty—to grant civil rights to blacks because of Philip's book, *Researches in South Africa.*

Missionaries of the LMS were also responsible for African exploration, which opened the road for missions. John Campbell (1776–1840) was sent to Africa to observe missionary work there for the LMS from 1812 to 1814. In his journeys north in 1812 Campbell "laid down the course of the Orange River and [on his second trip in 1819 with Moffat] discovered the source of the Limpopo."

David Livingstone (1813–73) was as famous an explorer as he was a missionary. Born in Blantyre, Scotland, he educated himself in Latin while he worked as a spinner. He took theology and medical courses in nearby Glasgow. Although he was inept in public prayer and preaching, the LMS accepted him, and Moffat persuaded him to go to Africa rather than to China, the country to which he had planned to go. He was ordained in 1840 and arrived at Cape Town the following year. Exploration to open the way for missions and lawful trade and later to fight Arab slave trading in East Africa appealed more to him than settled missionary work. Mary Moffat, whom he married, did not see a great deal of him.

Mrs. McRoberts, wife of the minister in Cambuslang, sent £12 to Livingstone to hire a native teacher. He engaged Mebalwe, who later saved his life at Mabotsa by shooting a lion who mangled his arm.

His first discovery was Lake Ngami in August 1842, in company with two English hunters, E. C. Oswell and Murray. In 1852 he sent his family home to England so that he could explore and open Africa to Christianity and commerce and undercut the slave trade. He went north to the upper Zambezi River in 1851. From 1853 to 1854 he traveled west with much hardship to Loanda in Portuguese East Africa. He did not go home, though ill, because he had promised a Makalolo chief that he would return his carriers to their chief. He crossed Africa from coast to coast between 1854 and 1856 and discovered and named Victoria Falls after Queen Victoria early in November 1855. His book, *Missionary Travels and Researches in South Africa,* described this trip and sold over thirty thousand copies. In 1857 he told students in the Cambridge Senate House, "I go back to try to make an open path for Christianity and commerce."

Between 1858 and 1864 he was leader of a government expedition to explore the Zambezi River sources. He discovered Lake Nyasa on September 16, 1859, and helped to settle Scottish Presbyterian missionaries in the vicinity of the lake. Because he looked upon "the geographic feat" as the beginning of the "missionary enterprise," he went back to Africa on his last trip (1866-73) to solve the problem of the African watershed. He wrote to James Young that he went to do missionary work and "do geography by the way." He discovered Lake Moero in 1867 and Lake Bangweolo in July 1868. He had reached Lake Tanganyika earlier in 1867. It was at Ujiji late in 1871 that Henry M. Stanley found him ill. Stanley provided him with medication and good food during a four-month stay with him. He said of Livingstone, "I never found a fault in him." Livingstone died on this trip in 1873.

Harry L. Johnston, a colonial explorer and administrator, said that Livingstone had "initiated the scientific exploration of Africa" in his travels of more than twenty-eight thousand miles in Africa. While he did not discover the sources of the Nile, he did map the Zambezi River system and the lake system of Central Africa. This opened Africa for missions and trade. In 1857 he challenged the Cambridge Senate House to evangelize Africa. The Universities' mission to Central Africa in 1860, the Kirk of Scotland Mission at Blantyre on Lake Nyasa, and the Free Church Mission were set up in response to that address.

Livingstone's high moral standards impressed the Africans. His exposure of the East African slave trade by Arabs led to legitimate trade and naval patrols which finally suppressed the trade. He wanted sale of cotton and other native products to replace the selling of slaves. His heart was appropriately buried in Africa by his loyal bearers, though his body lies in Westminster Abbey.

George Grenfell (1849-1906) of the Baptist Missionary Society explored and opened the Congo River basin just as Livingstone had done for the Zambezi. This Cornish missionary, after a term in the Cameroons (1875–78), dedicated his life to exploring and opening the Congo River basin to missions and trade. Between 1878 and 1906 he traveled fifteen thousand miles on the Congo and its tributaries in the steamer *Peace*, for which Robert Arthington of Leeds had given £10,000. He also discovered the Ubangi River in 1884 and put it on the map. The Royal Geographical Society recognized this geographical feat in 1887 by granting him its Founder's Medal. But Grenfell's main interest, like that of Livingstone, lay in the founding of mission stations.

The Church Missionary Society, founded in 1799 by Evangelicals in the Church of England, began work in India and East Africa. It grew out of discussions by the members of the Eclectic Society, founded in 1786. In a meeting of February 8, 1796, the members discussed a paper by Charles Simeon on "With What Propriety and in What Mode" they could get the gospel to foreign lands. John Venn, vicar of Clapham, who was in that meeting, chaired a meeting on April 12, 1799, in the Castle and Falcon Inn. Henry Thornton was appointed treasurer but William Wilberforce declined the presidency. The name of the society was adopted in 1812. Their best work was in East Africa. By 1819 they had sent out fifty-five missionaries and their income was £25,000.

Johann L. Krapf (1810–81), born in Germany and educated at the University of Tübingen and at the School of the Basel Mission in Switzerland, was sent to Abyssinia, now Ethiopia, in 1838. Roman Catholic opposition forced him to go to East Africa in 1843. He discovered Mount Kenya late in 1849 and got a full view of the snow-capped mountain. His associate Johannes Rebmann (c. 1819–76), sent out to help him in 1846, discovered Mount Kilimanjaro in 1848. Rebmann named and described the "beautiful snow mountain." Knowledge of the lake system of central Africa came from African tribesmen who described it to Arab traders. This report and their discoveries awakened wide interest in Britain for East Africa missions. Krapf also prepared a translation of the Bible in Swahili.

The work of Alexander Mackay and George Pilkington in Africa has been discussed earlier (see page 204).

Australia and New Zealand were not neglected by the English church. Samuel Marsden (1764–1838) was born in a farm home in Yorkshire. His education from 1786 to 1793 was subsidized by the Elland Society. This group had been founded in 1767 by Evangelical clerics to raise money to recruit and educate promising poor boys to the ministry. Marsden studied with Milner at Hull and then entered Magdalene College, Cambridge, in 1790 where he became a friend of Charles Simeon.

William Wilberforce offered him a chaplaincy in New South Wales in Australia in 1792. He was ordained in 1793 and went to Australia in 1794 where he served until 1838. He built St. John's Church and became "a gardener, a farmer, a magistrate, and minister" and supervisor of the mission to the Maoris in New Zealand. When he was in England from 1807 to 1810, George III gave him five ewes and two rams from his flock of merino sheep. This helped in the development of sheep farming in Australia.

On the way to Australia, Marsden met Ruatara, a Maori from New Zealand, and became interested in establishing a mission there. With personal funds and those of friends, he bought a ship for £1,500 and persuaded the Church Missionary Society to send Kendall and Hall to New Zealand in 1814. He took them in his ship to North Island to civilize and convert the Maoris. He had oversight of the work there until his death.

Through the work of these men and other missionaries many Maoris had become Christians by 1848 and given up tribal warfare and cannibalism. The missionary, Henry Williams, helped Captain William Hobson by interpreting when the Maoris accepted the draft treaty of James Stephen, Jr., as the Treaty of Waitangi in 1840. The treaty made New Zealand a British territory and provided that, if land was sold, it had to be to the British government, which would then sell it to settlers. Thus the nationals were protected from exploitation of their land. Maoris today have full and equal rights with the whites in New Zealand.

Between 1830 and 1880 the missionary societies held their annual meetings at Exeter Hall in the Strand. Usually either Wilberforce or Shaftesbury served as chairman, and James Stephen, Jr., as head of the colonial office. They had such great influence that government in England and in the colonies came to fear the power of "Exeter Hall" on behalf of missionaries and their native charges.

The China Inland Mission, now the Overseas Missionary Fellowship, owed its existence to the faith of J. Hudson Taylor (1832–1905). He was born in a godly home where Bible study and prayer were the order of the day and he was educated at home until 1845. Taylor had been exposed to a Methodist revival in 1839 but was not converted until 1846 through reading in a tract the words, "The finished work of Christ." He felt called to be a missionary the same year. A deep spiritual experience in December 1849 brought sanctification to him.

Books on China and a Chinese Mandarin Gospel of Luke opened up Chinese history and language to him. When he studied surgery with Dr. Richard Hardey of Hull for sixteen months, he began to live by faith and discipline himself. A sojourn in London to study medicine in 1852 ended because of an infection contracted in dissecting a corpse.

After a period of recuperation at home, he went to China in 1854 under the Chinese Evangelization Society. In 1855 he itinerated, did medical work, and preached with William Burns. He adopted Chinese dress and grew a queue. After 1857 his favorite words were *Jehovah-Jireh* ("The Lord will provide") and *Ebenezer* ("Hitherto hath the Lord helped us."). He soon broke with his mission society.

He returned to England in 1860 and remained there until 1866. During this time he worked on his NingPo New Testament. He won his diploma as a member of the Royal College of Surgeons in

1862. On Sunday, June 25, 1865, as he was walking on the sands at Brighton, he decided to give absolute obedience to Christ and to pray for twenty-four missionaries. He decided that the mission would be a faith mission named the China Inland Mission. Two days later he opened an account with £10 for the China Inland Mission.

In 1866 he returned to China with six men and nine women. They won 20 of the 34-member crew to Christ on the way. In 1887 he obtained 100 workers in one year by faith and prayer. He then asked God for 1,000 in the next five years, and 1,153 men and women joined his interdenominational faith mission. The Cambridge Seven served under the China Inland Mission in China. In 1853 there were about 300 Chinese Christians. Some years later 25,000 of 100,000 Protestant Chinese were in China Inland Mission churches.

The tremendous medical missionary activity of Wilfred Grenfell in Labrador was an outcome of revival with Grenfell's conversion in Moody's London meeting in 1885. Grenfell (1865–1940), born near Chester, was educated at Marlborough Public School on a scholarship. Here he was known as "The Beast" because of his readiness to fight. He studied medicine in London under the famous Frederick Treves. In 1888 Grenfell became a member of the Royal College of Surgeons and a surgeon at London Hospital, where his father was chaplain.

He attended a Moody meeting in London on February 2, 1885, in which Moody interrupted a long prayer by having the people sing. Intrigued by this, Grenfell listened to Moody's message. At another meeting he heard J. E. and C. T. Studd speak. He accepted Christ and began teaching a Sunday school class and preaching on Sunday nights in a lodging house.

His mentor, Treves, chairman of the medical work of the National Mission to Deep Sea Fishermen, asked him to serve on a mission vessel. Grenfell had loved the sea and fishermen from boyhood and this love led him to accept with pleasure. He sailed in January 1888 as a medical worker on a North Sea fishing boat. He joined the mission in December of that year and became its super-intendent within a year. He visited the Labrador coast of New-foundland in 1892, and the need of people after the burning of St. Johns led him to work in that area. That summer he treated nine hundred poverty-stricken patients.

The Mission Council bought a steam launch, the *Princess May,* so that he could carry on work in Labrador for the mission. He set up the first hospital at Battle Harbor during the 3,000-mile voyage.

Grenfell started a home for orphans and cooperatives for fishermen. Clarence Birdseye, who developed a quick-freeze pro-cess for keeping fish fresh, worked with Grenfell to help the fishermen. For forty-two years Grenfell served in Labrador, often with his life in danger. On one occasion when he was marooned on an ice floe going out to sea, he had to kill his dogs and use their skins to keep warm until he was rescued. At his request all this time his salary was only $1,500 per year.

This is only a sampling of the results of revival in English mis-sions. The Student Volunteer Movement provided most of the men from 1886 to World War I, and the Industrial Revolution pro-vided the money so generously expended for missions. The churches undergirded the whole process with prayer.

American Missionaries Abroad. We have already seen how the missionary enterprise began very early in America, with Euro-pean settlers eager to convert the Indians. The colonists also felt the need to do missionary work abroad.

Two eager proponents of missions were Thomas Coke in England and Samuel J. Mills, Jr., in the United States. Thomas Coke (1747–1814) was the son of a Welsh druggist in Brecon, Wales, who had provided medicines for Howel Harris and for Charles Wesley's wife. Coke was influenced by deism when he entered Jesus College, Cambridge, at the age of sixteen. After graduation, he was elected burgess and a member of the Common Council of Brecon in 1769 and a bailiff in 1770.

After his ordination as an Anglican priest in 1772, he continued to study for the M.A. and a doctorate in civil law. Thomas Maxfield, the first Methodist lay preacher, was instrumental in his conversion in 1773. From then on he worked with the Methodists. He had become a member of the annual conference by 1778. He was Wesley's right-hand man in London from 1778 to 1783. His impulsive, outspoken ways made trouble at times, but he helped Wesley with the legal work of the Deed of Declaration in 1784, which named one hundred men to hold Methodist property, such as chapels.

During the same year Wesley consecrated him as superintendent to be with Asbury, supervisor of the Methodists in America. From 1784 to 1803 Coke made nine trips to the United States and fifteen to the West Indies. He met Asbury in November 1783. He helped to found the Methodist Episcopal Church in America at a Christmas conference at Baltimore in 1784, a decade before the Methodists became a separate church in Britain. Coke toured the country from New York to the South. On this trip he became an enemy of slavery and pleaded for emancipation of slaves.

He expressed his interest in missions in 1783 in *A Plan . . . for the Establishment of Missions among the Heathen.* This work was written nearly ten years before Carey's appeal. Coke was responsible for Methodist missions in the West Indies and set up the first mission there in 1786. He worked with Sharp and Macauley to send ex-slaves to Liberia. He helped to send 1,200 blacks from Nova Scotia and Methodist missionaries to Liberia. In 1814 he set out for Ceylon and India to serve as a missionary there, but died on the way and was buried at sea. During his busy life he gave much of his income to missions. He also had time to write a six-volume *Commentary on the New Testament.*

Samuel J. Mills, Jr., (1783–1818) was the most ardent supporter of missions in the United States. He was the main mover in the founding of the interdenominational American Board of Commissioners for Foreign Missions, the American Bible Society, and the American Colonization Society.

Mills was born into a pastor's family in Torrington, Connecticut, and was of Dutch extraction and noble blood. He came under conviction in 1798 in a revival in his father's church, but did not find peace until the fall of 1801 on the way to Morris Academy. He decided to be a missionary a year later and entered Williams College during the revival of 1804 and 1806.

A group of five men met to pray for missions in a maple grove in Sloan's Meadow in August of 1806. They took shelter from a thunderstorm under a haystack one day. During this famous "haystack prayer meeting," Mills proposed a mission to Asia, saying, "We can do it if we will." In 1808 the group organized the "Brethren," as Mills titled it, a secret society to study and pray for missions.

While a student at Andover Seminary in 1810, Mills developed a "Brethren" society there for missions. Adoniram Judson became a member. In January 1811 he sponsored the Society of Inquiry on the subject of missions. The members wrote to David Bogue to see if they could become missionaries for the LMS.

Upon the advice of pastors and their teachers they decided to request the founding of a missionary society by the Congregational Church. They wanted to offer themselves as missionaries at the association meeting at Bradford on June 27, 1810. The request, drawn up by Judson, was read at the meeting, and on June 28 the Association founded the American Board of Commissioners for Foreign missions.

The board of the new society ordained five men—Judson, Mott, Hall, Newell, and Rice—as missionaries to India in February 1812. Mills was not ordained but was to "hold the ropes" at home. Hall remained in India, but Judson was expelled by the British East India Company after a short time in India and went to Burma.

In 1809 Mills met Henry Obookiah (Opukahaiah) (1795–1818), a Hawaiian, who had been brought to New York earlier that same year. While weeping on the steps of Yale because there was no one to teach him, Obookiah was befriended by Edwin S. Dwight. Mills took Obookiah to Litchfield, Connecticut, where the con-

ADONIRAM JUDSON (1788-1850), missionary and Bible translator. *(Courtesy of the Billy Graham Center Museum)*

sociation took him under its care. Prodded by Mills, the Congregationalists set up a Foreign Missions School in Cornwall (after
Obookiah's death in 1818) to train nationals to go back to their own
people as missionaries. The school opened with twelve pupils,
seven of whom were Hawaiians. Intermarriage between Indian
and white students caused the church to close the school in 1827.

Six families, led by Hiram Bingham, went to Hawaii in April
1820 under the ABCFM. The Hawaiians were won to Christianity. Thousands were converted in the revival from 1836 to 1838.

Mills, along with John Schermerhorn, took a 3,000-mile trip
through Ohio, Kentucky, Tennessee, Georgia, and South Carolina
in 1812 and 1813 to preach and to determine the spiritual needs of
the frontier. They wrote a fifty-page pamphlet on the needs as
they saw them. Mills urged Bible and tract distribution. He
scheduled a second trip (1814–15) with Daniel Smith. They went to
St. Louis and New Orleans and gave out six hundred English
Bibles, five thousand French New Testaments, and fifteen thousand tracts. Mills then organized state and city Bible societies
during 1885. The American Bible Society, a national organization,
was founded in 1886 largely as a result of Mills's efforts.

Mills was ordained in 1815 and promoted missions in Africa.
Through his efforts an African school was extablished in 1886 in
New Jersey to train blacks as missionaries to Africa.

Mills helped to found the American Colonization Society in 1817
and was a signer of its constitution. He volunteered to go to Africa
to find a suitable location for the colony of freed slaves and left for
Africa by way of London in 1818. He met Wilberforce and Macaulay in London. He visited their colony in Sierra Leone and went
on to Liberia, which he selected for the American blacks. He died
on the return trip and was buried at sea. The first freed slaves
went to Liberia in April 1822, and Liberia became an independent
republic in July 1847.

Adoniram Judson (1788–1850) was the apostle of Burmese missions. Born in Massachusetts, he read the Bible at three years of
age. He was educated at Brown University and graduated in 1807

with highest honors. For a time he wrote arithmetic and grammar texts and taught in a school which he opened.

He accepted deism in 1808. At an inn where he was staying he heard a dying man in the next room shriek, "Dead, lost, lost!" Upon inquiry he discovered that the dying man was the man who had led him into deism. Under deep conviction, he finally made public profession of his Christian faith in 1809. He read the sermon called "Star of the East," which Claudius Buchanan had preached in Bristol. This sermon led him to a decision to use his linguistic ability to translate the Bible into other languages in 1810.

He went to England in 1811 but was captured by the French and imprisoned for some months. When he was freed and arrived in London in May, the directors of the LMS told him to work with an American society instead of theirs.

The ABCFM appointed and ordained him in February 1812 to go to India with four other men. On the voyage he and Luther Rice became Baptists and were immersed in Calcutta by Carey. Because of the opposition of the British East India Company, Judson went to Burma in 1813, studied Burmese, and began preaching in Burmese in 1819. He was imprisoned as a spy during the Anglo-Burmese War, and both he and his wife suffered greatly. By 1834 Judson had translated the Bible into Burmese, and by 1842 he had published his Anglo-Burmese dictionary. He organized twenty churches with about five thousand converts before his death.

Gordon Hall (1784–1826), another member of Mills's missionary society, was a graduate of Williams College and Andover Seminary. He, too, went to India in 1872, studied Marathi at Bombay, and soon produced a Marathi New Testament.

Mills's contribution to American home and foreign missions laid foundations for missions in Hawaii, India, and Burma.

The next great impetus came with the Student Volunteer movement of 1889, beginning in the 1886 Northfield Conference with the "Mt. Hermon Hundred" volunteering to be missionaries. By

1930 about twenty thousand had become missionaries through this group. When Student Volunteers became liberal theologically and socially oriented after 1930, the Foreign Missions Fellowship and the Urbana conventions replaced it as sources for future missionaries. Over fifty-three thousand American Protestant missionaries were serving abroad in 1979, an increase of more than 50 percent from 1969.

9. SPIRITUAL, ETHICAL, AND ECUMENICAL IMPACT

THE previous chapter showed that revived Christians help the church expand through missions and evangelism. This chapter will focus on how revived Christians have helped to promote the spiritual life, a Christ-centered morality, and an ecumenical spirit.

THE DEEPER SPIRITUAL LIFE

Walter C. Palmer (1804–90), born in New Jersey, became a prosperous physician. He and his wife Phoebe (1807–74), whom he married in 1827, traveled widely to speak in churches and camp meetings. Phoebe claimed that twenty-five thousand got "pardon" or accepted Christ in their meetings. She also founded the Five-Point Mission in New York in 1850, a forerunner of settlement houses.

Her sister, Sarah Lankford, proposed interdenominational women's meetings to promote holiness. These were held every Tuesday for more than forty years, beginning in 1835, under Phoebe's leadership. Phoebe claimed an experience of "purity" or entire sanctification on July 26, 1837. Men were admitted to the meetings in 1839. The Palmers taught that the old nature was killed by a second work of grace.

They taught this doctrine in the United States, Canada, and Great Britain. Phoebe claimed that seventeen hundred were converted and more than two thousand sanctified during their ministry in Britain from 1859 to 1863. Their greatest success occurred in 1857 and 1858 in the prayer meeting revival. Their work was mainly among the Methodists. She was partly responsible for the founding of the National Association for the Promotion of Holiness at Vineland, New Jersey, in 1867. Some Methodists, the Church of the Nazarene, and the Salvation Army advocate this view of holiness.

A different approach to the deeper life grew out of the revival of 1857. This approach disdained any second work of blessing subsequent to salvation but declared that sanctification was both instantaneous (beginning with the New Birth) *and* progressive (by continually yielding to the Holy Spirit). This interpretation of Romans 6–8 is linked with the annual meetings at Keswick.

W. T. Boardman, who wrote *The Higher Christian Life* in 1860, and Hannah and Pearsall Smith carried this view to England in 1873. The Smiths were in England from 1873 to 1874 when Moody was holding his meetings. Hannah was converted in 1858 and entered into a deeper life experience in 1867. Her book, *The Christian's Secret of a Happy Life* (1870; enlarged edition, 1888), which sold widely, further propagated her ideas after the visit to England.

The Smiths and Boardman spoke on May 1, 1873, to a group of sixteen at Curzon Chapel in London on the life of victory. Evan Hopkins (1837–91) was converted by the testimony of a godly coastguardsman in 1858. He was the son of an engineer, who had worked in South America and the Far East for many years. He switched from an engineering career to theology at King's College, London, and was ordained in 1866 to serve St. John's

Church, Richmond. After seeing William Booth's East End work in London, he organized the Church Army, which Wilson Carlile later led. Hopkins had a victorious life experience on May 1, 1873, at Curzon Chapel. In 1893 he moved to St. Luke's, a parish of six thousand in London. He held a Keswick meeting in Jerusalem in 1892 and with £2,000 given to him walled off the Garden of Gethsemane and the tomb contained inside the garden. He became chairman of the committee that maintained this area. He was a perennial speaker at Keswick for forty years, beginning with the 1876 meeting.

Another meeting was held on July 17, 1874, at Broadlands, Palmerston's former estate, with one hundred present. The next meeting occurred at Oxford from August 30 to September 4. Canon Harford Battersby, vicar of St. John's Church in Keswick, was present. A graduate of Balliol College, he was ordained in 1847. At this meeting he, too, experienced a deeper spiritual experience.

The conference at Brighton from May 29 to June 7, 1875, drew seven thousand. Moody had Christians in London pray for this meeting, which was led by the Smiths. A meeting was scheduled to begin June 29 at Keswick with Harford Battersby as chairman. A tent with floorboards (now cement) was erected. Smith was to speak, but when he put his arm around an overwrought girl whom he was counseling in his hotel room, he was accused of adultery. This spurious accusation brought about a breakdown which kept him from speaking. H. W. Webb-Peploe and others filled in to speak to the six hundred present. Andrew Murray and F. B. Meyer became main speakers later.

The Keswick motto reflects the ecumenical spirit of the 1859 revival, "All One in Christ." Tents, holding 900 in 1886 and 2,250 in 1896 were secured. At the conference the message of Romans 6 and missions was proclaimed through scriptural exposition. Similar conferences were begun in Ontario, Canada, and Keswick, New Jersey, as well as other centers in British possessions.

MORALITY

Because Christian character follows commitment to Christ, revival has always been followed by moral living. Common sins of swearing, drunkenness, gambling, cheating, and domestic fighting were avoided. Jonathan Edwards testified how the Northampton revival stopped drinking and frivolous lives in the town. Camp meeting renewal in Kentucky changed fighters, who had been known to gouge out their opponents' eyes or bite off an ear, into peaceful citizens. The temperance movement was a direct result of revival. Many taverns in Wales were shut down for lack of business from the various revivals over the years. There were fewer cases in the courts. Sexual sins, such as prostitution, were less numerous after the 1859 revival in England. Family life was improved in numerous cases.

People who were revived or saved became more generous in meeting the needs of others. Lady Huntingdon gave away £100,000 and John Thornton £150,000 during their lifetimes. Henry Thornton, John's son, gave six-sevenths of his income to religious and charitable causes before his marriage and one-third after his marriage. Arthur and Lewis Tappan, wealthy New York merchants, gave thousands to the abolitionist cause and helped Finney's work. Wanamaker, Farwell, and McCormick generously backed Moody's enterprises. Thomas G. Ryman was the main backer in building Sam Jones's tabernacle in Nashville. The Church Missionary Society raised £16,000 in a short time to save Uganda missions. Robert Converse gave $8,000 a year to subsidize J. Wilbur Chapman's meetings.

Robert Arthington (1823–1900), whose father made a fortune in a brewery but quit it for conscience's sake, inherited £200,000 but lived like a miser on a loaf of bread and jug of milk daily for years. He made much money by careful investments and gave much to Baptist missions and to the LMS. He left over £943,000, which grew to nearly £1,120,000 before it could be distributed.

The church needs periodic revival because Christians lose their zeal for holiness and the deeper spiritual life. Where revival occurs, Christians experience a renewed appreciation for a holy and joyful life. *(Courtesy of the Billy Graham Center Museum)*

SCHISM AND ECUMENISM

Scripture suggests only three situations where separation becomes essential in churches. Doctrinal aberrations (Romans 16:17-18), sexual moral lapses (1 Corinthians 5:1, 4-5, 11), and refusal to work (2 Thessalonians 3:6-15) are legitimate cause for separation in the church. In most cases in revival, however, divisions or schisms occurred when a loveless majority forced out—or was estranged from—a minority seeking purer doctrine or deeper spiritual life.

The Great Awakening brought division because the Old Light Presbyterians resented itinerant revivalists and the ordination of men who had no college or seminary training. The Old Light men forced such New Light men as Gilbert Tennent out of the presbyteries. The New Light men in the middle colonies organized new presbyteries which grew more rapidly than those of the Old Light.

The revivalistic congregationalists in New England formed New Light—or Separate—Congregational churches, many of which eventually became Baptist churches. The Old Light churches, led by such figures as Charles Chauncy of Boston, gradually gave up the doctrine of depravity of man and by 1825 many of the Old Light churches had become Unitarian churches. The Dutch Reformed churches also had divisions over revival.

Methodism in England separated from the Moravians in 1740. Arminian Methodists under Wesley parted company with Calvinistic Methodists under Whitefield in 1741. The Welsh Calvinistic Methodist church and Wesley's followers also later left the established church.

During the Second Awakening the Primitive Methodists were forced out of the Methodist Church in England because Hugh Bourne used camp meetings as a tool in evangelism. In the United States many Christians followed Barton Stone (see page 000) after the Cane Ridge camp meeting when he separated from the Presbyterian Church. Thomas Campbell's Disciples formed a separate group until 1832, when the 10,000 Disciples united with Stone's followers to form the 12,000-strong Christian (Disciples of Christ) denomination. The Cumberland Presbyterian Church, which favored revival, broke from the Presbyterian Church in 1810.

Thomas Chalmers's Free Church of Scotland was formed in 1844 when 451 ministers left the Kirk of Scotland over the issues of revival and patronage. The Plymouth Brethren emerged in Ireland and England in this era (1831–46). Abraham Kuyper's group emerged out of the Dutch state church in Holland in 1849.

Although the revival from 1857 to 1895 was marked by ecumenicism, the Booths left the Methodist Church and founded the Salvation Army. The Christian and Missionary Alliance was formed in 1897 by A. B. Simpson. The Swedish Mission Covenant Church was founded in 1897. After 1900 many Pentecostals separated from denominations that would not countenance their activities and formed such groups as the Assemblies of God in the United States.

Despite these often forced divisions of revival groups from their parent denominations, revival generally promoted ecumenicity. Though an Anglican, George Whitefield preached in Presbyterian and Congregational churches in the colonies. His intercolonial and interdenominational itinerant ministry promoted a common religious interest which helped to unite the colonies. (Religion as well as politics was a factor behind the American Revolution.) In one of his sermons Whitefield dramatically called on Father Abraham to show that being a Methodist, Presbyterian, or any other denominational adherent would not be a badge of admission to heaven.

During the Second Awakening, Methodists, Baptists, and Presbyterians cooperated in camp meetings on the frontier. The same period was marked by the formation of voluntary interdenominational societies, such as the American Board of Commissioners for Foreign Missions (ABCFM). The Plan of Union from 1801 to 1856 ended duplication of work on the frontier by Presbyterians and Congregationalists. Ministers of one church could serve congregations of the other. Presbyterians profited more from this, and the policy was abrogated in 1856. Nondenominational groups such as the American Bible Society, Women's Christian Temperance Union, American Anti-Slavery Society, and Peace Society were formed for Christian cooperation in Christian service and reform.

Revivalistic evangelists, such as Beecher and Finney, who were both Congregational and Presbyterian at different times in their careers, cooperated across church lines in their revivals.

The Evangelical Alliance, devoted to creedal ecumenicity, was founded in England in 1846 and in America in 1867, largely as a result of the lay prayer revival. The preliminary meeting at Liverpool in October 1845 paved the way for the organizational meeting in London from August 19 to September 2, 1846. The nearly thirty Americans, one Canadian, one Frenchman, three Germans, and many English unanimously adopted the name, "The Evangelical Alliance." After much discussion the nine-point statement of faith, drawn up mainly by Edward Bickersteth, was adopted. About one thousand from fifty denominations and several countries were present. The Evangelical Alliance consisted of individuals who could accept this evangelical creed. The National Association of Evangelicals in America, founded at St. Louis in 1942, is a creedal descendant of this Alliance.

This ecumenicity was one of doctrine, spirit, and work in the organism of the church. Many times in modern ecumenism too much stress is laid upon organization, machinery, and social change. True ecumenism is of the Spirit, but it may indeed express itself in organization.

10. SOCIAL REFORM

REVIVAL and social reforms were described by J. L. and Barbara Hammond in their socialistic books as "a storm in a teacup." Novelist Charles Dickens caricatured Evangelical social reformers in the figure of Mrs. Jellyby in his *Bleak House*. She is pictured as a dirty, untidy woman who shamefully neglects her own family's material and spiritual welfare in order to support schemes for the cultivation of coffee in Africa by the Africans and for establishing surplus English settlers there.

The opposite was true, because social and political reform did not precede but inevitably followed the renewing of the church and the salvation of souls. J. W. Bready said, "reformation of the soul" is the "soul of reformation." The fruit of Christianity has been cultural revitalization and humanization of life. Revival goes hand in hand with the application of Christian principles to government and with antislavery, antiwar, and temperance activities.

Evangelicals have adopted the principle—stated in Ephesians 2:10 and Titus 3:8—that those who are saved must serve God by good works. Those who love God will love and serve men (Colossians 1:4-5; 1 Thessalonians 1:3, 9-10). The efforts of the voluntary missionary, Bible, and reform societies and the generosity of wealthy Christians have fostered care for the physical as well as the spiritual needs of men. In past revivals there was no dichotomy—no "either/or"—between soul saving and meeting the material needs of men. It was a case of "both/and," but priority was given to spiritual needs. In all their reforms, many of them realized they could achieve only proximate solutions to social problems. They knew that only Christ's Second Coming could bring final solutions.

BATTLING SOCIAL PROBLEMS

Ending the Black Slave Trade and Slavery in England. The English slave trade had begun about 1652 when John Hawkins took three hundred slaves from Spanish slave ships and sold them in the Spanish colony of Santo Domingo. The Royal Company of Adventurers of England Trading with Africa was chartered to get slaves from West Africa to sell in the West Indian sugar-growing colonies. The Asiento agreement in the Treaty of Utrecht (1713) allowed England to supply 4,800 slaves a year to Spanish colonies.

Between 1680 and 1700 more than 300,000 slaves were taken to the colonies in British ships. Liverpool ships alone carried 300,000 slaves, about six-sevenths of all slaves carried, to the West Indies and the thirteen colonies. These were sold for more than £1,500,000 between 1789 and 1793. Between 1680 and 1786 well over 2 million slaves were carried to the thirteen colonies to work on sugar, indigo, tobacco, and, later, cotton plantations. The use of sugar by the English rose from 800,000 pounds in 1730 to 4.4 million pounds in 1774. In 1787 the British West Indies exported £2,600,000 worth of raw sugar and £237,000 worth of cotton. In 1791 Colonel Tarleton said in the House of Commons that ending the slave trade would idle about 1,600 ships and 5,500 sailors. It would end a trade in slaves worth £800,000 and trade in exports and imports (from and to the West Indies) worth £6,000,000.

While the slave trade was undeniably profitable, it was also undeniably cruel. Many slaves died in the process of capture in inland Africa, on the march to the coast, or on the long ship passage to the colonies. For every slave delivered to the ship at the coast, another died on the way, and one in four died on the trip to the colonies. African losses in life amounted to about 475,000 a year, 100,000 in the Arab slave trade from East Africa and 375,000 in the European slave trade from West Africa.

In the established and dissenting churches both clergy and laity sought to end the slave trade and slavery in England. As early as 1671 George Fox, the leader of the Quakers, advocated in his *Journal* and in a book on slavery that Quakers should free their slaves. Anthony Benezet's book on the evils of slavery was read by Wesley in 1772 and by other Evangelicals as well as by the Quakers. Initially Quakers formed the majority of those working with Sharp to end slavery in England.

Although George Whitefield had purchased a plantation in South Carolina to help support his Bethesda orphanage, he had urged slave owners to treat their slaves kindly.

Wesley also took an early and active stand against the slave trade and slavery. His pamphlet, "Thoughts Upon Slavery," published in 1774, was a "careful argument and eloquent plea" against the slave trade or slave-holding. Three editions were sold in the first year. He wrote a long letter opposing slavery which was printed in the *Arminian Magazine* in 1787. Earlier he had supported Oglethorpe's decision to exclude slavery from Georgia. On March 3, 1738, he had preached against the slave trade to a large crowd in Bristol, the home port of many slave traders.

Wesley's Methodists provided the troops under the upper-class Evangelical leaders in the fight against the slave trade and slavery. Over 229,000 names on petitions to the House of Commons in 1792 against the trade were of Methodists. Only 123,000 of other religious groups signed. In 1833 in a petition urging abolition of slavery, 224,000 of the 354,000 dissenters sign-ing the petition were Methodists. The evils of the slave trade pro-vided both Evangelicals and Dissenters with cause to oppose it.

The most influential and effective leaders in the fight against the slave trade were the upper-class men who formed the Clapham Sect. Granville Sharp (1735–1813), the oldest of the Clapham Sect, was born at Durham in a minister's family.

In 1755 he met a black slave named Jonathan Strong in his brother William Strong's medical office. William was treating Jonathan, who had been brutally beaten by his owner, David Lisle, a lawyer from Barbados. Two years later Lisle claimed Jonathan and sold him for £30 to James Kerr, a Jamaica planter. Sharp refused to give up Jonathan and was sued by Kerr. Sharp then studied law for two years. In an early edition of Blackstone's legal commentaries he found a case in which a slave had been freed when he entered England. Sharp drew up a long paper and sent twenty copies to the Inns of Court. In fear, Kerr delayed his suit and had to pay triple costs to Sharp. Sharp published his paper in 1769 under the title, "The Injustice of Tolerating Slavery in England." The courts, fearing the effect of this case on the ownership of slaves, dismissed it.

James Somerset, a slave, was rescued from a ship bound for Jamaica where his new owner lived. Because his master owned him, the courts had to act. Lord Mansfield declared Somerset to be free in 1772 since by common law slaves setting foot on the soil of England were free. This principle freed about 14,000 other slaves in England.

Sharp developed the idea of a colony in Africa for freed slaves in 1783. Dr. Henry Smeathman, a naturalist who had been in Sierra Leone, proposed it as a colony for freed slaves. Sharp received government aid to transport and relocate 400 black slaves from England in 1787 and accompanied them to Sierra Leone. In 1787 the Clapham Sect formed the St. George's Bay Association with Sharp as president. Henry Thornton, who gave much financial support to the Clapham Sect, reorganized it in 1791 as the Sierra

Leone Company. Lieutenant John Clarkson took more than 1,000 black slaves who served in the British army in the American Revolution from Nova Scotia to Sierra Leone and then served as governor of the colony. The colony had 1,400 settlers by 1794, but £10,000 worth of goods were taken the same year when it was sacked by the French. Zachary Macaulay served as governor from 1793 to 1799. The Evangelicals couldn't continue to finance this private colony because they lost £240,000 of capital. The British government took Sierra Leone over in 1807, and by 1825 it was the home of 180,000 freed slaves.

William Wilberforce (1759–1833) was the main leader of the Clapham Sect's fight against the slave trade. Born at Hull, he was a puny, short, weak-eyed, hot-tempered man with a tipped-up nose. He was influenced for good in the Hull grammar school of Joseph Milner. When his father died in 1768, he was sent to live with an aunt and uncle, friends of Whitefield and Newton. His mother, a socialite who feared they would make him a Methodist, sent him to Pocklington boarding school from 1771 to 1776.

He went to St. John's College, Cambridge, where he did little but gamble and entertain as an excellent mimic. He graduated in 1780 and was elected as a member of the House of Commons from Hull after spending over £8,000. He remained in the House until 1825. He joined the exclusive Brooks Club, but gave up gambling when he won £600 from a boy who could not afford to lose that much money. He was an excellent orator and was dubbed "the nightingale" of the House of Commons for his good voice and oratorical ability. He became a good friend of William Pitt the Younger.

When he traveled to Italy with Isaac Milner from October 1784 to February 1785, the two read Philip Doddridge's *The Rise and Progress of Religion in the Soul*. During a second trip in June 1785, they read and discussed the Greek New Testament. Wilberforce, under deep conviction, went to see John Newton on December 7, 1785. Newton helped to guide him to faith in Christ. Later that same day John Newton wrote him that he felt God had raised him up for the good of the church and the nation. By April 1786, Wilberforce experienced salvation and gave up many of his former practices. He gave one-quarter of his income for charitable and religious purposes.

Lady Diana and Charles Middleton introduced Wilberforce to James Ramsay, a ship's surgeon and missionary at St. Kitts. Ramsay told him of the evils of the slave trade and slavery in the Caribbean. Thomas Clarkson, a member of his own school, St. John's College, Cambridge, who had written a prize essay on the evils of the trade, helped to deepen his interest in the subject. He had agreed to lead the battle by 1786. On October 28, 1787, he wrote in his diary that God had given him two tasks: "the suppression of the slave trade and the reformation of manners." John Wesley's last letter (February 4, 1791) urged Wilberforce to stand like Athanasius against the planters and slave traders.

On April 12, 1797, Wilberforce published his *Practical View*, which in six months sold seven thousand copies. The essential idea was that the biblical New Birth meant that one who was saved must serve society in any way possible. The members of the Clapham Sect agreed with Wilberforce's idea and were dedicated to abolishing the slave trade.

To plan their campaign, the members of the Clapham Sect met in the home of Henry Thornton in the oval library built along the lines suggested by William Pitt. They all lived in Clapham Common and attended John Venn's church. They were leaders in business and politics.

Wilberforce spent nine hours a day studying the ten thousand pages of evidence that Thomas Clarkson and Zachary Macaulay obtained for him. After years of agitation, resolutions, bills in the House of Commons, and a boycott against slave-grown sugar, he succeeded in 1807 in getting a law passed to end slave trade by the British. During the long battle he developed severe headaches for which he had to use opium in small doses for the rest of his life.

Wilberforce continued to struggle against the trade after 1807 with the founding of the African Institution to oppose other ways of trading in slaves. Castelreagh, the foreign secretary in the House of Commons, was pressured by petitions into getting the Congress of Vienna to outlaw the slave trade in principle by Europeans in 1815. The British government gave £700,000 to Spain and Portugal to quit the trade. Wilberforce lived long enough to see the Act of 1833 end slavery in the British Empire. In the struggle, he lost most of his money and died relatively poor.

Zachary Macaulay (1768–1838) and Thomas Clarkson were Wilberforce's chief researchers for information. Macaulay was born in Inverary, Scotland, in a minister's family with an inherited defect: one eye blind from birth. At the age of sixteen he became a bookkeeper on an estate in Jamaica. Later he became the manager. There he saw the miseries and cruelty of slavery firsthand.

Macaulay returned to England in 1792. From 1793 to 1799 he was governor of Sierra Leone. Broken in health, in 1794 he went home for a short time in a slave ship, the *Anna*, which was taking slaves to Barbados. He took this longer route in order to see the evils of the Middle Passage. Thus he knew the true state of the trade and slavery from beginning to end. When he finally returned to England in 1799, he had with him children of African chiefs whom Robert Haldane was going to educate at his own expense. When he desired to bring them up in the Church of England, Haldane backed out, and Henry Thornton bore much of the expense.

Macaulay began trading as a merchant with Africa, but in 1802 became editor of the *Christian Observer*, a position he held until 1816. The paper was devoted to abolition. He was also secretary of the African Institution from 1807 to 1823. He became Wilberforce's source of information about the slave trade. Whenever Wilberforce needed facts about the trade, he would say facetiously, "Let us look in Macaulay."

Macaulay's trading enterprise failed because his incompetent relative, T. B. Babington, mismanaged the venture until at one point they were £100,000 in debt. Macaulay had devoted so much time to finding facts on the slave trade that he did not oversee his partner enough and died poor. He was a great help to both Wilberforce and Buxton in all their work.

The poet Coleridge declared Thomas Clarkson (1760–1846) "the giant with one idea" and "the Moral Steam Engine" against slavery. With Macaulay he served both Wilberforce and Buxton in the struggle against the slave trade and slavery.

During his years at St. John's, Cambridge, he won a prize for a 1785 essay entitled, "Is It Lawful to Make Slaves of Them Against Their Free Will?" He got off his horse on the way home in the summer of 1785 and on his knees dedicated his life to fighting slavery. He collected information on the trade in 1780 with the help of James Ramsay.

Told of a sailor who could give him information on the slave trade, Clarkson traveled one thousand miles in three weeks in 1790 and boarded over 350 ships to find the sailor whose name he did not have. He finally found him, Isaac Parker, on the *Melampus* and got the data firsthand. He got witnesses and accurate data for Wilberforce's speeches, and he planned propaganda.

The poet William Cowper aided the antislavery propaganda effort with a song called "The Negroes' Complaint." The potter Josiah Wedgwood sold cameo snuffboxes and brooches in 1788 with a picture of a Negro kneeling in chains with upraised hands and the words, "Am I not a man and a brother?"

The Clapham leaders obtained about eight hundred petitions with about 1 million names, asking the British government to take action to end the trade at the Vienna Peace Conference. The Congress of Vienna on February 8, 1815, stated the desire of the powers for "universal abolition" of the slave trade. In 1815 Portugal gave up the trade in return for £300,000 and remission of a £600,000 war debt to England, and in 1817 Spain gave up the trade for £400,000 payment. A naval squadron, set up at an annual cost of £750,000, rescued approximately three thousand slaves a year from sneak slave traders.

Between 1823 and 1833 the Evangelicals kept fighting to end

slavery in the British Empire. They were now led by Buxton with Macaulay and James Stephen, Jr., securing information, because Wilberforce and Clarkson were too old. They formed the Anti-Slavery Society in 1823 and began publishing *The Anti-Slavery Reporter* with Macaulay as editor in 1825. This paper sold as many as twenty thousand copies a month.

T. Fowell Buxton (1786–1845), called "Elephant Buxton" by his classmates because of his six-foot-four stature, was born in a Quaker home in Essex. He loved country life and sports, but earned a gold medal and other academic honors at the University of Dublin. His uncle, Samson Hanbury, helped him to get a position in the Truman, Hanbury, and Company brewery in 1808. He made a fortune until he retired early for conscience's sake. In 1813 he became a Christian. He supported the Bible society and charity work from 1808 to 1816. He was elected to the House of Commons in 1818, and from 1818 to 1822 he aided his sister-in-law, Elizabeth Fry, in her prison reform work.

He devoted a year and a half to the study of slavery in response to the dying wish of another sister-in-law, Priscilla Gurney, and a letter from Wilberforce, dated May 24, 1821, asking him to be the "leader in this holy enterprise." In the fall of 1822 he was finally convinced that he should assume leadership of the struggle for abolition of slavery. He and his friends met each night to study the Bible and to pray.

Buxton moved a resolution for the gradual abolition of slavery in the British colonies on May 15, 1823. George Stephen (1794–1871) and the more radical abolitionists formed the Agency Committee to promote public meetings and petitions for abolition in 1831. Buxton called on the churches to set aside January 16, 1833, as a day of prayer to pray for the passage of the abolition bill. On May 14, 1833, he presented petitions with 187,000 names advocating abolition. These petitions had been secured by ladies in ten days.

James Stephen, Jr., was asked to draw up an abolition bill. Even though he had religious scruples against Sunday work, he drew up the long, long bill with sixty-six sections between Saturday noon and Monday noon. The bill passed on July 23, became law with the king's signature on July 23, 1833, and took effect on August 1, 1834.

James Stephen, Jr. (1789–1859), who graduated in law from Trinity College, Cambridge, in 1812, was legal advisor to the colonial office from 1813 to 1834, assistant undersecretary from 1834 to 1836, and permanent undersecretary from 1836 to 1847. He ruled the colonial office for years and aided missionaries and the Clapham Sect in their fight for civil rights for slaves and natives. In addition to drafting the 1833 bill to abolish slavery, he helped to set up responsible government in Canada and drafted the document which became the Treaty of Waitangi in 1840. This treaty protected the Maoris of New Zealand. From 1849 to 1859 he served as professor of modern history at Cambridge. He was nicknamed "Mr. Over-Secretary" because of his strong stand for human rights.

His bill, which became the Emancipation Act of 1833, freed about 781,000 slaves in the British colonies at a cost of £20,000,000 to compensate owners. By 1845 the money had been paid out at an administrative cost of £150,000. The slaves were valued at £45,282,000.

Wilberforce, who heard the news of the Emancipation Act just before his death on July 29, 1833, rejoiced to see the day when England set aside "twenty millions sterling for the abolition of slavery." In a speech in May 1833 Buxton said that God was the author and Christians the instruments of abolition of slavery.

Not satisfied, Buxton and his friends formed the Aborigines Protection Society in 1837 to protect the native peoples in the colonies from exploitation by settlers. Naval patrols were also set up to end the Arab slave trade in East Africa after Livingstone's revelations on the evils of that trade became known through his books.

Much of the money needed to finance the ventures of the Clapham Sect came from John Thornton (1720–90) and his son Henry.

John had grown rich in the Russian trade and was able to give away £150,000 during his lifetime. He had Russian Bibles printed and sent to Russia. His generosity is illustrated by his gifts of £600 to Hannah More for her schools and £700 for the founding of Dartmouth College. When Henry was born in 1760, John had amassed a fortune of £600,000.

Henry Thornton (1760-1815) was a banker whose home, Battersea Rise House in Clapham, was the meeting place of the Clapham Sect. He was first secretary of the Church Missionary Society and the first treasurer of the Bible Society in England. He reorganized the St. George's Bay of Association of 1787 into the Sierra Leone Company which ran the Sierra Leone colony of freed slaves from 1787 to 1807. His integrity was demonstrated by the loss he sustained through the company and by paying £20,000 (which he was not legally obligated to pay) when relatives failed in business.

Ending Slavery in the United States. Slavery was ended by war in the United States rather than by legislation. This was not because Christians in the United States had not tried to abolish slavery. The slave trade was ended in 1808 when the ban written into the Constitution took effect, but cotton-growing in the new lands of the South and West created a new vested interest in the continuance of slavery. This struggle against slavery went through various stages. Christians used amelioration with emancipation and colonization until 1830, abolition from 1831 to 1861, arms in the Civil War, and amendments to the Constitution from 1861 to 1865.

John Woolman (1720-72), a Quaker tailor and preacher, traveled in the thirteen colonies after 1757 and called on Quakers to free their slaves. Quakers in the American colonies gave up slaveholding in 1761. Woolman's *Journal* describes his efforts against slavery. He died in England when he went there to attack slavery at its center in 1772.

Anthony Benezet (1713-84) was born in France and moved to

Philadelphia where he taught school from 1742 to 1784. His book *A Caution to Britain and Her Colonies* on the sad condition of slaves was read by Wesley in 1772 and Evangelicals in England.

Samuel Hopkins (1721–1803), a product of the Great Awakening, received his education at Yale and studied theology for four months under his friend and mentor, Jonathan Edwards. He was brought under conviction in his room by the earnest pleading of David Brainerd and by the preaching of Gilbert Tennent. He became pastor at Housatonic, Massachusetts, and was ordained in 1743. From the spring of 1770 until 1803 he was pastor of the First Congregational Church of Newport, Rhode Island. He usually spent each Saturday in prayer.

Newport had a vested interest in the slave trade, which Hopkins opposed. Before 1776, Newporters had 150 ships in the American slave trade. Between 1704 and 1708 Newport traders were responsible for transporting 3,488 of the 17,048 slaves brought to the thirteen colonies. Newport also had twenty distilleries of rum, some of which were owned by church members.

Hopkins wrote and preached against their slave trade, which was ended in Rhode Island legislation in 1774. Shipowners in his congregation had sold rum for slaves in Africa, but his church voted against the trade in 1784. In 1776 he published his *Dialogue Concerning the Slavery of the Africans* in which he opposed the buying and owning of slaves.

He sent a copy to each member of the Continental Congress. He urged good treatment of slaves and even emancipation. The English Sierra Leone experiment led him to favor colonization of freed slaves in Africa, an idea which he advocated as early as 1773.

The American Colonization Society was founded in 1817 by Samuel J. Mills, Jr., and William Lloyd Garrison. Between 1817 and 1867 it settled 13,000 freed slaves in Liberia.

From 1831 to 1861 the revival forces insisted increasingly on immediate abolition. In 1831 William Lloyd Garrison (1805–79), publisher of the *Liberator,* called for immediate abolition to end the sin of slavery. He also helped to found the American Anti-Slavery Society in 1833 at Philadelphia. There were a thousand auxiliary groups by 1838.

Finney supported the abolitionist cause. Oberlin College, where Finney taught after 1825, was a key point on the "underground railway."

Theodore D. Weld (1803–95), a tall, unkempt, muscular man, was born in Hampton, Connecticut. He worked on the family farm from the time he was twelve until he was fifteen. He went to Andover Academy at the age of fifteen, but hurt his eyes by too much study. After two years, he left to travel for another two years as a lecturer on mnemonics, but he gave it up for study at Hamilton College at Utica.

He was tricked into attending Finney's meeting by his Aunt Sophia but was convicted by Finney's statement that "one sinner destroyeth much good." The next day he abused Finney verbally in a store but later apologized to him. He became blasphemous when his aunt asked him to pray in evening prayers. This so upset him that late that night he was converted. He referred to Finney as "my dear father in Christ."

Weld helped Finney in meetings in 1826 and 1827. He also spent some time in Labrador in 1827. He went in 1827 to George Gale's Oneida Institute, where he led two sons of Lewis Tappan to Christ and studied for the ministry. When Weld met Lewis Tappan at Oneida, Tappan hired him as a general agent for the Society for Promotion of Manual Labor in Literary Institutions to find a site for such a school. He traveled nearly 4,600 miles in 1831 and 1832 and decided that Lane Seminary in Cincinnati would be the best choice. Twenty-one of forty students in the first class of Lane Seminary were from Oneida Institute.

By 1832, when he went to study at Lane Seminary, he was a convinced abolitionist. He helped the Tappans to organize the American Anti-Slavery Society in 1833. He became secretary in

1833 and publicity director in 1836. He was its first antislavery lobbyist in Washington from late 1841 to early 1843. He even helped John Quincy Adams on research for his speeches.

Weld sponsored a debate on slavery at Lane Seminary that ran for two-and-a-half hours each night for eighteen nights. After this debate, which was partly a revival, more than fifty of the rebels against the faculty and board went to Oberlin College with Asa Mahan, one of the professors.

Lewis Tappan subsidized Weld to lecture on abolition between 1834 and 1836 and to recruit other lecturers later in 1836. He married another militant abolitionist, Angelina Grimké, in 1838. He wrote *American Slavery as It Is*, which was published and distributed by the American Anti-Slavery Society in May 1839. The more than 100,000 copies sold stressed the cruelties of slavery. From 1840 to 1854 he farmed in New Jersey and from 1854 to 1895 he was an educator.

Harriet Beecher Stowe (1811–96), a daughter of Lyman Beecher, the revivalist and educator, was converted in 1825 and married Calvin Stowe, a melancholy and gluttonous Lane professor of Hebrew in the late thirties. She admitted that many of the ideas for *Uncle Tom's Cabin* came from Theodore Weld's book on slavery. Her book ran as a serial in the *National Era* in 1851 and was published complete in 1852. The book sold 500,000 copies in five years in the United States, and 1.5 million were sold in Britain and the colonies. Lincoln was reported to have said on meeting Stowe, "So this is the little lady who made this big war." She traveled in England, France, Switzerland, Germany, and Belgium from April to September 1853 and promoted the idea of abolition.

Church colleges agitated for abolition and helped freed slaves reach Canada. Examples of such colleges were Knox College at Galesburg, Illinois, and Wheaton College, both of which Jonathan Blanchard served as president. But because of vested interests, a resort to arms and the Thirteenth Amendment to the Constitution were necessary to end slavery.

Reforms for White Laborers. Evangelicals were not guilty of being alert only to the needs of blacks. They also expended much time and treasure to help white laborers. They left economic and political reforms to others.

Michael T. Sadler (1780–1835), an assiduous fact-finder and lobbyist for social reform, was born in an Anglican family sympathetic with Methodism. He was mostly self-taught through extensive reading in his father's library. He became wealthy through importing Irish linen. In 1829 he became a member of the House of Commons for Newcastle and for the rest of his life he devoted much of his time to religion and public service. Although he remained in the Church of England, he was superintendent of a large Methodist Sunday school in Leeds for many years.

As an unpaid chairman of a House of Commons committee in 1832, he examined eighty-nine witnesses, half of them workers, on conditions in factories and proposed a bill to mandate a ten-hour working day. In 1832 mass meetings of 16,000 in York and 100,000 in Manchester were held to support the bill, but it was defeated. Sadler's health broke because of overwork and his loss of his seat in the House by the Reform Bill of 1832. His mantle fell on Shaftesbury. He continued to support the cause by getting information on the need for reform.

Richard Oastler (1789–1861) took Sadler's place in getting information and propagandizing on behalf of the workers. He was a Methodist who as a boy had been blessed by John Wesley, who was a guest in his father's home. He was educated at a Moravian school and apprenticed to an architect. He became wealthy but lost his money in 1821 and became a steward at Fixby for £300 a year. He was unjustly imprisoned for three years from 1841–43 for £3000 that Thornhill of Fixby said he owed to him. Friends raised money to pay the sum and he was released. Even in prison he put in ten-hour days writing letters to editors and having petitions circulated.

He was visiting in the home of godly John Wood, a worsted spinning mill owner in Bradford who some claim spent £40,000 to help in social reform. Wood told him of evils in the factory system and asked him to lead the struggle for remedial legislation. On September 29, 1830, he wrote a letter to the Leeds *Mercury* in which he spoke of "Yorkshire slavery" in the mills. He soon became known as "The Factory Child's King" because of his propaganda on behalf of child laborers.

Anthony A. Cooper, Lord Shaftesbury (1801–85), became the leader in obtaining legislation on behalf of workers. He was a second-generation Evangelical born in London. His father was an ambitious politician and his mother a socialite. Both parents ignored him. Fortunately he had one godly friend, Maria Millis, the housekeeper at whose knee he learned to pray and read the Bible. After her death he would tell friends that she had been the "best friend I ever had" and show the gold watch she had willed to him and which he always wore.

He was educated at Harrow from 1813 to 1817. One day about 1813 while he was a student at Harrow he saw a band of shouting, cursing drunks carrying a coffin to the cemetery. When they let it fall to the ground, Shaftesbury, shocked at this callous treatment of a body, vowed to serve God by helping the poor and friendless.

Shaftesbury lived for a while in the home of a clergyman who enjoyed horses and dogs. He then went to Christ Church College, Oxford, and earned his degree with first-class honors in the classics. Between 1822 and 1826 he furthered his education by touring Europe.

In 1826 he became a member of Parliament for Woodstock. In his diary for December 13, 1825, he wrote that he would found his "policy on the Bible" and practice "active benevolence in public life" in order to advance religion and "increase human happiness."

His first efforts were on behalf of the insane who were badly treated and in some cases unjustly put in asylums by callous relatives. As a member of a committee on conditions in asylums Shaftesbury obtained legislation in 1828 to take supervision of asylums away from doctors and put them under a committee. Shaftesbury was chairman of that committee from 1829 to 1855. Two other acts in 1845 made it impossible to commit sane people to asylums and to abuse the insane. (Keepers of Bedlam asylum near London often charged fees for people to see the insane. Such abuses were ended by Shaftesbury's legislation.)

Shaftesbury devoted most of his time to fighting evils in factories. (Robert Southey, the poet laureate, referred to factories as "our white slave trade.") Michael Sadler's committee revealed that workdays of thirteen to sixteen hours for children were common. Children would be whipped by supervisors if they were unable to perform at a sufficient rate. Many children were crippled in accidents resulting from fatigue coupled with the lack of guards on machines. G. S. Bull asked Shaftesbury to take over Sadler's work. Shaftesbury followed Sadler's pattern of obtaining the facts about the evils of factories, coal mines, or lodging houses to convince Parliament of the need for action. His practice was to investigate the facts, legislate, and inspect to enforce the law.

In 1833 Shaftesbury introduced a bill limiting work for those under age eighteen to a ten-hour day. Factory owners substituted a milder bill that limited work for those aged thirteen to eighteen to twelve hours of work a day, or sixty-nine hours a week, setting aside two hours a day for education. But Shaftesbury finally got his ten-hour day for women and children in textile factories; the Ten-Hour Act became law in 1847.

He also took up the cause of women and children in mines. His committee found women working as "hurriers" and children as "pushers." The "hurriers" were women who crawled on their hands and knees, pulling 200-pound coal carts by belts fastened around their waists. The "pushers" were children who pushed the carts with their heads. The children had actually worn bald spots on their heads. He also found children aged four to eight spending twelve to fourteen hours a day in the dark mines, opening and closing ventilation doors when the coal carts passed. Upon hearing this evidence, secured by personal investigation, the House was so shocked that Shaftesbury's bill easily passed in 1842. It prohibited children under age ten and women from working in the mines and set up inspection for enforcement.

Shaftesbury also became interested in the lot of chimney sweeps. Most of them were orphans as young as eight years of age. Their skins were often hardened by soaking in brine. In some cases fires of damp straw lit under them forced them to go up dark chimneys. In 1864 he sponsored a bill declaring that no assistant sweep could be under sixteen. In 1875 another bill banned the use of boys in sweeping chimneys.

Brickyards had child workers from under four to seventeen years of age. They alternated between working outside with cold clay and inside near the hot kilns. In 1871 Shaftesbury was able to persuade the House to pass legislation to protect them.

Shaftesbury's interest in the poor led him to investigate lodging houses. He found nearly a thousand families in London with one small room per family. In one case, five families lived in one room. One room, thirty-three-feet-by-twenty-feet, held one hundred people, along with assorted lice and bedbugs. Shaftesbury secured legislation that improved conditions in such lodging houses.

He also had a city mission worker, Thomas Jackson, arrange for him to meet four hundred thieves in the East End of London. After he had read the Bible and prayed, he asked each of the thieves to state his specialty in thieving. Shaftesbury discovered that they had resorted to theft because they could not get work and that they would have preferred to go to Canada or Australia. He had the government set aside money to help them emigrate, and three hundred emigrated in one year.

He also became interested in the "ragged schools" for educating poor children. In 1844 he founded a Ragged School Union. He supported the setting up of a Sanitary Commission during the Crimean War. Florence Nightingale, who was in the Crimea, said that the commission "saved the British army." He also tried to improve the lot of people on his estate.

A crowd of about ten thousand attended his funeral to show their love for this "Evangelical of Evangelicals," whose aims in life were to honor God and promote human happiness. He claimed that God called him "to relief of the factory population." He lived up to the family motto, "Love, Serve." In a speech in the House on May 10, 1844, he said that what was morally right would never be politically wrong and what was politically wrong could never be morally right.

He held the Bible to be an inspired, infallible rule for faith and life. He saw justification by faith in Christ's atoning blood as the "Keystone of the Reformation" and saw good works as an evidence of personal faith. For him, life and property were stewardships from God. He firmly believed in the premillennial coming of Christ; the words, "Even so, come, Lord Jesus" were engraved on the flaps of his envelopes, and "Oh, pray for the peace of Jerusalem" was engraved on his ring. He did all that he could to help the Jews to return to Palestine through Prime Minister Palmerston, his stepfather-in-law. Good deeds which he performed were only for the glory of God and proximate solutions to the evils which only the Second Coming and Christ's kingdom would end.

Samuel Plimsoll (1824–98), another Evangelical from Bristol, became a member of the House of Commons from Derby. He wrote *Our Seamen* early in the 1870s to show how sailors were exploited. So-called coffin ships were often overinsured by their owners and then intentionally sunk along with the crew so that the owners could collect the insurance. The Merchant's Shipping Act in 1876, which Shaftesbury helped Plimsoll to get through Parliament, set a limit on ships called the "Plimsoll Line" beyond which they could not be loaded.

Prison Reform. In Britain, people might be imprisoned and executed for debt or for such minor offenses as poaching a rabbit or stealing a loaf of bread. One could be executed for any of more than two hundred crimes in the early nineteenth century. Jailers did not receive salaries but exacted fees from their prisoners. Conditions in prisons were filthy and immoral.

John Wesley, who had visited prisons as a member of the Holy Club in Oxford, began to visit felons and debtors in prison in 1742. Silas Todd (1711–79), a profane and indifferent sailor and later a schoolmaster at Wesley's Foundery in London, met Wesley in 1740 and was converted in 1748. He visited Newgate prison in the fall of 1748 and was an unofficial chaplain for the prisoners until 1779. He often rode to the gallows in the cart with a condemned man to provide comfort. Bristol's Newgate prison was cleaned up by the jailer Dagge, a Methodist converted under George Whitefield. In 1759 Wesley took up an offering of £24 in Bristol to get clothes for 1,100 French prisoners and persuaded the city fathers to provide blankets to protect them from the cold.

John Howard (1726–90), who Wesley said was "one of the greatest men in Europe," was encouraged by Wesley in his work of prison reform. Howard was sickly as a child, but was born into a well-to-do home and received £15,000 at his father's death during his teen years.

When he went to Portugal in 1756 to help people suffering from a severe earthquake, he was captured and imprisoned in France for a time. In February 1773 he became high sheriff of Bedfordshire and found many prisoners had been imprisoned without a trial and were starving because they could not pay the jailer's fees. Others were ill with jail fever, while still others, including women and children, were crowded into the same filthy rooms with degenerate criminals. He obtained salaries for the keepers and cleaned up the prisons.

After tours of inspection of British prisons from 1774 to 1777, Howard published a book about the bad conditions in British prisons and gave evidence before a committee of the House of Commons. In 1774 an act was passed to provide pay for jailers and make prisons more sanitary.

He spent £30,000 of his own money and traveled more than forty-two thousand miles in ten years, visiting prisons to get hard facts. He visited the Netherlands, France, Germany, and Russia. He died in Kherson, Russia, of a fever which he contracted from a girl he had tried to help medically.

Elizabeth Fry (1780–1845) was converted from a life of gaiety by William Savery, a Quaker preacher. She married Joseph Fry, had eleven children, became a Quaker preacher, and was a prison reformer. Before her marriage she taught a school for seventy children called "Betsy's Imps." Stephen Grellet, a Quaker French noble, told her of the terrible conditions in Newgate prison in London and from 1813 on she made almost daily visits there. She found three hundred women and children crowded into four rooms. She read the Bible to the prisoners, provided food and clothing, and started schools to teach literacy, sewing, and knitting. In 1817 she was called upon to testify before the House of Commons. She also visited transports leaving England for the convict colonies from 1818 to 1841. Her travels in Europe in 1838 influenced Wichern in his prison work and brought better conditions to European prisons. She wished to segregate prisoners according to the gravity of their crimes and sponsored efforts to rehabilitate prisoners by religion and useful work.

The YMCA. Other reformers, like George Williams (1821–1905), sought to create a better social environment that would help people keep out of prison. This farm lad, impressed as an apprentice with the need for good diversions after work for apprentices, began the YMCA in 1844.

Born in a well-off farmer's house in Dulverton, Somerset, he was apprenticed for £30 a year to Holmes, a draper in Bridgewater, to learn the cloth business. Converted in 1837, he became an ardent Sunday school worker and a man of prayer through reading Finney's books on revival. He got a job in London in the cloth business with Hitchcock and Rogers in 1841. Seeing the need of the boys, he organized a meeting for prayer and Bible study among the apprentices.

On June 6, 1844, about a dozen Baptist, Anglican, Congregational, and Methodist young men joined with him and started what became known as the Young Men's Christian Association. The organization received its name from Christopher Smith, Williams's roommate. The group emphasized prayer, Bible study, and "mental culture." Physical development was added later. The "Y" committed itself to "Jesus Christ as Lord and Savior" in the Paris Platform of 1855.

Williams soon had a fortune through faithful work and his marriage to Helen Hitchcock. He devoted this money to extension of "Y" work and other endeavors. The "Y" work began in Montreal, Canada, late in 1851 and shortly after that in Boston. These institutions provided religious services and culture in "a home away from home."

The Temperance Movement. Temperance to forestall people from falling into drunkenness and crime came about through individuals touched by revival. Dr. Benjamin Rush, an American evangelical, pointed out the evil impact of alcohol on the mind and body in 1784. Lyman Beecher's six sermons denouncing alcohol in 1826 were published and distributed in many languages. Finney also opposed liquor interests.

The American Temperance Union was formed in 1836. The Washington Temperance Society was organized on a basis of total abstinence and enlisted two thousand former drinkers in Baltimore alone. State prohibition was legislated in Maine in 1851 through the efforts of a businessman, Neal Dow. In 1874 the Women's Christian Temperance Union (WCTU) was organized. Under the presidency of Frances Willard (1839–98) it became a powerful force against liquor.

Frances Willard's family moved from New York to Ohio, then to Wisconsin where she was educated. When she was ill with typhoid in 1859, she heard a voice saying, "You will get well if you become a Christian." She became a Christian when she went forward in an Evanston Methodist church in June. After graduating from college, she taught in colleges in Pennsylvania and New York from 1862 to 1868 and toured Europe until 1870. She held meetings for women in Moody's campaign in Boston for three months. In 1879 she became president of the WCTU and traveled much. She founded the World WCTU in 1883 and served as president from 1891 to 1898. She spent much time in England and on the Continent fighting alcohol abuse. She usually gave four hundred lectures and traveled five thousand miles each year.

Billy Sunday vehemently opposed the use of liquor in his revival meetings and had a favorite sermon titled "Booze." The work of Willard, Sunday, and the churches finally resulted in the outlawing of liquor by the Eighteenth Amendment, which became effective in 1920. It was repealed during the early days of Roosevelt's "New Deal."

Rescue Missions. Some felt that the down and outers could be helped best by rescue missions. Jerry McAuley (1839–84), who was born in the home of an Irish counterfeiter in Kerry, Ireland, came to the United States at the age of fourteen to stay with his married sister. He was arrested at the age of nineteen for a robbery he did not commit, but because of his reputation he was sentenced to fifteen years in Sing Sing. He was convicted one Sunday when Orville Gardner spoke in the prison chapel. He read the Bible and, after three weeks under conviction, he felt God's presence and knew he was saved. He was released from prison long before his term was up because of prayer on his part.

Lacking Christian fellowship, he fell into his old ways upon his release. On one occasion he fell into the water and was nearly drowned during a robbery. A man asked him to go to the Howard Mission in the Bowery, and A. S. Hatch, a Wall Street banker, followed him and helped him.

McAuley believed God had called him to rescue work for men, and he began a rescue mission at 316 Water Street, which Hatch purchased for him, in October 1872. He cleaned it up and hung out his sign with the words, "Helpful Hand." Maria, who became his wife, was saved in the mission from a dissolute life. When he died in 1884, she continued the work of the mission until 1892. He opened the Cremorne-McAuley Mission in 1882, and after his death Samuel Hadley, an 1882 convert, managed that mission until 1906. Hadley is credited with seventy-five thousand converts. Thus the prayer meeting revival of 1859 in which Gardner was converted bore fruit in McAuley.

Sarah Clarke (1835–1917) and George Clarke (1827–92) founded the Pacific Garden Mission in Chicago. Clarke, who had been a colonel in the Civil War and a lawyer, made money in real estate. It was his wife's prayer that he would give up business. Her prayer was answered when he did that on a trip to Denver. They opened the mission in 1877, and it is estimated that more than twenty-five thousand have knelt at its altar. Billy Sunday was one of their most notable converts.

Orphanages. Orphanages were a direct result of revival in order to rescue orphans. Charles Wesley first mentioned the need for an orphanage to Whitefield. This was reinforced when he saw the need of numerous orphans on his trip to the thirteen colonies in 1738.

He returned to England, got a charter, and raised £1000 in 1739. The trustees for Georgia gave him five hundred acres ten miles from Savannah. On March 25, 1740, Whitefield, with surveyors and carpenters, laid the first bricks of the large sixty-by-forty-foot building with twenty rooms. By June he had raised another £500 in the colonies for the Bethesda orphanage, which soon housed 150 orphans. Altogether he raised £15,000 and gave about £3,300 himself.

The responsibility and debts for it gave him much concern. He routinely took collections in his meetings for the orphans. On one occasion, Benjamin Franklin determined that he would give

Mrs. Sarah J. Bird at her Sunday morning meeting and breakfast with her boys at the Bowery Mission. Revival in the church has led to concern for the destitute, particularly in urban areas. *(Courtesy of the Billy Graham Center Museum)*

nothing. As Whitefield pled for his orphans, Franklin was so moved that he emptied his pockets.

Whitefield gave Lady Huntingdon charge of the orphanage in his will. A fire caused by lightning destroyed the house in 1773. When Lady Huntingdon died, the legislature of Georgia took it over.

Johannes H. Wichern (1808–81) was born in Hamburg and educated at the Universities of Berlin and Göttingen. In 1833 he set up his first *Ruhe Haus* ("rough house") for orphans. The boys were placed in cottages with about a dozen boys in each cottage under a mentor. This work developed into a large organization. During the 1860s he also engaged in prison reform.

On November 10, 1848, he organized the "Innere Mission" to use the laity in the social work of the church in relief and welfare and to have the winning of souls a main aim. All of these Germans were evangelicals who saw the spiritual as well as material needs of the poor, sick, prisoners, orphans, and natives of other lands.

George Müller (1805–98) was a wayward dissolute Prussian youth who stole from his father and defrauded others. He even stole nearly all of the confirmation fees his father had given him. When he graduated form the University of Halle in 1828, the school, formerly a bastion of Pietism, had become rationalistic. In mid-November 1825 he went to a meeting where the Bible was read, an LMS missionary from Africa spoke, and the group kneeled to pray. He was converted and on January 1, 1826, he decided to be a missionary.

He studied Hebrew to prepare to work with Jews and, through Professor Tholuck of Halle, he was invited to London to train for Jewish work. He began the course in March 1829, but became ill in May and went to Teignmouth for his health. There he met Henry Craik, a classical graduate of St. Andrews University, and he gave up training for Jewish work.

In 1830 he and Craik became ministers of the Plymouth Brethren Ebenezer Chapel at Teignmouth. He was baptized by immersion, married Mary Groves, and decided to live by faith. He and

Craik went on to Bristol in 1832 as pastor of Bethesda and Gideon Chapels.

The needy orphans that he observed in Bristol—and his memory of a two-month stay in Francke's orphan house in Halle—became a call of God to open an orphan house in the early winter of 1835. He had many applicants for his first house, opened for girls aged seven to twelve, in April 1836. He opened a second home for children under seven and a third home for boys over seven in 1837. By 1844 he had opened his fourth house.

Müller then asked God to give him £10,000. He bought seven acres on Ashley Down, then in the country, with the money and opened a building to house 300 orphans in 1849. About 1850 he opened a second building holding 700. By 1870 there were five houses, costing over £100,000 and housing 2,050 orphans. James Wright, who married Müller's daughter Lydia in 1871, was made codirector of the homes in 1872 and director in 1875. The centralized buildings have now been replaced by ten small homes with houseparents. All this was and is done by faith in God without any pleas for money.

Müller began preaching tours that took him all over the world from 1875 to 1892. This involved 200,000 miles of travel. His *Autobiography*, describing his life of faith, has inspired many. About 18,000 children had been cared for in his home from its founding until 1980.

He also founded the Scriptural Knowledge Institution in 1834 to support day schools, to provide Bible teaching, to distribute Bibles, and to support missionaries. By 1975 about £300,000 had been given to missionaries. Müller's organization, his preaching tours, and his orphanages gave help to thousands.

Thomas J. Barnardo (1845–1905), a product of the revival in 1859, was born in Dublin. He was a little man (five-foot-five) who was somewhat of a dandy in dress. He was to rescue thousands of abandoned or destitute children in London during his life.

When he was two, the doctor pronounced him dead, but the mortician felt his heart flutter. He grew up to be a hot-tempered, self-willed, and imperious boy who loved to read and swim. Though confirmed in the Church of Ireland, he became a deist during his four years in business.

He came under conviction in a house meeting. Some weeks later after hearing the converted actor, John Hambleton, preach, he knelt by his bed and accepted Christ on May 26, 1862. He began to teach in a Ragged School in Dublin and held Bible classes and evangelistic services. He was immersed in 1862 and became a Plymouth Brethren.

When J. Hudson Taylor spoke to Grattan Guiness's class on February 19, 1866, Barnardo felt called to go to China. He decided that if a man as small as Taylor could serve Christ, then he could serve Christ too. He went to London to train for medicine in the London Hospital in 1866. In his spare time he taught in one of Shaftesbury's Ragged Schools.

Barnardo soon opened his own school in a donkey shed. He found James Jarvis with no home one night in 1866. Jarvis showed him many sleeping on a roof in the cold night. He got Jarvis into a foster home.

When a speaker didn't come as arranged to the Agricultural Hall in Islington, Chairman Davidson asked Barnardo to speak. For an hour he spoke about his waifs. Shaftesbury read his speech and asked him to speak to over fifteen rich people who took carriages to see if what he told them was true. In a short time Barnardo found seventy-three boys from seven to thirteen years of age. They took the boys to a cafe at 3:00 A.M. to eat. Shaftesbury influenced Barnardo to be a missionary to the slums.

Barnardo proposed the need of a room to hold six hundred waifs while they heard the gospel in an article in the *Revival* of July 25, 1867. Soon £200 was raised for a room over the King's Arms, a public house. Nearly 2,350 boys were fed at a meeting on November 5, 1867. He moved to Hope Place on March 2, 1868, and founded his East End Juvenile Mission with church, Bible classes, and prayer meetings on Sunday and three nights a week. He set up a lending library, penny bank, and classes in shoe blacking and sewing. Boys and girls were placed in foster homes.

Early in 1870 he had no room to take in "Carrots" Jim Somers, who died of exposure. It was then that he put the sign over the door, "No Destitute Child Ever Refused Admission." His first home for boys was opened at 18 Stepney Causeway on December 8, 1870. He found that 85 percent of the children were homeless because of drinking parents. "The Edinburgh Castle," a former pub, was purchased in October 1872 for £4,200 and was made into a Coffee Palace and People's Church.

By 1873 he was caring for 130 boys, but his recognition of the needs of girls and a gift from John Sands of Mosspore Lodge in Essex enabled him to open a girls' home in October. In 1876 he built thirteen cottages because he felt that decentralized homes were better for the children. Before he died he had cared for 60,000 children, of whom 24,000 were girls. By 1966 about 170,000 children had gone through his homes. A house given to him in Kent was made into a "Babies' Castle" in 1844. He completed his medical work in 1876 so that he could serve as a doctor for the children.

When Roman Catholics claimed some of his children, he was responsible for getting "The Barnardo Act," the children's act, through Parliament in October 1891. This act permitted the taking of children from parents who were neglectful, criminal, or immoral. He incorporated his homes in 1899 with the Bible as "our chief textbook." The children were also taught trades and helped to emigrate. In 1882 he sent one thousand boys to Canada with Annie McPherson, who placed a total of twenty thousand children in Canada in Christian homes. He then began his own emigration of boys to British colonies.

Wilson Carlile (1847-1942) helped to found the Church Army of the Anglican Church in 1884. He helped many boys as well as men to get a fresh start in life by emigration.

Help for the Urban Poor. William Booth (1829-1912), after successful pastorates and evangelism, also began to minister to the poor of the East End of London in 1865. Booth was born in Nottingham and apprenticed to a Unitarian pawnbroker. He was converted in 1844 in a Methodist chapel. He determined that "God should have all there was of him" when he heard the American Methodist revivalist James Caughey preach in Wesley Chapel in Nottingham in 1846. Booth also learned that Caughey's success in spiritual work came because he used methods that involved "Common sense, the Holy Spirit, and the Word of God." From that time he knew that evangelism was his mission.

He became a lay Methodist preacher at age seventeen and went to London in 1849. Edward Rabbits encouraged him to quit business in 1851 and supported him when he joined the Methodist New Connexion and married Catherine Mumford in 1849. Catherine took on the unusual role for a woman of preaching as early as 1860. In 1861 they left the Methodist New Connexion. In 1861 and 1862 they ministered successfully in revivals in Cornwall and Wales. They had convicted sinners kneel at a penitent bench. Booth was invited to hold tent meetings in the East End of London in July 1865. Their East End Mission was renamed "Christian Mission" in 1870. Then in January 1877 a military organization was used in his work. Booth had called his work "Salvation Army" by Christmas 1877 and the title was officially adopted in 1878. The general was the autocratic leader. Their movement, which soon spread all over the world, reached the down-and-out and poor with the gospel and social services.

Christian Nursing of Soldiers. Florence Nightingale (1820–1910), who was born in Italy of wealthy English parents, believed that on February 7, 1837, God had called her in an audible voice to help the sick. She read a yearbook of the Deaconess Institution at Kaiserswerth in October 1846, and visited the Institution for a month in August 1850 to see the work. Between June and September of 1851 she worked there with the nurses and learned much about caring for the sick.

Between 1854 and 1856 she and thirty-eight other nurses cared for British soldiers in the Crimea. Her work cut the death rate from wounds from 42 percent to about 2 percent. The soldiers called her "The Lady with the Lamp" because of her nightly rounds. When she was given £50,000 in recognition of her public service, she built the Nightingale Home and School in 1860 for training nurses.

The United States Christian Commission, which emerged from the YMCA and the prayer revival of 1857, was organized in 1861. Until 1866 the Commission evangelized soldiers, distributed Bibles and Christian literature, and met temporal needs with medicines and hospital care. George C. Stuart, a leader in the Philadelphia revival, was chairman and supervised the spending of over $6,291,000 during the war. Moody served as one of the five thousand workers, did personal work, and helped the sick and wounded.

Henri Dunant, who was born into an evangelical Swiss family, founded the Red Cross after caring for the wounded at the battle of Solferino. This Swiss Red Cross became an international work to relieve the suffering of soldiers in war and civilians in disasters.

Protection of Animals. Proverbs 12:10 suggests that a good man will treat his animals well. Arthur Broome, an Anglican cleric, founded the Royal Society for the Prevention of Cruelty to Animals in England in 1824 with the aid of Wilberforce and friends.

Fight against Prostitution. Josephine Butler (1828–1906), a product of the revival of 1859 in England, worked to stop exploitation of women for immoral purposes. Settling with her husband in Liverpool in 1866, she began to work for the rehabilitation of prostitutes. She became involved in the campaign against the Contagious Diseases Acts, which had been passed in 1864, 1866, and 1869, supposedly to prevent the spread of venereal disease in garrison towns and naval stations. The acts permitted the arrest of any suspected women and required compulsory medical examination and hospitalization if the women were found affected. Butler organized the Ladies National Association for Repeal, which agitated for repeal of the acts on the grounds that they deprived the most defenseless members of society of their constitutional rights and also failed as health measures. Because of her petitions, her appeals to working men, her intervention in elections, and her debates, the acts were repealed in 1886. She also founded an international organization to urge governments to abolish licensed brothels and state regulation of prostitution. She revealed to the public that licensed brothels were markets for white-slave traffic and for child prostitution. She had many notable supporters, including the French author Victor Hugo and the American abolitionist William Lloyd Garrison.

EVANGELICALS IN POLITICAL ACTIVITY

The British Evangelicals gave more attention to social than to political and economic reforms, such as widening the franchise and getting the Corn Laws repealed so that food would be less expensive. William Wilberforce, however, as well as Shaftesbury, believed that Christianity should influence politics for justice and compassion. Wilberforce wrote A Practical View, published on April 12, 1797; in it he compared the religious and political views of the middle and upper classes with real Christianity. The work was a sensation at Bath, a fashionable social center, and went through fifteen impressions and two editions in England and twenty-five in the United States. It was translated into French, German, Italian, Spanish, and Dutch.

Wilberforce believed that politics should be based on Christianity. He recognized that man was depraved by nature and would be judged for sin unless he experienced salvation by faith in Christ's shed blood. The Scriptures should also be foundational in political life. True religion would promote public welfare and motivate ethical action. Political problems were basically moral and spiritual problems. Shaftesbury had similar ideas.

Many historians believe that England was spared much civil

unrest and possibly even revolution by revival. Elie Halévy believed that the "operative principle of British liberalism" was to be found in the Evangelical and Methodist groups. Lecky thinks that Wesleyanism saved England from "the horrors of a French Revolution."

Revival leaders joined with others to plead for religious toleration. One such leader was Francis Makemie (1658–1708). Born in Ireland and educated at Glasgow University, he became the founder of American Presbyterianism. In 1706 Lord Cornbury, the governor of New York, had Makemie arrested for unlicensed preaching. After six weeks in jail, Makemie won his own case by arguing that his license to preach, granted in Barbados and validated in Virginia, was good in any colony. Like many other colonial preachers, Makemie was opposed to a state church and any coercion of the conscience by the state.

Through John Leland the Baptist General Association asked the General Assembly of Virginia for religious toleration in 1754. With the Presbyterians, the Baptists supported Thomas Jefferson's bill which ended the establishment of the Episcopal Church in Virginia in 1786.

In New England, Isaac Backus drew up memorials to the Continental Congress, and, representing the Warren Baptist Association before it, pleaded for toleration of New Light Congregationalists and Baptists who suffered under the law banning itinerant preachers speaking in parishes without the consent of the resident minister.

Missionaries motivated by revival sought to protect the natives from rapacious traders and colonists who sold them guns and liquor to get their land. Missionaries did not espouse imperialism, but believed that the welfare of the natives would be better served if signs banning "Hottentots and dogs" from white churches were eliminated.

James Stephen, Jr., head of the English colonial office, drafted a treaty between England and the New Zealand Maoris (who had been evanglized by Samuel Marsden) and sent Captain William

Hobson to negotiate it. Henry Williams, a missionary, was interpreter for Hobson, and the Maori chiefs signed the Treaty of
Waitangi in 1840. Thus were the Maoris protected from predatory
land-hungry settlers.

John Mackenzie (1838–99) was converted in 1853. In 1858, when
he was serving in Africa as a missionary under the LMS, he
sought to stop the Boer takeover of Bechuanaland by getting
England to annex it. He campaigned in England through speeches
and his two-volume book, *Austral Africa*. He and the Evangelicals and Dissenters of Exeter Hall pressured the British government into making Bechuanaland a protectorate in 1885. According
to the agreement, the British residents would control foreign
affairs, but the autonomous native chiefs enforcing tribal law
would control domestic relations.

In 1875 and 1876 missionaries of the Scottish Free Church and
Kirk of Scotland had opened work in Nyasaland through Livingstone's influence in the mid-nineteenth century. They opposed the
Arab slave trade by substituting legitimate trade. In 1878 Scottish merchants, led by James Stevenson as chairman, founded the
Central African Company, Ltd., with the two Moir brothers to
supervise the African end. Capital, initially £20,000, was raised to
£100,000. The Edinburgh Botanical Gardens sent out coffee plants
to John Buchanan who started the coffee plantations of the highlands of Nyasaland. Eleven hundred tons of coffee had been exported by 1899 and coffee growing had spread to Kenya.

James C. E. Stewart (?–1883), a civil service engineer in India,
vacationed in Africa. He returned to Africa in 1881 to build a road
between the north end of Lake Nyasa and the south end of Lake
Tanganyika. With the road built, the missionaries could help the
gospel advance and the company could substitute legitimate trade
for the Arab slave trade. James Stevenson gave £4,000 to pay the
cost of building the road. Stewart built over 50 miles of the
hardest part of the 250-mile road. The road was then completed by
others.

When the Portuguese threatened to take over the area, Robert Laws of the Free Church and others of the Kirk aroused the churches in Scotland to the danger that Portuguese annexation would increase the spread of the slave trade. A Scottish delegation of ministers and peers visited Prime Minister Salisbury on May 17, 1889. The leader, Scott, placed a petition on the table with names of 110,000 elders and ministers asking for annexation and said that this was "the voice of Scotland." The British government informally annexed Nyasaland in 1889 and made it a formal protectorate in 1893. Scottish missionaries were then free to continue work in that area.

Uganda became a protectorate on April 1, 1893, through the efforts of CMS missionaries led by Bishop Alfred Tucker. The CMS raised £16,000 to enable the Imperial British East Africa Company to remain another year until Christian public opinion could force the government to declare a protectorate. The formal announcement of the protectorate was made in 1894. The Anglican Church in Uganda, revived by the awakening of the 1930s, is today one of the strongest churches in Africa.

These missionaries and reformers were anything but flag-waving imperialists. For them, politics was always a tool, a means to a spiritual end. These people did not expect perfection in their work because of the downward pull of the world, the flesh, and the devil. They believed that the task of the church was to equip Christians spiritually for witness and the task of the Christian citizen to do good works.

CHRISTIAN EDUCATION

Elementary and High Schools. Many revivalistic pastors and itinerant revivalists became educators or founded schools. George Whitefield founded a school for miners' children before 1738. Griffith Jones established his Welsh Circulating Schools as early as

1730 to teach people to read the Welsh Bible. Charles of Bala later picked up his work in Wales.

Andrew Bell (1763–1838), educated at St. Andrews University and ordained in 1784, became a missionary in India. In 1789 he used the older Tamil boys in his orphanage to monitor and teach younger boys. He used this system in St. Botolph's Charity School in England and in the United States after 1818. Joseph Lancaster used monitors in his London School in 1801, received royal patronage in 1809, and eventually enrolled over twenty-five thousand in his ninety-five schools. James Thomson developed the same system in several South American and Caribbean countries between 1824 and 1842. He was for a time copastor with James Haldane in Edinburgh before he went to South America as a Bible society colporteur. He developed the schools to teach people to read the Bibles he sold. All three of these men were Evangelicals.

Industrial Education. Lovedale and Blythswood were founded in South Africa in 1841 and 1877 respectively. They were examples of industrial schools organized to train natives in printing, carpentry, nursing, and other occupations.

Colleges. Colleges were promised by proponents of revival to be "nurseries of ministers." This was why Harvard and Yale were founded by the Puritans. The College of New Jersey, now Princeton University, was founded in 1746 by New Light men after David Brainerd was expelled from Yale in 1742. Jonathan Dickinson was the first president and the college met in his home. Jonathan Edwards was president for a time. James Witherspoon (1723–94), a Scot who won his B.A. at age thirteen and his M.A. at sixteen from Edinburgh University, was a pastor in Scotland until 1768, when he was asked to be president of Princeton. He was a five-year member of the Continental Congress and trained men such as James Madison. He helped to organize a national Presbyterian Church in 1789, wrote most of its Directory of Worship, and was its first moderator. Colleges such as this replaced the "log colleges" of Gilbert Tennent, Samuel Blair, and John McMillan.

Whitefield's Philadelphia tabernacle, erected for his meetings, became the center of a charity school which eventually became the University of Pennsylvania.

The revival party in the Dutch Reformed Church founded Queen's College (now Rutgers University) in 1756.

The College of Rhode Island (now Brown University) was founded in 1764 by Baptists. The notable revivalist Isaac Backus served on its board for nearly thirty years.

After Methodist students were expelled from St. Edmund College, Oxford, in 1768, Lady Huntingdon set up Trevecca College in that year to train ministers.

Dartmouth College was born in revival and developed from Joshua Moor's Indian school, with generous help from John Ryland and others.

Hampden-Sydney College was founded in 1776, and until 1916 half of those graduating became ministers.

Seminaries. Many seminaries originated in revival. Andover Seminary was founded in 1808 with thirty-six students to provide an orthodox seminary for Congregationalists when the Unitarian Henry Ware was made professor of theology at Harvard. Moses Stuart (1780–1852), a pupil of Timothy Dwight, was its famous professor from 1808 to 1848 and trained such men as Mills and Judson. The home missionary Iowa Band, formed in 1832 to minister on the frontier in Iowa, came from Andover. Neesima Hardy, who founded Doshisha University in Japan, was one of Andover's students. For a long time it was a center of revival and missions. Princeton Seminary was also founded in 1812. Hartford Seminary was founded by revival leaders in 1833 in East Windsor, Connecticut.

An American Education Society founded in 1815 was, like the Elland Society in England, established to raise money to provide financial aid for poor pious men to train as ministers. It had its headquarters in Andover Seminary until it was moved to Boston. By 1819 it had helped 190 men.

Far from being ignorant, most of the revivalists who founded or taught in "log colleges," colleges, and seminaries were learned men whose learning had been set on fire in revival. Edwards, a Yale graduate, was president of Princeton. Nettleton lectured on revival in what became Hartford Seminary in his later years. Finney served as professor of theology and later as president of Oberlin.

Bible Schools. Bible institutes to train the laity as "gap men," Moody's term, sprang up in the late nineteenth century and blossomed into a large movement in the twentieth century. They were born in revival and in opposition to the liberals' takeover of the mainline denominational schools and seminaries.

We have seen how Johannes Gossner set up a school in Germany in 1842 to train missionaries. By the time of his death, 141 missionaries had been trained in the school. The East London Institute for Home and Foreign Missions, founded by H. Gratian Guinness, a revivalistic evangelist, trained over five hundred workers in sixteen years in the Bible and related subjects to work in the church at home and on the foreign field. A. B. Simpson, who had heard Guinness speak on schools when he was a young man, founded Nyack as a Bible school in 1883 in New York. In 1897 the school was moved to Nyack. Moody Bible Institute, which began in 1886, became a full-fledged Bible institute with its own building in 1889. Thousands of graduates of Bible schools have become earnest evangelical ministers, missionaries, or teachers. In 1976 Bible schools attracted about 50,000 students, with 35,000 in the one hundred schools accredited by the American Association of Bible Colleges.

Sunday Schools. Griffith Jones's Welsh Circulating Schools were forerunners of the Sunday school. They were in operation as early as 1730 and used the Bible as a text to teach people to read. In 1769 Hannah Ball (1733–92) started the first Sunday school in High Wycombe, thirty-five miles west of London. She taught reading and writing in order to train them in the Bible and to understand the Anglican service. Wesley was very pleased when he visited these Sunday schools and wrote of them that they might become "nurseries for Christians."

Robert Raikes (1735–1811) did not start the Sunday school, but first popularized it in 1784 in his *Gloucester Journal*. He worked first with older men in jail. When he saw how hardened they were, he started his first school in 1780 in Sooty Alley near the jail and engaged Mrs. Meredith to teach it. He then paid Mrs. Mary Critchley to hold it in her home. The movement spread all over England, and the Sunday School Union was founded in 1803.

Hannah More (1745–1833), a leading London dramatic and poetic writer, had Samuel Johnson the lexicographer, Joshua Reynolds the painter, and David Garrick the actor as her friends in the 1770s. After she was converted, partly through John Newton's sermons, she was so shocked at the ignorance and distress in Cheddar, a town near Bristol, in August 1789, that she decided to open a Sunday school. She rented a house and paid a teacher £30 a year. By the end of 1789 she had five hundred in her schools to learn the Bible and catechism. And at the end of twenty-five years twenty-five thousand had been through her schools.

CHRISTIAN LITERATURE

The Methodists founded a Naval and Military Bible Society in 1799 to provide pocket Bibles for soldiers and sailors. The Evangelicals founded the British and Foreign Bible Society in 1804 to provide Bibles for the Welsh and others converted during the Second Awakening. Thomas Charles of Bala in Wales saw the great need for Welsh Bibles for those trained in his schools. In 1799 he persuaded the Society for the Promotion of Christian Knowledge to print ten thousand Bibles and two thousand New Testaments in Welsh. This met only a quarter of the need. When he went to London in 1802 for his annual period of supply in Lady Huntingdon's Spa Field's Chapel, he met with the Religious Tract Society on December 2 to try to get Welsh Bibles. Joseph Hughes proposed a society to print and sell Bibles. Finally on March 7, 1804, at a meeting of three hundred at the London Tavern with Granville Sharp presiding, the nondenominational British and Foreign Bible Society was founded. The founders subscribed £700 at the meeting to produce only the King James version "without notes or comment."

The American Bible Society was founded because Samuel J. Mills found great need for Bibles on the frontier on two trips to the South and West in 1812 and 1814. He enlisted Elias Boudinot (1740–1821), a wealthy lawyer, a member of the Continental Congress in 1778, a legislator and director of the mint, and president of the New Jersey Bible Society, to issue a call in 1816 for a meeting to found a national society. The meeting in New York formed a national society on May 10 and elected Boudinot as president and formed a constitution on May 11. Boudinot gave $10,000 to the society to print and distribute Bibles.

The production of other helpful Christian literature was not ignored. In 1795 Hannah More founded the *Cheap Repository* to distribute tracts to instruct in morals and religion. She wrote 114 tracts, some of which had a circulation of 2 million in one year. She gave most of the $150,000 she earned from her dramas and poetry to this organization and other worthy causes.

George Burder, who served a Congregational church at Coventry, was secretary of the LMS, a founder of the Bible Society, and the editor of the *Evangelical Magazine.* He invited ministers to a meeting in May 1799, and on May 10 the Religious Tract Society was organized. The American Tract Society, influenced by the success of Hannah More's *Cheap Repository* and the Religious Tract Society, came into being in the United States in 1824.

Moody also founded the Bible Institute Colportage Association in 1894 to provide inexpensive Christian literature for Christians.

It can readily be seen from this study of the results of revival that it touched every area of life for good. People were renewed and won to Christ and then went about as Jesus did, doing good for God's glory.

PART THREE *The Faith of Revival*

11. THE THEOLOGY AND HYMNOLOGY OF REVIVAL

THEOLOGY OF REVIVAL

The theology of revival has tended to be biblical and practical rather than speculative or systematic. Revival leaders, with the exception of Jonathan Edwards and some others, have usually emphasized doing rather than thinking. This is not to say that the revivalists were theologically ignorant. The Holy Club at Oxford carefully studied the works of the church fathers and later theologians. Most of the leaders were college graduates. If not, they read widely to educate themselves in the faith. They went from the Puritan theologians back to the thinkers of the Reformation and the early church and ultimately to the Bible.

They were indeed men of the Book, the Bible. They took it as a fully inspired revelation from God, written by men who were inspired by the Holy Spirit. The Holy Spirit would illuminate the Word to believers so that the Bible could serve as an infallible rule of faith and practice. To them the Bible was a "self-contained and self-interpreting revelation" given by God. It was a complete, final, and binding authority on the church. Scripture was to be interpreted by Scripture in order to find the original meaning, which could then be applied in the revivalist's day.

All the revivalists, whether Calvinists or Arminians, declared the sovereignty of God as Creator and Redeemer. They emphasized God's holiness and justice, before which sinful man must quake as the Israelites did before Sinai. Revivalists had no difficulty with the idea that all men are sinners. Most looked upon man as depraved through Adam's sin and incapable of fulfilling God's righteousness. Finney and others, however, held that each man was a sinner by choice and that the will was free to choose good or evil. But the sermons of Calvinists and Arminians alike pointed out the wrath of God against all sin, while preaching that men could experience the love of God in Christ's atonement if they repented of their sins and believed God. Any reading of the sermons of the revivalists makes clear that in most cases they believed man was guilty of original *and* actual sin and thus a sinner by birth and choice.

But if, as Moody preached, man is ruined by the Fall, there is redemption through the death of Christ on the cross. God had made salvation for the sinner possible in the virgin-born Christ, who was true man as well as true God.

The revivalists preached the law so that men might be convicted of sin. A man might then repent and have faith in Christ as his substitutionary sin-bearer who took the sin of man upon himself. Faith would bring justification before God and regeneration, the New Birth which all the revivalists proclaimed. The Wesleyans also emphasized the *assurance* of the saved man, the awareness that one's sin is forgiven.

Devereux Jarratt's sermon on Galatians 3:22, entitled "The Miserable State of Man by Nature, and the Way of Recovery by Faith in Christ Jesus," elaborated on the points already made. Asahel Nettleton's sermons, strongly doctrinal and with few illustrations, emphasized the total depravity of man, the awfulness of sin against a holy and majestic sovereign God, and the Cross as the only remedy for sin. Edwards's sermon "Sinners in the Hands of an Angry God" made people conscious of their lost state. Apart from Christ there was only future judgment and hell. Moody did perhaps preach God's love more than most, but he prefaced it with the idea that man was ruined by the Fall. This was a necessary prelude to Calvary in the thinking and preaching of revival leaders.

Their preaching of man redeemed by Christ would lead to a transformation of character. The Christian would morally become more like his Savior in his character. Wesley and Finney laid more stress than the Calvinists on Christian perfection. In his pamphlet *Christian Perfection*, Wesley wrote that because the love of Christ in the consecrated heart would drive out sin and let Christ's love fill the heart, perfection was possible in this life. There might be "mistakes" of ignorance and omission but not sins of commission. That is, the Christian's essential inclination is to consciously oppose and resist sin, resulting in a life that excludes actual sins.

Finney and the Palmers and their holiness followers went even farther in asserting that the evil nature of man was eradicated completely in a second work after conversion. Perfection should be expected in this life. The holiness movements, the Salvation Army, and the Nazarenes reflect this view today.

More revivalists followed the third pattern of the Keswick conventions. Sanctification, according to Keswick supporters, is instantaneous with the New Birth, but also progressive through life as the Christian reckoned by faith that in Christ he was dead to sin. Keswick does not claim that the Christian's tendency to sin is completely extinguished. Rather, sin is counteracted by victorious living in the Spirit.

All the revivalists, however, believed that holiness of life and the development of Christian character was important. They also believed that the Christian who was transformed in character and personal life would in turn help to transform society. Wesley and others insisted that Christianity was a social religion. Reform of the individual would bring reform of society. Passages such as Ephesians 2:10 and Titus 3:8 convinced revivalists that the saved man should do the "good work" of reforming society.

Until the middle of the nineteenth century most revivalists

were evangelical postmillennialists and asserted that the changes regenerated man would bring in society would produce the millenium after which Christ would come. But after the prayer revival of 1857–59, such revivalists as Moody, Chapman, Sunday, and Torrey, and laymen such as Shaftesbury, were premillennialists. They did not believe that the church would create a perfect order on earth. They, like Wesley, Whitefield, Haldane, and Finney, worked for reforms to improve the social order while admitting that their solutions would be proximate and not final.

Differences such as those between Wesley and Whitefield over election and sanctification and between Finney and Nettleton over Finney's "New Measures" did not stop them from agreeing on the main doctrines just discussed. They disagreed finally in love and went on preaching salvation.

The creed of the Evangelical Alliance of 1846 set forth the major doctrine of revival leaders. The Niagara Conference, beginning in 1878, gave rise to a fourteen-point platform in 1890, drawn up in large part by James H. Brookes (1830–97), the Presbyterian pastor of Walnut Street Presbyterian Church in St. Louis. This so-called "Five Points" was published in 1895. It proclaimed an inerrant Bible, the Virgin Birth and deity of Christ, the substitutionary atonement, the resurrection of Christ, and his bodily return to earth.

The greatest attempt to proclaim the major doctrines of revival took place form 1910 to 1915 with the publication of *The Fundamentals: A Testimony of the Truth.* A. C. Dixon (1854–1925), a Baptist pastor with several pastorates after 1876, including Moody Church from 1906 to 1911, spoke on the subject of liberalism as a threat to the church on a trip to the west coast in August 1909. Lyman Stewart, who had already formulated his own creed of seven ideas (similar to those set forth in this chapter), thought it was time for the fundamental doctrines of Christianity to be set forth clearly. After hearing Dixon, he talked at length with him about editing twelve volumes of the basic principles of the faith. These principles would be presented by sixty-four of the best American and British evangelical scholars and would be sent free to ministers, missionaries, evangelists, Sunday school superintendents, and YMCA workers all over the English-speaking world.

Dixon agreed to head up the project, and Lyman and Milton Stewart gave $300,000 in securities to finance it. Dixon was only to receive his expenses. After conferring and praying with prominent evangelicals in Chicago, Dixon organized the Testimony Publishing Company. The first volume came out in February 1910 and was sent to 175,000 persons, later expanded to 200,000. Dixon edited the first five volumes in eighteen months. Louis Meyer edited the next five volumes. After Meyer died in 1913, R. A. Torrey completed the last two volumes by 1915. Three million individual volumes in all were sent all over the world to Christian leaders, and about 200,000 letters of commendation were received.

The Fundamentals were republished in 1917 in a four-volume edition and again in 1958 by Charles Feinberg in a two-volume edition. The doctrines, set forth in nearly one hundred articles, codified the basic doctrines the revival preachers had been proclaiming since 1726. The volumes were scholarly, rational, and ecumenical in authorship.

MUSIC OF REVIVAL

The music used in revivals is closely related to the doctrines of revivals. The revivalists continued Luther's practice of congregational singing and created a new hymnology. Their theology and experiences were expressed in joyful song. A perusal of any hymnal will reveal how indebted we are to revivalists, such as Charles Wesley and others.

Before the Reformation, congregations listened passively to the great music of the organ and the complicated polyphonic singing of trained choirs. A few of our hymns come from the Greek and Latin Fathers, but more come from the Reformation and post-

Reformation Germany, and from England and America after 1700.

John Hus wrote hymns for congregational singing by his followers. Luther, an able musician himself, wanted to express biblical truth in songs written in the vernacular. Congregations would actively participate in singing these hymns. His great hymn of faith, "A Mighty Fortress Is Our God," is based on Psalm 46. The Reformed churches also had congregational singing, but restricted it to metrical unison Psalms because Calvin would not use trained choirs, instruments, or part singing. Some of the Psalm tunes written by Calvin's friend Louis Bourgeois are still in use.

The Pietist revival, especially its Moravian expression, and the Wesleyan revival had a more subjective view of Christ and emphasis upon subjective personal Christian experience. They composed hymns to be sung by the congregation with, in the case of Moravians, accompaniment by musical instruments which they made. The Moravian Museum at Winston-Salem, North Carolina, reveals the variety of fine instruments they made and used.

The Lutheran pastor Paul Gerhardt (1607–76) was the "Charles Wesley" of Germany. He wrote many fine hymns, including the famous Christmas song "All My Heart This Night Rejoices." Count Zinzendorf, the Moravian leader, who gave us the lovely hymn "Jesus, Thy Blood and Righteousness," wrote about two thousand hymns, many of them still in use. John Cennick (1718–55), who became the leader of the Moravian revival in Yorkshire, wrote "Children of the Heavenly King" and "Lo, He Comes with Clouds Descending."

The great hymn-writer Isaac Watts (1674–1748), a little man with a feeble body, was mainly educated in Southampton by his father. He had done well in Greek by the time he was four, in French by age nine, and in Latin and Hebrew by age thirteen. He became a tutor in the family of Sir John Hartopp in 1696. He joined the dissenting Mark Lane Church in London, became its assistant pastor in 1698, and became its pastor in 1702. He lived with Thomas Abney at Theobald near London for many years.

Watts began writing hymns at the age of twenty. When he complained about the versified Psalms (which were the only hymns used in the service), he was challenged to write one of his own. In all, he wrote about six hundred hymns, including "O God, Our Help in Ages Past," "When I Survey the Wondrous Cross," "Joy to the World," and the first real missionary hymn, "Jesus Shall Reign." He published his *Hymns and Spiritual Songs* in 1707. He knew and appreciated the work of Charles Wesley. The doctrines of revival, such as a sovereign God, sin, depravity, and Christ as Savior, are in his hymns. His little child's prayer, "Now I lay me down to sleep," has been the prayer of thousands of little children since then.

William Williams (1717-91), who preached and traveled 96,000 miles all over Wales, decided to enter the ministry and was ordained as a deacon in 1740 to serve two mountain parishes. He resigned in 1743 to become Daniel Rowland's assistant in the Welsh Methodist Church. He made many evangelistic tours of the country. The greatest of the eight hundred hymns he wrote, almost the Welsh national anthem, was "Guide Me, O Thou Great Jehovah." The Welsh church always sang in revival. In 1904 Evan Roberts had his "Singing Sisters" to help in that revival.

Augustus M. Toplady (1740-78), the son of an army officer, was converted in a revival in a barn in Ireland. He received his B.A. and M.A. degrees from Dublin University, was ordained in 1704, and served as a pastor from 1762 to 1778. An ardent Calvinist, he supported Whitefield in the dispute with Wesley and attacked Wesley bitterly. His great hymn, "Rock of Ages," written in March 1776 while he was sheltering from a bad storm in the protection of a great rock in a gorge, has been loved by English-speaking people.

In the same era Philip Doddridge (1702-51) produced a hymn, "O Happy Day," that has been a favorite hymn, one widely used in revivals. Doddridge also wrote the devotional classic *The Rise and Progress of Religion in the Soul.*

Charles Wesley was an able revivalistic evangelist but is better known for his hymns that made the Methodists a joyful, singing people. He often used folk songs, opera melodies, and psalm tunes for his hymns. He is credited with over six thousand hymns, and may have written seven thousand. Best known and loved are "Hark, the Herald Angels Sing," "Christ the Lord Is Risen Today," "Love Divine, All Loves Excelling," "O, For a Heart to Praise My God," and "A Charge to Keep I Have." His hymns are objective in exalting God's love and mercy and subjective in expressing man's praise.

Mention should also be made of John Newton and William Cowper (1731–1800). Both lost their mothers at an early age and were dissolute in youth. Newton came to Christ because of his sins and Cowper because of his mental torment over disappointment in love and the deaths of loved ones.

Newton spent forty-three years as minister at Olney and at St. Mary's Church in London. Together with Cowper he produced the 280 hymns, published as *Olney Hymns* in 1779. The best known and loved of his hymns are "How Sweet the Name of Jesus Sounds," "Amazing Grace," and "Glorious Things of Thee Are Spoken."

Cowper, who was shy and melancholic to the point of contemplating suicide three times, was cared for by Mary Unwin in her home near Newton's home. Newton was able to help Cowper keep his mental balance. "God Moves in a Mysterious Way," "O For a Closer Walk with God," and "There Is a Fountain Filled with Blood" are favorites written by Cowper. The last was used very often in revivals. Both men were the product of revival forces, and their hymns reflect hearts opened to God.

The hymns of Watts, Wesley, Cowper, and Newton speak more of objective truth about the sovereign God, but the American camp meeting hymns almost universally reflect the subjective expression of feelings of the sorrow of conviction and joy of conversion. Printed songbooks used in camp meetings show that these songs took up and repeated a simple refrain which could be easily remembered. They expressed subjectively (and often ungrammatically) the believer's experience of the Cross and assurance of salvation. Sometimes independent choruses were used. Secular tunes were used in these spontaneous "plain folk songs." These songs, often improvised, were termed "spiritual" songs or choruses. Many of these songs were collected in *The Southern Harmony*, published in 1835, which sold about 600,000 copies in twenty-five years. Written often in intimate and devotional terms, they saw life as a warfare to reject the world, pressed for decision for Christ, and expressed their hope of heavenly joy.

Finney, a musician himself, used Thomas Hastings of Utica as the first soloist and leader of music in revivals. Finney also made an early use of songbooks in his meetings.

The gospel song came out of the urban mass meetings through men like Sankey, whom Moody used as a soloist and song leader during the period from 1873 to 1899. The often simple, lifting, rhythmic music, easily sung by nonprofessionals, usually had a repetitive chorus or refrain unlike the earlier praise hymns. These songs used the subjective "I" more frequently than addressing God. (It has been said that hymns are the words of groups singing *to God*, while gospel songs are the words of an individual singing *about his experience of God*. "We" is more common in hymns, while "I" is more common in gospel songs. These are generalizations, of course, and there are many exceptions.) They expressed personal and emotional human experience and called for decision. Examples are "Almost Persuaded," "The Old Rugged Cross," and "Rescue the Perishing."

Ira D. Sankey (1840–1908) led music for Moody and sang solos accompanied by his portable reed organ between 1873 and 1895. He was born in Pennsylvania and converted in a revival when he was sixteen years of age. He entered banking but kept up his musical interest by leading a choir. He met Moody while a delegate to an international YMCA convention in Indianapolis in 1870. He accompanied Moody to Britain from 1873 to 1875 and published his sixteen-page edition of *Sacred Songs and Solos* in 1873.

In 1875 he and Philip P. Bliss (who wrote many popular songs still in use) published *Gospel Hymns and Sacred Songs*. By 1900 from 50 to 80 million copies of these books had been sold all over the world. The royalties, which amounted to well over $1,250,000, were donated to religious works. He put Elizabeth Clephane's poem, "The Ninety and Nine" to music and used it with acceptance in the Edinburgh meeting. Emotional hymns, such as "Just As I Am" and "Where Is My Wandering Boy Tonight?" were used in altar calls.

Fanny Crosby (1823–1915), blinded from early childhood through a doctor's wrong prescription, had a conversion experience at Broadway Tabernacle in New York in 1850. She rejoiced in Moody's and Sankey's revival work and wrote many of the gospel songs used in their meetings. She is credited with nine thousand hymns in her long life. Her hymns were personal, informal, and subjective. Examples of her best hymns were "I Am Thine, O Lord," "Safe in the Arms of Jesus," "Blessed Assurance," "Jesus, Keep Me Near the Cross," "Pass Me Not, O Gentle Savior," "All the Way My Savior Leads Me," "To God Be the Glory," and "Rescue the Perishing." These were gospel songs born in the period of revival in which Fanny Crosby exulted and served from 1857 to 1895. Sankey used many of her hymns over and over again in the Moody meetings with great blessing to people.

Charles Alexander (1867–1920) was born in Tennessee of Irish descent. He taught music at Maryville College and at other colleges until he went to Moody Bible Institute in 1892. After traveling for some years with the YMCA evangelist Milan Williams, he accompanied R. A. Torrey on his world tour from 1902 to 1908. The song, "O That Will Be Glory for Me," became a trademark of their meetings. Between 1908 and 1913 he made other world tours as a song leader and soloist for J. Wilbur Chapman.

Billy Sunday also had Homer Rodeheaver and his trumpet to lead the song service and sing solos. Cliff Barrows and George Beverly Shea fulfill the same function for Billy Graham.

FANNY CROSBY (1823-1915), blind composer of over two thousand hymns, many of which are still commonly used. *(Courtesy of the Billy Graham Center Museum)*

These leaders in revival recognized that God spoke to the people through the Word as it was preached, but that the people need to respond in prayer and song to prepare their hearts. Gospel songs reflected the emotion of revival as people responded in joyous praise in song for what God had done for them. The experience of Isaiah (chapter 6) suggests the nature of an ideal song. Isaiah saw God's holiness in contrast with his sin which he confessed. After he was cleansed he was commissioned to serve God. Hymns that came out of revival reflected this experience, repeated again and again in the lives of believers.

PART FOUR *The Forms of Revival*

12. METHODS, MANIFESTATIONS, AND MEANS OF REVIVAL

METHODS OF REVIVAL

Organization. The gospel may be communicated—both to lukewarm Christians and to the unsaved—by personal witness (one person to another), by proclamation in stated meetings, or by the presence of Christians engaged in doing good, which opens hearts to hearing the gospel. Extemporaneous proclamation by pastors or itinerant pastors and revivalistic evangelists has been used most in revival.

ITINERANT PREACHING. During the Great Awakening, Griffith Jones extended the range of revival by itinerating in Wales. Whitefield itinerated widely with his extensive travels in Britain and thirteen Atlantic crossings to the thirteen colonies. Wesley made Britain his parish. When parish ministers closed their churches to them, Harris, Whitefield, and Wesley began open-air preaching. Methodist circuit-riders and Baptist farmer-preachers constituted another type of itinerant preacher.

Coupled with this itinerancy (which often provoked settled ministers to protest what they saw as an intrusion into their parishes) was the practice of extemporaneous preaching and prayer.

LAY PREACHERS. The use of lay preachers by revival leaders in order to meet the needs of the new congregations created by revival involved an extension of this itinerancy. Wycliffe had his Lollard lay preachers. John Wesley used local lay preachers, beginning with Thomas Maxfield, and Francis Asbury perfected Wesley's system of circuit riders in the thirteen colonies. Frelinghuysen made use of lay leaders to conduct meetings for prayer and Bible study. Hauge had his lay "readers" in the Norwegian revival.

THE CAMP MEETING. The camp meeting, which originated in Kentucky, was at first used by Baptists, Presbyterians, and Methodists. In its heyday from 1800 to 1840 it was used mainly by Methodists. Lorenzo Dow, who described the techniques and defended camp meetings in his book, carried the idea to England, where Hugh Bourne began to hold camp meetings. The Primitive Methodist Church came out of this practice.

Camp meetings began with James McGready's Gasper River sacramental meeting (July 1800) in which people first camped out. Cane Ridge was organized in early August 1801 by Barton Stone and drew a crowd estimated to be between ten thousand and twenty-five thousand. James Finley, a frontier hunter and doctor, and David Purviance, who lived three miles from Cane Ridge, wrote firsthand accounts of that meeting. Finley spoke of the "vast crowd" and the noise like the "roaring of Niagara" and experienced "a strong, supernatural power." He was so convicted that an older German Christian was able to lead him to Christ as Finley was on the road home. The meetings were usually held after the harvest from July to October, but most of them were in September. They were held frequently until 1840.

ITINERANT PARISH MINISTRY. Asahel Nettleton gave himself to an itinerant ministry in churches in small towns or villages at the invitation of the pastor or more often went to churches which had no pastor. He would stay several weeks and even months preaching and counseling in the revival that followed.

PROFESSIONAL URBAN ITINERANT MISSIONS. Finney was itinerant, but also carried on his work in cities in New York and the Northeast rather than in one parish. He was a pioneer of "professional" urban itinerant missions. His revival meetings were more structured and were the forerunner of the mass urban revival and evangelistic meetings of Moody and his successors. Although his stress was on prayer and preaching, he did use a soloist and had congregational singing. He believed that by following proper rules the church, guided by the Holy Spirit, could "provoke" revival rather than passively waiting for the sovereign God to give in his own time a spontaneous awakening such as in New England in Edwards's time or England in Whitefield's day. He set forth these rules in his *Lectures on Revival*. These became known as his "New Measures" which upset older revival leaders such as Beecher and Nettleton.

URBAN MASS REVIVALISTIC EVANGELISM. Urban mass revivalistic evangelism, outside the churches and organized by professional leaders, began after the Civil War. Although Finney's famous Rochester meeting in 1830 was held in the churches, it marked the transition from pastoral revivals in that it was conducted by professional leaders of revival with more stress on evangelism. It has been a prominent pattern from the days of Moody in the North and Sam Jones in the South to Billy Graham. These centralized meetings have involved the careful preparation of counselors, choirs, ushers, prayer groups, and follow-up work to get those reclaimed or saved into the church.

B. Fay Mills and J. Wilbur Chapman decentralized their meetings. The city would be divided into sections in which an associate speaker and song leader would hold meetings, with the main speaker either alternating in the various sections or speaking in a central meeting. Later in his career Chapman abandoned this method for the centralized meeting.

Evangelism-in-Depth, developed by Kenneth Strachan in 1958, was another variation of urban revivalism. Strachan (1910–65) was a missionary in Costa Rica and director of the Latin American Mission from 1950 to 1965. He wanted to mobilize the "total constituency in continuous evangelistic action" on a national level.

Evangelism-in-Depth was first tried in Nicaragua in 1960 and then used in other Central and South American countries and later throughout the world.

The meeting in Nicaragua resulted in 2,000 trained believers sharing their faith with 65,000 families and won 2,600 converts. In 1962, 1,000 churches in thirty-three denominations in Guatemala united in 600 prayer cells, and thousands of trained workers shared their faith and had 15,000 decisions. It is estimated that in the 1960s in Latin America 47,000 churches formed 35,000 prayer cells, trained 160,000 workers, and visited 1,320,700 homes with 140,000 professions of faith.

With Evangelism-in-Depth the total national church is mobilized to witness. After conferences of pastors to enlist their support, believers are gathered into prayer cells and trained in witnessing to their neighbors all across the nation. Religious parades and special meetings are held in cities, with the capital city being given the most attention.

The so-called electronic church engages in mass revivalism through radio and television.

Mass children's meetings in cities began with E. P. Hammond. He had one meeting in Spurgeon's Tabernacle which 8,000 children attended with many decisions for Christ. Hammond held many such meetings in the British Isles, Europe, and North America. Moody also held special children's meetings during his campaigns. The Children's Special Service Mission of England and Child Evangelism Fellowship continue this thrust in camps and homes on a smaller scale.

REVIVAL AND EVANGELISM AMONG YOUNG PEOPLE. Christians practice revival and evangelism both individually and in group meetings in trying to reach high school and college youths. Youth for Christ and Young Life seek to strengthen Christians and win unsaved high school young people in Bible clubs and other meetings. Inter-Varsity Christian Fellowship, Navigators, and Campus Crusade for Christ reach Christian and unsaved young people in colleges by cultivating personal friendships and by Bible studies.

Decision. Ever since the days of Elijah, who sought with his action sermon to get Israel to decide for God by asking how long they would halt between two opinions, revivalists have used different methods to help people decide for Christ.

PASTORAL COUNSELING. During the Great Awakening and Second Awakening the main technique for helping those convicted was counseling by the pastor or elders or by home visitation. Asahel Nettleton counseled in an office or at his boarding house and visited from home to home to help the anxious in their spiritual experience. Sometimes "inquiry meetings" were held to instruct and help the convicted.

THE ALTAR CALL. Those convicted of sin in the camp meeting revivals were invited to a special area at the front in altar-call fashion. Here other Christians prayed for them and helped them. Some who were prostrated needed little help as they rose to their feet with the assurance of salvation. The "call to the altar" was used by the Methodists even earlier than the camp meeting era.

THE INQUIRY ROOM. Finney used the "anxious bench" at the front; there, those convicted could go for counsel and prayer after the meeting. He used this technique for the first time during his Rochester meeting in 1830. Here he or helpers dealt with those who came to the bench.

Use of the inquiry room, especially in England, started in the era from 1813 to 1846. Moody asked people to rise in his meetings and then go to the inquiry room for prayer and counsel. It was in one such inquiry meeting that he was able to help J. Wilbur Chapman to assurance of salvation.

DECISION CARDS AND INSTRUCTIVE LITERATURE. B. Fay Mills made use of decision cards which inquirers were asked to sign. Billy Sunday had a part of the platform built lower so that he could shake hands with those who "hit the sawdust trail."

Workers would then deal with them and give them Sunday's useful sheet of instructions on how to be saved and lead a successful Christian life.

Billy Graham utilizes a combination of these methods for getting decisions. At the conclusion of the message he invites people to come forward to an area in front of the platform where trained counselors stand beside them. After some words of instruction from him and prayer by him, the counselors help people with their questions, pray with them, help them fill out cards indicating salvation or reconsecration, and give them literature to help them in their Christian lives. Counseling for his television programs is also done over the telephone when people phone in to central banks of phones manned by specially trained counselors.

Various methods of organization and decision have been used during the history of revivalism. The crux of the matter is renewal of the Christian life or, if the inquirer is a convicted sinner, the acceptance of Christ. All of these leaders of revival we have surveyed tried to help both Christians and non-Christians. The older New England method of letting the sinner under conviction agonize and pray for days, weeks, months, and even years until he experienced peace with God gave way to these newer methods.

MANIFESTATIONS OF REVIVAL

Revival has been characterized by common manifestations during its long history. *Conviction of sin* after personal witness of a Christian by life or word or the preaching of the Word is one such characteristic. This may bring about an emotional reaction with tears and crying (as in Scottish revivals or Wesley's meetings), or with physical actions, such as prostration, leaping, jerking, or other forms of action (as in the camp meetings). The duration of conviction today seems to be shortened, perhaps unduly, by modern methods of decision. Deep remorse for sin and sincere repentance might create stronger Christians.

Confession of sin, coupled with asking forgiveness of another individual or several individuals, or with the making of restitution, has followed in every revival. This was true of the Welsh revival of 1904, the Korean revival of 1904-7, and the Wheaton College revival of 1950, which the author witnessed. Confession was usually oral or by letter and was as wide as the sin. It may have involved one person, several people, or a whole group. Sometimes even elders, pastors, or missionaries were prodded by the Holy Spirit to confess sin to their followers.

Conversion follows confession and conviction. Multiplied millions have experienced this sovereign work of the Holy Spirit as they have become conscious of being "born again." Joy always came with faith in Christ. The Welsh would break into spontaneous group singing after reconciliation with Christ in their revivals.

Christlike character results from revival. Cursing, gambling drunkards become reverent and sober. Immoral people break with their immoral associates. The proud become humble. It is true that in Christ people become new creations (2 Corinthians 5:17). Christlikeness becomes the aim of life (Romans 8:28-29; 2 Corinthians 3:18).

Godly conduct, spurred on by the love of Christ and involving Christlike service to others, becomes a way of life to one touched by revival. People become involved in social service of various types in the community. We have already seen that this service takes many forms.

MEANS OF REVIVAL

Our times need revival perhaps more desperately than in the past. Secular humanism is fast gaining a hold on the world. Belief in God as Creator of the world and man has been replaced by belief that everything comes from a chance concatenation of atoms. The Christian ethic based upon the absolute commandments of a sovereign God is being replaced by a relativistic ethic of doing what seems good in a particular situation. Instead of being rooted in unchanging right and wrong and written by God, law is relativistic and sociological, written and rewritten by men in the courts. The cheap manner in which life is held is clearly illustrated by the more than 15 million abortions since the *Roe v. Wade* Supreme Court decision in 1973. The former revival pattern—God's glory and man's good as the aim of life—is being replaced with a pattern in which one is not accountable to God or man but seeks what is best for himself. Only revival and revived Christians who act as responsible citizens can stem the tide.

This leads one to ask if there are means which lead to revival. Although revival is a sovereign activity of the Holy Spirit, this study has revealed certain patterns preceding revival.

Prayer. Prayer and the Word were the functions of leaders in the infant church (Acts 6:2). Prayer ranks first in the coming of revival.

A Concert of Prayer was organized in Britain before revival came in the 1790s. Isaac Backus organized a Concert of Prayer in the United States in the same period. Conventions of Presbyterian ministers in Pittsburgh in 1857 and Baptists in New York played an important part in the coming of the lay prayer revival.

Individuals have also consecrated themselves to pray for revival. "Father" Nash traveled with Finney for years and prayed for his meetings. A godly nurse, Pearl Good, has traveled to the cities where Billy Graham holds crusades in order to spend most of her time in prayer for him and the meetings. The "effectual fervent prayer" of the godly has done much and can do much in bringing revival.

Revivalists from 1726 to the present have organized prayer groups or cells to pray for revival. Prayer preceded the Scottish revivals of 1742 and 1839. Moody, Chapman, and other nineteenth-century evangelists had many organized prayer groups praying for their work. Mrs. Warren organized thousands to pray for the Torrey meetings in Australia and then for his meetings in Britain. Indeed, Torrey's call to lead in worldwide revival came in a prayer meeting at Moody Bible Institute. There cannot be revival unless Christians pray for it.

Preaching of the Word. Prayer is a prelude to the faithful preaching of the Word. Paul believed that the Word of God was profitable as well as inspired and that conversion and Christian conduct would come from studying the Word (2 Timothy 3:14-17). Millions have been saved by "the foolishness of preaching." Witness to the Word and to Christ led to salvation in the early church.

M'Culloch and Robe in Scotland in 1742 and Edwards in Massachusetts in 1734 preached for a long time on justification by faith, and revival broke out in their congregations. Nettleton's doctrinal sermons based on the Bible brought deep conviction of sin. Moody became a more effective preacher after Henry Moorhouse helped him to study the Bible inductively and to stress the love of Christ. All of the revival leaders proclaimed from the Word man's depravity and sin, Christ's atonement, and the regenerating work of the Holy Spirit. Indeed, as Paul said, faith came by hearing and hearing by the Word of God (Romans 10:17).

Discipling. Consolidation, conservation, or discipling of converts has been practiced by leaders of revival. They wanted to have the people touched by revival to develop into mature Christians, be indoctrinated in Christian truth, have fellowship with other Christians, and serve God. Billy Graham has an elaborate follow-up program to refer new Christians to churches. This was originally developed by the Navigator staff. Back in the time of Whitefield and Wesley, class meetings helped in the discipling of new Christians.

This account of revival has repeatedly demonstrated that spiritual falling away and deadness brought personal or national crises which aroused some to a deep sense of sin. Their longing for a better spiritual life and the conversion of the unsaved was met by ardent continued prayer and the study of the Word. God then sent his leader to be the human instrument of revival in the hands of the Holy Spirit. Then revival would come with renewal and salvation which would bring praise, joy, and singing.

The longing for revival is expressed very well by the Psalmist (Ps. 85:6-7) and by the prophet Habakkuk (3:2), with the request for God to renew his people. God is the ultimate source of revival.

This account of revival suggests that God's formula for revival (2 Chron. 7:14) has been the experience of the church when revival has come. His first requirement for those who "are called by my name" is to "humble themselves." One notes that all of the great revival leaders have been very humble men who have desired to give God the glory for their success. There can be no revival where there is pride and people do not see their need.

No revival has come without prayer. The lay revival of 1857 to 1859 came because of prayer and prayer only. The "effectual fervent prayer" of Christians (James 5:16) will be answered.

God said that his people should seek his face. This seems to involve study of the Word to discover the nature and will of God. The Bible had an important role in the Korean revival as Christians sought God.

Repentance is demonstrated when men "turn from their wicked ways." Even evangelicals who have been caught up in the relativistic spirit of our age and the seeking of affluence need to repent if they are to be salt and light in the world. Then, and only then will God forgive sin and bring healing to their land. They are not again to "turn to folly" (Ps. 85:8).

The formula in 2 Chronicles is certainly to be followed by the individual or church that wants to see revival. Many believe on the basis of Joel 2:28 and Acts 2:17-18 that major revival will precede Christ's Second Coming, and Acts 3:19 suggests that "times of refreshing" from God will occur before Christ returns.

Signs of spiritual coldness and doctrinal indifference are evident even in many evangelical churches and institutions. Evidence of lessened belief in the full inspiration and authority of Scripture, the evil effects of affluence, overconfidence in learning, faith in man instead of God, and preoccupation with social action at the expense of the priority of evangelism have appeared. These factors are similar to those which led to the decay of evangelicalism in the formerly evangelical denominations and seminaries and the rise of liberalism in the late nineteenth and early twentieth centuries.

Only zeal on the part of Christians in Bible study and prayer will break the vicious rhythm of spiritual decline followed by revival. Revival is a perennial need. One can only hope and pray that the church of today will not fail God but be as faithful today as so often it was in the past.

BIBLIOGRAPHY I have made exten-
sive use of these primary and secondary books and theses but
have not listed newspaper and periodical articles I have read. This
bibliography will make it possible for the reader who wishes to
study revival in-depth to pursue the subject further.

Aarflot, Andreas. *Hans Nielsen Hauge.* Minneapolis: Augsburg, 1979. His
  life and message are ably presented.
Abzug, Robert H. *Passionate Liberator: Theodore Dwight Weld and the
  Dilemma of Reform.* New York: Oxford University Press, 1980.
The Advance Guard. London: Moravian Bookroom, ca. 1932. The story of
  Moravian Missions.
Ahlstrom, Sidney E. *A Religious History of the American People.* New
  Haven: Yale University Press, 1972. A voluminous history of the church in
  America, with considerable material on revival.
Alexander, Archibald. *The Log College.* London: Banner of Truth, 1968. A
  reprint of an 1851 book discussing the log colleges.
Alexander, Helen C., and J. K. *Charles M. Alexander.* 3rd. ed. London:
  Marshall Brothers, n.d.
Allen, William E. *The History of Revivals of Religion.* Lisburn, Ulster:
  Revival Publishing, 1951.
Allis, William T. *Billy Sunday.* Philadelphia: Universal Book and Bible
  House, 1914. Billy Sunday's personality, message, and samples of his
  sermons are presented.
Anderson, Courtney. *To the Golden Shore: The Life of Adoniram Judson.*
  Grand Rapids: Zondervan, 1977.
Antbff, Wick. *The Life of the Venerable Hugh Bourne.* London: George
  Lamb, 1872.
Armstrong, Anthony. *The Church of England, the Methodists and Society,
  1700–1850.* London: University of London Press, 1973.
Armstong, Maurice. *The Great Awakening in Nova Scotia, 1776–1809.* Hart-
  ford, Conn.: The American Society of Church History, 1948.

Asbury, Herbert. *A Methodist Saint.* New York: Alfred A. Knopf, 1927. A somewhat cynical, although accurate, biography of Francis Asbury.

Atter, Gordon F. *The Third Force.* 2nd rev. and enl. ed. Peterborough, Ontario: Gordon F. Atter, 1965. An account of the rise of Pentecostal churches all over the world, with special attention to Canada.

Autrey, C. E. *Revivals of the Old Testament.* Grand Rapids: Zondervan, 1960.

Awake! London: Church Missionary Society, 1937. Story of Blasio Kigosi's life.

Babbage, S. Barton, and Ian Siggins. *Light Beneath the Cross.* Garden City, N.Y.: Doubleday, 1960. Describes Billy Graham's 1959 crusade in Australia.

Backus, Issac. *A History of New England.* Newton, Mass.: Backus Historical Society, 1871.

Bainton, Roland. *Yale and the Ministry.* New York: Harpers, 1957.

Baker, Daniel. *Revival Sermons.* Philadelphia: Alfred Martin, 1879. Sermons from the 1813–46 era of revival.

Baker, Frank. *William Grimshaw, 1708-1763.* London: Epworth, 1963.

Balleine, G. R. *A History of the Evangelical Party in the Church of England.* New York: Longmans, Green, 1911.

Barnes, Gilbert. *The Antislavery Impulse.* Gloucester, Mass.: Peter Smith, 1957. Much data on Weld and antislavery activities.

Bartleman, Frank. *Azusa Street.* Plainfield, N.J.: Logos, 1980. A contemporary diary by a newsman of the Azusa Street renewal, originally published in 1925.

Batt, John H. *Dr. Barnardo.* London: S. W. Partridge, 1904.

Bayliss, Edward E. *The Gypsy Smith Missions in America.* Boston: Interdenominational Publishing, 1907. A full account of his sixth visit in 1906 and 1907.

Bazikian, Daniel A. "The United States Christian Commission." Master's thesis, Trinity Evangelical Divinity School, 1976.

Beardsley, Frank G. *A History of American Revivals.* 2nd rev. and enl. ed. New York: American Tract Society, 1912. A useful survey of revivals in the United States.

——————. *A Mighty Winner of Souls, C. G. Finney.* Philadelphia: American Tract Society, 1937.

——————. *Christian Achievement in America.* Chicago: Winona, 1907.

——————. *Religious Progress Through Revivals.* New York: American Tract Society, 1943. Helpful on outcomes of revival.

Bedell, George, Leo Sandon, Jr., and Charles T. Wellborn. *Religion in America.* 2nd. ed. New York: Macmillan, 1982. Helpful text with relevant documents interspersed.

Begbie, Harold. *The Life of William Booth.* 2 vols. London: Macmillan, 1953.

Belden, Albert D. *George Whitefield the Awakener.* New York: Macmillan, 1953.

Bell, Marion L. *Crusade in the City: Revivalism in Nineteenth-Century Philadelphia.* Lewisburg, Pa.: Bucknell University Press, 1977. Revivals

in Philadelphia in the nineteenth century, with emphasis upon those of
Finney and Moody.

Bennet, Richard. *The Early Life of Howell Harris.* London: Banner of
Truth, 1962.

Bennett, William W. *A Narrative of the Great Revival Which Prevailed in
the Southern Armies.* Harrisonburg, Va.: Sprinkle, 1976. First published
about 1877, this is a firsthand account by a chaplain.

Blake, W. O. *The History of Slavery and the Slave Trade.* 2 vols. New
York: Haskell House, 1970. An account of the cruelties of the slave trade
and the fight to end it.

Boles, John B. *Religion in Antebellum Kentucky.* Lexington, Ky.: University of Kentucky Press, 1976.

_____. *The Great Revival, 1787-1805: The Origins of the Southern
Evangelical Mind.* Lexington, Ky.: University of Kentucky Press, 1972. A
scholarly account of the Second Awakening, mainly in the South.

Booth, Frank. *Robert Raikes of Gloucester.* Nutfield, Redhill Surrey,
England: National Christian Education Council, 1980.

Boulton, Ernest. *George Jeffreys.* London: Elim Publishing Office, 1928.

Boyd, George A. *Elias Boudinot, Patriot and Statesman, 1740-1821.*
Princeton University Press, 1952. An authoritative account of his life and
his part in the founding of the American Bible Society.

Bradford, Gamaliel. *D. L. Moody: A Mighty Worker in Souls.* New York:
Doran, 1929.

Brainerd, Thomas. *The Life of John Brainerd.* Philadelphia: Presbyterian
Publication Committee, 1865.

Brauer, Jerald C. *Patriotism in America.* Rev. ed. Philadelphia:
Westminster, 1965.

_____, ed. *Religion and the American Revolution.* Philadelphia: For-
tress, 1976.

Bready, John W. *Doctor Barnardo: Physician, Pioneer, Prophet.* London:
George Allen and Unwin, 1930. All of Bready's books are sympathetic
discussions of the results of revivals in areas other than soul-saving.

_____. *England Before and After Wesley: The Evangelical Revival
and Social Reform.* New York: Harpers, n.d.

_____. *Faith and Freedom.* New York: American Tract Society,
1946. This does not include the footnotes of the preceding book but is
otherwise the same.

_____. *Lord Shaftesbury and Social-Industrial Progress.* London:
George Allen and Unwin, 1926.

_____. *Wesley and Democracy.* Toronto: Thorn, 1939.

Broomhall, A. J. *Hudson Taylor and China's Open Century.* London:
Hodder and Stoughton, 1982.

Broomhall, Marshall. *Hudson Taylor.* London: C.I.M., n.d. Contains a useful
chronology of Taylor's life.

_____. *Robert Morrison.* London: C.M.S., 1924.

Brown, Elijah P. *The Real Billy Sunday.* New York: Revell, 1914.

Brown, Ford H. *Fathers of the Victorian Age.* Cambridge: Cambridge
University Press, 1981.

Brumback, Carl. *Suddenly . . . From Heaven.* Springfield, Mo.: Gospel Publishing House, 1961. A history of the Assemblies of God and related Pentecostal movements.

Bull, John. *John Newton of Olney.* 2nd ed. London: Religious Tract Society, 1868.

Bumsted, J. M. *Henry Alline, 1748–1784.* Toronto: University of Toronto Press, 1971. A scholarly biography of the Nova Scotia revivalist.

——————, ed. *The Great Awakening.* Waltham, Mass.: Blaisdell, 1970. Documents of that revival.

—————— and John E. Van de Wetering. *What Must I Do to Be Saved?* Hinsdale, Ill.: Dryden, 1976. An accurate account of the Great Awakening in colonial America.

Bunting, Thomas P. *The Life of Jabez Bunting, D.D.* London: T. Woolmer, 1887. A biography of John Wesley's successor, with much source material.

Burns, Islay. *Memoir of the Rev. William C. Burns.* New York: Robert Carter, 1870.

Burns, James. *Revivals: Their Laws and Leaders.* London: Hodder and Stoughton, 1909.

Burr, Nelson R., et al. *A Critical Bibliography of Religion in America.* 2 vols. Princeton, N.J.: Princeton University Press, 1961. Has a helpful bibliography of American revival.

Burtner, Robert W., and Robert E. Chiles, eds. *A Compend of Wesley's Theology.* New York: Abingdon, 1954.

Bushman, Richard L. *From Puritan to Yankee: Character and the Social Order in Connecticut.* Cambridge, Mass: Harvard University Press, 1980.

——————. *The Great Awakening: Documents on the Revival of Religion, 1740–1745.* Chapel Hill, N.C.: University of North Carolina Press, 1970. Documents pertaining to the Great Awakening.

Buxton, T. F. *The African Slave Trade.* 2nd ed. London: John Murray, 1839.

Cameron, Richard. *Methodism and Society.* 4 vols. New York: Abingdon, 1961.

Candler, Warren A. *Great Revivals and the Great Republic.* Nashville: Methodist Episcopal Church, South, 1924. A helpful general survey of revivals.

Cantor, William. *A History of the British and Foreign Bible Society.* London: John Murray, 1904.

Carey, S. Pearce. *William Carey.* New York: Doran, 1923.

Carlberg, Gustav. *China in Revival.* Rock Island, Ill.: Augustana, 1936. Discusses revivals in 1932 and 1933.

Carson, John S. *God's River in Spate.* Belfast: Publication Board of the Presbyterian Church in Ireland, 1958. An excellent account of the Ulster revival of 1857–59.

Cartwright, Peter. *Autobiography of Peter Cartwright.* Nashville: Abingdon, 1956.

Carus, William. *Memoirs of the Life of the Rev. Charles Simeon, M.A.* London: Hatchard and Son, 1848.

Carwardine, Richard. *Transatlantic Revivalism: Popular Evangelicalism in Britain and America, 1790–1865.* Westport, Conn.: Greenwood, 1978. The author ably analyzes revival in the United States and Britain from 1776 to 1858.

Caskey, Marie. *Chariot of Fire: Religion and the Beecher Family*. New Haven: Yale University Press, 1978.

Caughey, James. *Earnest Christianity Illustrated*. London: Partridge, 1857. Consists of selections from Caughey's *Journal*.

Chapman, J. Wilbur. *The Life and Work of Dwight L. Moody*. W. E. Scull, 1900.

Chirguin, A. M. *Arthington's Millions*. London: Carey Press, n.d. An account of his life and giving to missions.

Church, John E. *Jesus Satisfies*. Achimoto, Ghana: African Christian Press, 1973. Church's account of the work he led in Uganda.

_____. *Quest for the Highest*. Exeter: Paternoster, 1981. Church's account of East African revival from 1927.

Clark, Allen D. *A History of the Church in Korea*. Seoul: Christian Literature Society of Korea, 1971.

Clark, Henry W. *History of English Nonconformity from Wiclif to the Close of the Nineteenth Century*. 2 vols. New York: Russell and Russell, 1965.

Clark, John, W. Dendy, and J. M. Philipp. *The Voice of Jubilee*. London: John Snow, 1865. Biographical accounts of Baptist missions, with many documents included.

Clark, Rufus W. *The Work of God in Great Britain Under Messers Moody and Sankey, 1873 to 1875*. London: Sampson, Low, Marsten, Low and Searle, 1875.

Clark, Samuel D. *Church and Sect in Canada*. Toronto: University of Toronto Press, 1948.

Clarke, W. K. Lowther. *A History of the SPCK*. London: SPCK, 1959.

Cleveland, Catherine C. *The Great Revival in the West, 1797–1805*. Gloucester, Mass.: Peter Smith, 1916. A helpful account of that revival.

Coan, Lydia B. *Titus Coan*. Chicago: Revell, 1884.

Coan, Titus. *Life in Hawaii*. New York: Anson D. F. Randolph, 1882.

Coggan, F. D. *Christ and the Colleges*. London: Intervarsity Fellowship of Evangelical Union, 1934. The account of IVF in England and dominions.

Cohen, Daniel. *The Spirit of the Lord*. New York: Four Winds, 1975. History of revival from 1800 to 1975.

Cole, Charles, Jr. *The Social Ideas of the Northern Evangelists, 1826–1860*. New York: Octagon, 1966.

Coleman, Robert C., ed. *One Divine Moment*. Old Tappan, N.J.: Revell, 1970. A useful account of the 1970 Asbury revival.

Conant, William C. *Narratives of Remarkable Conversions and Revival Incidents*. New York: Derby and Jackson, 1858. Documents from the 1857 prayer revival.

Conrad, Arcturus Z., ed. *Boston's Awakening*. Boston: The King's Business, 1909.

Cook, Charles T. *The Billy Graham Story*. Wheaton, Ill.: Van Kampen, 1954.

Cooper, L. Orman. *John Havard, the Prisoner's Friend*. London: National Sunday School Union, n.d.

Cragg, George C. *Grimshaw of Haworth*. London: Canterbury, 1947. An able biography from sources.

Cross, Joseph. *Sermons from Christmas Evans*. Philadelphia: W. A. Leary, 1849.

Cross, Whitney R. *The Burned-over District: The Social and Intellectual History of Enthusiastic Religion in Western New York, 1800–1850*. Ithaca, N.Y.: Cornell University Press, 1982. The problems of revival in western New York from 1800 to 1850.

Cunningham, Charles E. *Timothy Dwight*. New York: Macmillan, 1942.

Curtis, Richard K. *They Called Him Mr. Moody*. Garden City, N.Y.: Doubleday, 1962.

Dallimore, Arnold A. *George Whitefield: The Life and Times of the Great Evangelist of the Eighteenth-Century Revival*. 2 vols. London: Banner of Truth, 1970. A definitive biography based on careful study of sources.

——————. *Spurgeon*. Chicago: Moody, 1984.

Dargan, Edwin C. *A History of Preaching*. 2 vols. New York: Doran, 1905–1912.

Davies, Rosina. *The Story of My Life*. Llandyssul, Wales: Gomerian, 1942.

Davis, George T. B. *Torrey and Alexander*. New York: Revell, 1905.

Davis, Raymond J. *Fire on the Mountains*. Grand Rapids: Zondervan, 1966. Revival in the Wallamo tribe of Ethiopia, 1936–48.

Days of Grace in Manchuria. Kilmarnock, Scotland: John Ritchie, n.d. Describes 1908 revival.

The Dealings of God, Man and the Devil as Exemplified in the Life, Experience and Travels of Lorenzo Dow. New York: Sheldon, Lamport and Blakeman, 1849.

Dekar, Paul R., and Joseph D. Ban, eds. *The Great Tradition*. Valley Forge, Pa.: Judson, 1982.

Detzler, Wayne A. "British and American Contributions to the *Erweckung* in Germany, 1815–1848." Ph.D. thesis, University of Manchester, n.d.

Dickson, D. Bruce, Jr. *And They Sang Hallelujah*. Knoxville: University of Tennessee Press, 1974. Camp meeting revivals and their hymnology.

Dixon, Helen A. *A. C. Dixon: A Romance of Preaching*. New York: Putnam's, ca. 1931.

Doggett, L. L. *History of the YMCA*. 2 vols. New York: International Committee of the YMCA, 1916.

Dolan, Jay P. *Catholic Revivalism: The American Experience, 1830–1900*. South Bend, Ind.: University of Notre Dame Press, 1978.

Dorough, C. Dwight. *The Bible Belt Mystique*. Philadelphia: Westminster, 1974.

Douglas, J. D., Earle E. Cairns, and James E. Ruark, eds. *The New International Dictionary of the Christian Church*. Rev. ed. Grand Rapids: Zondervan, 1978.

Douglas, William D. *Andrew Murray and His Message*. Ft. Washington, Pa.: Christian Literature Crusade, 1926.

Dow, Lorenzo. *Vicissitudes in the Wilderness*. 5th ed. Norwich, Conn.: William Faulkner, 1833. Peggy Dow's journal describing her life with Lorenzo.

Drevery, Mary. *William Carey*. Grand Rapids: Zondervan, 1978. Helpful maps, genealogy, and dates of Carey's life.

du Plessis, J. *The Life of Andrew Murray of South Africa*. London: Marshall Brothers, 1919.

Durasoff, Steve. *Bright Wind of the Spirit*. Englewood Cliffs, N.J.: Prentice-Hall, 1972. Account of Pentecostal movement, including neo-Pentecostals.

Dwight, Henry O. *The Centennial History of the Bible Society*. 2 vols. New York: Macmillan, 1916.

Dyer, Helen S. *Pandita Ramabai*. New York: Revell, 1900.

Edwards, Jonathan. *A Faithful Narrative of the Surprising Work of God*. n.p. 1735. Edwards's account of the 1734–35 revival.

Elliott-Binns, Leonard E. *The Early Evangelicals*. London: Lutterworth, 1953. Excellent account of early Evangelicals.

Ellsworth, Donald Paul. *Christian Music in Contemporary Witness*. Grand Rapids: Baker Book House, 1980.

Ellwood, Robert J., Jr. *One Way*. Englewood Cliffs, N.J.: Prentice-Hall, 1973. Account of the Jesus People.

Enroth, Ronald, Edward E. Ericson, and C. B. Peters. *The Jesus People*. Grand Rapids: Eerdmans, 1972. The best account.

Erb, Peter C., ed. *The Pietists: Selected Writings*. New York: Paulist, 1983. Writings of Spener, Francke, and other Pietists.

Ervine, St. John. *God's Soldier*. 2 vols. New York: Macmillan, 1935. William Booth's life.

Evangelical Alliance. London: Partridge and Oakey, 1847. A detailed account of the founding of the Alliance.

Evans, D. M. *Christmas Evans, A Memoir*. London: J. Heaton and Son, 1863.

Evans, Eifion. *Revival Comes to Wales*. Bryntirion, Wales: Evangelical Press of Wales, 1979.

_____. *The Welsh Revival of 1904*. Bryntirion, Wales: Evangelical Press of Wales, 1969. Accurate account of 1904 revival.

Falk, Peter. *The Growth of the Church in Africa*. Grand Rapids: Zondervan, 1979.

Farwell, John V. *Early Recollections of Dwight L. Moody*. Chicago: Bible Institute Colportage Association, n.d. A firsthand account by a friend and supporter.

Fawcett, Arthur. *The Cambuslang Revival*. London: Banner of Truth, 1971.

Findlay, James F., Jr. *Dwight L. Moody*. Chicago: University of Chicago Press, 1969. A scholarly account of Moody's life, message, and work.

Finney, Charles G. *Finney's Lectures on Systematic Theology*, edited by J. H. Fairchild. Grand Rapids: Eerdmans, 1951.

_____. *Lectures on Revivals of Religion*. New York: Revell, 1888.

_____. *Memoirs of Rev. Charles G. Finney*. London: Hodder and Stoughton, 1876.

Fischer, Harold A. *Reviving Revivals*. Springfield, Mo.: Gospel Publishing House, 1950. A helpful survey of revival.

Fitt, Arthur P. *Moody Still Lives*. New York: Revell, 1936. Favorable survey of Moody's life by his son-in-law.

Foster, Charles I. *An Errand of Mercy*. Chapel Hill, N.C.: University of North Carolina Press, 1960. An able account of the united front of American and English evangelicals from 1790 to 1832.

Frady, Marshall. *Billy Graham*. Boston: Little, Brown, 1979. Critical yet fairly objective account based on sources such as newspapers.

Frodsham, Stanley. *With Signs Following*. Rev. ed. Springfield, Mo.: Gospel Publishing House, 1944. Account of the rise of the Assemblies of God by one of the early leaders.

Fuller, Daniel P. *The Story of Charles Fuller*. Waco, Texas: Word, 1972. His son's account of his life.

Gamble, Thomas. *Bethesda*. Savannah: Morning News Print, 1902. An account of Whitefield's orphanage at Savannah.

Garré, E. G., ed. *Praying Hyde*. London: Pickering and Inglis, n.d.

Garton, Nancy. *George Müller and His Orphans*. New York: Revell, 1963.

Gasper, Louis. *The Fundamentalist Movement*. Grand Rapids: Baker Book House, 1981.

Gaustad, Edwin S. *The Great Awakening in New England*. New York: Harper, 1957.

_____. *A Religious History of America*. New York: Harper and Row, 1974. Combines firsthand sources with the history.

_____. *The Rise of Adventism*. New York: Harper and Row, 1974. Has considerable discussion on revival in chapter 8.

Gee, Donald. *Wind and Flame*. Luton, England: Assemblies of God Publishing House, 1967.

Getz, Gene. *MBI: The Story of Moody Bible Institute*. Chicago: Moody, 1969.

Gewehr, Wesley M. *The Great Awakening in Virginia, 1740-90*. Durham, N.C.: Duke University Press, 1930.

Gibson, William. *The Year of Grace*. London: Oliphant, Anderson and Fernier, 1909. A helpful account of the awakening in Ulster in 1858.

Gill, Frederick C. *Charles Wesley: The First Methodist*. New York: Abingdon, 1964.

Gillies, John, comp. *Historical Collections of Accounts*. Glasgow: Robert and Andrew Foulis, 1754. Account of revivals.

Gingrich, Gerald I. *Protestant Renewal Yesterday and Today*. New York: Exposition, 1959.

Goen, C. C. *Revivalism and Separation in New England, 1740-1800*. New Haven: Yale University Press, 1962.

Goforth, Jonathan. *By My Spirit*. London: Marshall, Morgan, and Scott, n.d. Story of Manchurian revival, 1907-1908.

_____. *When the Spirit's Fire Swept Korea*. Grand Rapids: Zondervan, 1943.

Goforth, Rosalind. *Goforth of China*. Grand Rapids: Zondervan, 1937. A useful biography of Goforth by his wife.

Goodrich, Arthur, et al. *The Story of the Welsh Renewal*. New York: Revell, 1905.

Gordon, Anna H. *Frances Willard*. Chicago: Illinois Temperance Publication Association, 1898. Biography of Willard by her secretary of over twenty years.

Gorham, W. B. *Camp Meeting Manual*. Boston: H. B. Degen, 1855.
Describes the rules for such meetings.

Gow, Bonar A. *Madagascar and the Protestant Impact*. New York: African
Publishing Company, 1979.

Greenbie, Sydney, and Marjorie B. *Peter Cartwright, Hoof Beats to Heaven*.
Penobscot, Maine: Traversity, 1935. Fictional, but based on historical
sources.

Grenfell, Wilfred T. *A Labrador Doctor*. London: Hodder and Stoughton,
1948. His autobiography.

Grubb, Norman P. *C. T. Studd, Cricketeer and Pioneer*. London: Religious
Tract Society, 1933.

Gullen, Karen, ed. *Billy Sunday Speaks*. New York: Chelsea House, 1970.
Includes several of his sermons.

Gundry, Stanley. *Love Them In: The Proclamation Theology of D. L.
Moody*. Grand Rapids: Baker Book House, 1982. Scholarly account of
Moody's theology.

Hadden, Jeffrey K., and Charles E. Swain. *Prime Time Preachers: The Rising Power of Televangelism*. Readon, Mass.: Addison-Wesley, 1981.

Hadley, Samuel H. *Down in Water Street*. New York: Revell, 1902–06.

Haldane, Robert. *Memoirs of the Times of Robert Haldane of Airthrey and
His Brother James Alexander Haldane*. New York: Carter and Brothers,
1857.

Hale, Charles. *The Early History of the Church Missionary Society for
Africa and the East*. London: Church Missionary Society, 1896.

The Half Can Never Be Told. Atlantic City, N.J.: The Worldwide Revival
Prayer Movement, 1927. Account of 1858 and 1859 revival.

Hall, Gordon L. *The Sawdust Trail*. Philadelphia: MacRae Smith, 1964. A
popular account of American revival.

Halliday, S. B., and D. S. Gregory. *The Church in America and Its Baptism
of Fire*. New York: Funk and Wagnalls, 1896. Useful history of revival.

Ham, Edward E. *Fifty Years on the Battlefront with Christ*. Louisville, Ky.:
Old Kentucky Home revivalist, 1950.

Hammond, J. L. and Barbara. *Lord Shaftesbury*. London: Constable, 1923.

Harding, William H. *The Life of George Müller*. London: Morgan and Scott,
1914.

Hardman, Keith J. *The Spiritual Awakeners*. Chicago: Moody, 1983. A
scholarly, sympathetic account of American revival and revival leaders.

Hardy, Arthur S. *Life and Letters of Joseph Hardy Neesima*. Boston:
Houghton Mifflin, 1892.

Harford-Battersby, Charles F. *Pilkington of Uganda*. New York: Revell, c.
1899. Mostly based on Pilkington's letters.

Harper, Michael. *As at the Beginning*. London: Hodder and Stoughton, 1965.
Useful for British and European Pentecostal history.

Harrell, David E., Jr. *All Things Are Possible: The Healing and Charismatic Revivals in Modern America*. Bloomington, Ind.: Indiana University
Press, 1976. The history of recent charismatic and healing leaders.

Harris, J. C. *Couriers of Christ*. London: Livingstone, 1949. History of the
work of the London Missionary Society.

Harrison, W. Archibald. *The Evangelical Revival and Christian Reunion.* London: Epworth, 1942.

Hastings, Shirley A. *The Life and Times of Selina, Countess of Huntingdon.* 2 vols. London: William E. Painter, 1841-1844.

Hayden, Eric W. *Spurgeon on Renewal.* Grand Rapids: Zondervan, 1962.

Headley, R. C., ed. *The Harvest Work of the Holy Spirit.* Boston: Henry Hoyt, 1862. Life and sermons of E. P. Hammond from sources.

Heasman, Kathleen. *Evangelicals in Action.* London: Geoffrey Bles, 1962.

Heimert, Alan, and Perry Miller. *The Great Awakening: Documents Illustrating the Crisis and Its Consequences.* Indianapolis: Bobbs-Merrill, 1967.

Helps to a Life of Holiness and Usefulness. 3rd ed. Boston, 1852. Contains some of Caughey's sermons.

Henry, Stuart C. *George Whitefield, Wayfaring Witness.* New York: Abingdon, 1957.

_____. *Unvanquished Puritan.* Grand Rapids: Eerdmans, 1973. Life of Lyman Beecher based on sources.

Hervey, G. W. *Manual of Revivals.* New York: Funk and Wagnalls, 1884.

Hewett, John H. *Williams College and Foreign Missions.* Boston: Pilgrim, 1914.

High, Stanley. *Billy Graham.* New York: McGraw-Hill, 1956.

Hildebrand, Jonathan. *History of the Church in Africa.* Achimata, Ghana: African Christian Press, 1981.

Hill, Samuel S., Jr. *The South and the North in American Religion.* Athens, Ga.: University of Georgia Press, 1980.

Hills, A. M. *Life of Charles G. Finney.* Cincinnati: God's Revivalist, 1902.

History of Cosmopolite. n.p., n.d. Lorenzo Dow's travels and experience.

History of Revivals of Religion in the British Isles. Edinburgh: Olliphant, 1836. Good collection of sources.

Hoffman, Fred W. *Revival Times in America.* Boston: W. A. Welde, 1956.

Holcomb, Walt. *Sam Jones.* Nashville: Methodist Publishing House, 1947. Jones's life by a coworker.

Hood, Edwin P. *Christmas Evans.* London: Hodder and Stoughton, 1883.

Hopkins, C. Howard. *History of the YMCA in North America.* New York: Association, 1951.

Hopkins, Hugh E. *Charles Simeon of Cambridge.* Grand Rapids: Eerdmans, 1977. Scholarly biography.

Horne, Silvester. *The Story of the LMS, 1795-1895.* London: London Missionary Society, 1895.

Houghton, Frank. *Amy Carmichael of Dohnavur.* London: SPCK, 1955. Biography based on sources.

Hovey, Alvah. *A Memoir of the Life and Times of the Rev. Isaac Backus.* New York: Da Capo, 1972. Reprint of 1858 edition.

Howard, David. *Student Power in World Evangelism.* Downers Grove, Ill.: InterVarsity Press, 1970.

Hudson, Winthrop S. *Religion in America.* 3rd ed. New York: Scribner's, 1981. Scholarly survey of American church history.

Hughes, George. *The Beloved Physician: Walter C. Palmer, M.D.* New York: Palmer and Hughes, 1884.

Hughes, William. *Life of the Rev. Thomas Charles, B.A.* Bala, Wales: Davies and Evans, 1909.

Hunter, James. *American Evangelicalism: Conservative Religion and the Quandary of Modernity.* New Brunswick, N.J.: Rutgers University Press, 1983.

Hustad, Donald P. *Jubilate! Church Music in the Evangelical Tradition.* Carol Stream, Ill.: Hope Publishing, 1981. Survey of the history of evangelical hymnody.

Huxley, Elspeth. *Livingstone and His African Journeys.* Elspeth Huxley, 1974.

Jamison, Wallace N. *Religion in New Jersey.* Princeton: D. Van Nostrand, 1964.

Jarratt, Devereux. *Sermons.* Raleigh, N. C.: William M. Glendenning, 1805.
_____. *The Life of the Reverend Dr. Jarratt.* Baltimore: Warner and Hanna, 1806.

Jeal, Tim. *Livingstone.* New York: Putnam's, 1973. Objective and based on firsthand documents.

Jeffreys, Edward. *Stephen Jeffreys the Beloved Evangelist.* London: Elim Publishing, 1946.

Jenkins, D. E. *The Life of the Rev. Thomas Charles of Bala.* 3 vols. Denbigh, Wales: Llewelyn Jenkins, 1908.

Johnson, Charles A. *The Frontier Camp Meeting: Religion's Harvest Time.* Dallas: Southern Methodist University Press, 1984. The most helpful history of camp meetings.

Johnson, Henry. *Stories of Great Revivals.* London: Religious Tract Society, 1900.

Johnson, Paul E. *A Shopkeeper's Millennium: Society and revivals in Rochester, New York., 1815–1837.* New York: Hill and Wang, 1978.

Jones, Charles C. *The History of Georgia.* 2 vols. Boston: Houghton-Mifflin, 1883. Useful for its account of Whitefield's orphanage.

Jones, Laura M. *The Life and Sayings of Sam P. Jones.* Atlanta: Franklin-Turner, 1907.

Jorstad, Erling. *That New-Time Religion.* Minneapolis: Augsburg, 1972. Account of the Jesus movement and of classic and neo-Pentecostal movements.

Katarikawe, James, and John Wilson. "The East African Movement." M.A. thesis, Fuller School of Missions, 1975.

Keller, Charles K. *The Second Great Awakening in Connecticut.* New Haven: Yale University Press, 1942.

Kennedy, James W. K., ed. *Henry Drummond.* New York: Harper, 1953.

Kent, John. *Holding the Fort.* London: Epworth, 1978. Critical account of English revival from 1859 to 1875.

Kerr, J. Lennox. *Wilfred Grenfell.* New York: Dodd, Mead, 1949.

Kittler, Glenn. *The Jesus Kids and Their Leaders.* New York: Warner, 1972.

Knapp, Jacob. *Autobiography of Jacob Knapp*. New York: Sheldon and Company, 1868.

Knapp, James. *The Life of Hugh Bourne*. London: 1892.

Knight, Helen C. *A New Memoir of Hannah More*. New York: M. W. Dodd, 1853.

───────. *Lady Huntingdon and Her Friends*. Grand Rapids: Baker Book House, 1978. Reprint of 1853 edition.

Knight, William. *Memoir of Henry Venn*. London: Seeley, Jackson, and Halliday, 1882.

───────. *The Missionary Secretarial of Henry Venn, B.D.* London: Longmans, Green, 1880.

Koch, Kurt. *Revival Fires in Canada*. Grand Rapids: Kregel, 1975. Account of the revival in Saskatoon.

───────. *The Revival in Indonesia*. Grand Rapids: Kregel, 1972. Koch's books are somewhat credulous.

Lacy, R., Jr. *Revivals in the Midst of the Years*. Richmond: John Knox, 1943. Mostly on Southern Presbyterian renewal.

Lancaster, John. *The Life of D'Arcy, Lady Maxwell*. London: J. Kershaw, 1826.

Latourette, Kenneth S. *A History of Christian Missions in China*. New York: Macmillan, 1929. A classic by a master historian.

Laws, Robert. *Reminiscences of Livingstone*. Edinburgh: n.p., 1934.

Lee, Jesse. *The Memoir of the New Jesse Lee*. New York: Arono, 1969.

Lennox, Cuthbert. *Henry Drummond*. London: Andrew Melrose, n.d.

Lesick, Laurence T. *The Lane Rebels: Evangelism and Antislavery in Antebellum America*. Metuchen, N.J.: Scarecrow, 1980.

Lewis, H. Elnet. *Howell Harris and the Welsh Revivalists*. National Council of Churches of the Evangelical Free Church, n.d.

───────. *With Christ Among the Miners*. London: Hodder and Stoughton, 1906.

Littell, Franklin H. *The Macmillan Atlas History of Christianity*. Macmillan, 1976. Excellent maps, diagram, and charts on the history of the church.

Livingstone, Judith. *The Other Livingstone*. New York: Scribner's, 1973.

Loane, Marcus. *Oxford and the Evangelical Succession*. London: Lutterworth, 1950.

Lockard, David. *The Unheard Billy Graham*. Waco, Texas: Word, 1971.

Lockerbie, D. Bruce. *Billy Sunday*. Waco, Texas: Word, 1965.

Lorenz, Ellen J. *Glory Hallelujah: The Story of the Camp Meeting Spirituals*. Nashville: Abingdon, 1980.

Loud, Grover C. *Evangelized America*. New York: Dial, 1928. A history of revivals.

Love, W. DeLoss. *Samson Occom and the Indians of New England*. Boston: Pilgrim, 1899. Much material from Occom's diary.

Loveland, Anne C. *Southern Evangelicals and the Social Order, 1800–1860.*

Baton Rouge: Louisiana State University Press, 1980.

Lumpkin, William C. *Baptist Foundations in the South*. Nashville: Broadman, 1961.

Lutzer, Erwin. *Flames of Freedom*. Chicago: Moody, 1976.

Lyall, Leslie. *A Passion for the Impossible*. Chicago: Moody, 1965. A useful history of the China Inland Mission, 1865 to 1965.

McAllister, Lester G., and William E. Tucker. *Journey in Faith*. St. Louis, Mo.: Bethany, 1975. A helpful history of the Christian Church (Disciples).

_____. *Thomas Campbell: Man of the Book*. St. Louis, Mo.: Bethany 1954.

McLoughlin, William O., Jr. *Billy Graham*. New York: Ronald, 1960. Somewhat critical of Graham.

_____. *Billy Sunday Was His Real Name*. Chicago: University of Chicago Press, 1955. Critical of Sunday.

_____. *Modern Revivalism*. New York: Ronald 1959.

_____. *Revivals, Awakening, and Reform*. Chicago: University of Chicago Press, 1978.

M'Nemar, Richard. *The Kentucky Revival*. New York: Edward O. Jenkins, 1846. Firsthand account.

MacPherson, John. *Henry Moorhouse*. Kilmarnock, Scotland: John Ritchie, n.d.

McQuaid, Ina D. *Miss Hannah Ball, a Lady of High Wycombe*. New York: Vantage, 1964.

Magnuson, Norris. *Salvation in the Slums*. Metuchen, N. J.: American Theological Library Association, 1977. Useful account of evangelical social work since 1859.

Mahan, Asa. *Autobiography*. London: T. Woolmer, 1882.

Marsden, George M. *Fundamentalism and American Culture: The Shaping of Twentieth-Century Evangelism*. New York: Oxford University Press, 1980.

Martin, K. L. P. *Missionaries and Annexation in the Pacific*. London: Oxford University Press, 1924.

Martin, Roger. *R. A. Torrey, the Apostle of Certainty*. Murfreesboro, Tenn.: Sword of the Lord, 1976.

Matthewman, Phyllis. *William C. Burns*. Grand Rapids: Zondervan, 1953.

Matthews, Donald G. *Religion in the Old South*. Chicago: University of Chicago Press, 1977.

Maxson, Charles H. *The Great Awakening in the Middle Colonies*. Gloucester, Mass.: Peter Smith, 1978.

Meacham, Standish. *Henry Thornton of Clapham, 1760-1815*. Cambridge, Mass.: Harvard University Press, 1964.

Mears, David O. *The Life of Edward Norris Kirk, D.D.* Boston: Lockwood, Brook, 1877.

Menzies, William W. *Anointed to Serve: The Story of the Assemblies of God*. Springfield, Mo.: Gospel Publishing House, 1971. Scholarly history of the Assemblies of God.

Miller, Perry. *Jonathan Edwards*. Amherst, Mass.: University of Massachusetts Press, 1981. A classic study of Edwards's thought, originally published in 1949.

Miller, R. Edward. *Thy God Reigneth*. Fontana, Cal.: World Missionary Assistance Plan, 1964. Revival in Argentina.

Mitchell, Curtis. *Billy Graham—Saint or Sinner*. New York: Revell, 1979. Friendly but accurate defense of Graham against false accusations.

———. *God in the Garden*. Garden City, N.Y.: Doubleday, 1957. Full account of Graham's 1957 New York crusade.

Miyawaka, T. Scott. *Priests and Pioneers*. Chicago: University of Chicago Press, 1964.

Mode, Peter G. *Source Book and Bibliographical Guide for American Church History*. Menasha, Wis.: Peter Mode, 1921. Contains many useful documents on revival.

Monod, Renê. *The Korean Revival*. London: Hodder and Stoughton, 1969.

Monsen, Marie. *The Awakening*. London: China Inland Mission, 1961. Revival in northern China, 1927–37.

Moody, William R. *D. L. Moody*. New York: Macmillan, 1930.

Moore, Samuel J. *The Great Revival in Ireland (1859)*. London: Marshall Brothers, n.d.

Morgan, Edward. *John Elias: Life and Letters*. London: Banner of Truth, 1973.

———. *Memoir of the Reverend John Elias*. Liverpool: Jones, 1844.

Morgan, J. J. *The 'Fifty-nine Revival in Wales*. Mold: J. J. Morgan, 1909.

Morgan, J. Vyrnwy. *The Welsh Revival*. London: Chapman and Hall, 1909. Critical of Evan Roberts.

Morgan, R. C. *The Life of Richard Weaver*. London: Morgan and Scott, 1861.

Morison, John. *The Fathers and Founders of the L.M.S.* London: Caxton, 1884.

Moule, Handley C. G. *Charles Simeon*. Chicago: InterVarsity Press, 1892.

Moyer, Elgin. *Wycliffe Biographical Dictionary of the Church*. Rev. and enl. by Earle E. Cairns. Chicago: Moody, 1982.

Mulder, John, and John F. Wilson, eds. *Religion in American History*. Englewood Cliffs, N.J.: Prentice-Hall, 1978.

Muncy, W. L., Jr. *Evangelism in the U.S.* Kansas City, Kans.: Central Seminary Press, 1945. A history of revival and evangelism.

Neill, Stephen C., and Hans-Reudi Weber, eds. *The Layman in Christian History*. Philadelphia: Westminster, 1963.

Nevius, Helen S. C. *The Life of John Livingstone Nevius*. New York: Revell, 1895.

Nevius, John L. *The Planting and Development of Missionary Churches*. Grand Rapids: Baker Book House, 1958.

New, Alfred. *The Coronet and the Cross*. London: Partridge, 1857. Biography of Lady Huntingdon.

Nichol, John T. *Pentecostalism*. New York: Harper and Row, 1966. Early scholarly history of Pentecostalism.

Nissenbaum, Stephen. *The Great Awakening at Yale College.* Belmont, Cal.: Wadsworth, 1972. Documents.

Northcote, Cecil. *Glorious Company.* London: Livingstone, 1945. History of revival.

Norton, Herman. *Rebel Religion.* St. Louis: Bethany, 1961. Account of work of Confederate chaplains.

Nyus, Joel M., trans. *Autobiographical Writings of Hans Nielsen Hauge.* Minneapolis: Augsburg, 1954.

O'Brien, T. C., ed. *Corpus Dictionary of the Western Churches.* Washington: Corpus Publications, 1970. Concise, accurate treatment of topics and individuals.

Offord, Robert M., ed. *Jerry McAuley, an Apostle to the Lost.* New York: Doran, 1885.

Ogilvie, J. N. *Our Empire's Debt to Missions.* London: Hodder and Stoughton, ca. 1924.

Olford, Stephen F. *Lord, Open the Heavens: A Heartcry for Revival.* Wheaton, Ill.: Harold Shaw, 1980.

Ollson, Karl A. *By One Spirit.* Chicago: Covenant, 1962.

Olmstead, Clifton E. *History of Religion in the United States.* Englewood Cliffs, N.J.: Prentice-Hall, 1960. Still a useful text on American church history.

Omulogoli, Watson A. "The S.V.M.: Its History and Contribution." M.A. thesis, Wheaton College, 1967.

Orr, J. Edwin. *America's Great Revival.* Elizabethtown, Pa.: n.p., 1937. An account of the 1857 revival. Orr, the dean of historians of revival, draws most of his material from contemporary newspapers.

_____. *Campus Aflame.* Glendale, Cal.: Regal Books, 1971.

_____. *Evangelical Awakenings in Africa.* Minneapolis: Bethany Fellowship, 1975.

_____. *Evangelical Awakenings in Latin America.* Minneapolis: Bethany Fellowship, 1978.

_____. *Evangelical Awakenings in Southern Asia.* Minneapolis: Bethany Fellowship, 1975.

_____. *Evangelical Awakenings Worldwide.* J. E. Orr, 1968. Account of awakenings from 1900.

_____. *Good News in Bad Times.* Grand Rapids: Zondervan, 1953.

_____. *The Eager Feet.* Chicago: Moody, 1975. Account of revivals from 1787 to 1842.

_____. *The Fervent Prayer.* Chicago: Moody, 1974. Revivals from 1857 to 1895.

_____. *The Flaming Tongue.* 2nd rev. ed. Chicago: Moody, 1973.

_____. *The Ready Tongue.* London: J. E. Orr, 1968. This and the preceding book are on the revivals from 1900.

_____. *The Light of the Nations.* Grand Rapids: Eerdmans, 1961. Good survey of revival from 1795 to 1914.

_____. *The Second Evangelical Awakening in America.* London: Marshall, Morgan, and Scott, 1952.

_____. *The Second Evangelical Awakening in Britain.* London: Marshall, Morgan, and Scott, 1949.

Ottman, Ford C. *J. Wilbur Chapman.* Garden City, N.Y.: Doubleday, Page, 1920.

Overton, John H. *The Evangelical Revival in the Eighteenth Century.* London: Longmans, Green, 1886.

Pachai, Brigdal, ed. *Livingstone: Man of Africa.* London: Longmans, Green, 1973.

Padwick, Constance F. *Henry Martyn.* New York: Doran, n.d.

Paisley, Ian R. K. *The "Fifty-Nine" Revival.* Belfast: Free Press, 1958.

Palmer, Phoebe. *Four Years in the Old World.* New York: Walter C. Palmer, 1869. Firsthand account of their travels and work in the British Isles.

Parham, Mrs. Charles F. *The Life of Charles F. Parham, Founder of the Apostolic Faith Movement.* Birmingham, Ala.: Mrs. Charles F. Parham, 1930.

Park, Arthur. *Sadhu Sundar Singh.* New York: Revell, 1920.

Park, Edward A. *Memoir of the Life and Character of Samuel Hopkins, D.D.* Boston: Doctrinal Tract and Book Society, 1854.

Patten, John A. *These Remarkable Men.* London: Lutterworth, 1945. Helpful account of men of the Clapham Sect.

Paul, Ronald C. *Billy Graham.* New York: Ballantine, 1978.

Peters, George W. *Indonesian Revival.* Grand Rapids: Zondervan, 1973. Balanced account of that revival.

Philip, John. *Researches in South Africa.* 2 vols. London: James Denman, 1828.

Pierson, Arthur T. *George Müller of Bristol.* London: Nesbet, 1901.

Pilcher, George W. *Samuel Davies, Apostle of Dissent in Colonial Virginia.* Knoxville: University of Tennessee Press, 1971.

_____, ed. *The Reverend Samuel Davies Abroad.* Urbana, Ill.: University of Illinois Press, 1967. Davies's diary.

Pilkington, Walter, ed. *The Journals of Samuel Kirkland.* Clinton, N.Y.: Hamilton College, 1980.

Plowman, Edward E. *The Jesus Movement in America.* New York: Pyramid, 1971.

Poling, Daniel. *Why Billy Graham?* Grand Rapids: Zondervan, 1977.

Pollock, John C. *A Cambridge Movement.* London: Murray, 1953.

_____. *Billy Graham.* New York: McGraw-Hill, 1966.

_____. *Billy Graham, Evangelist to the World: An Authorized Biography.* San Francisco: Harper and Row, 1980.

_____. *Crusades.* Minneapolis: Worldwide, 1969.

_____. *The Keswick Story.* London: Hodder and Stoughton, 1964.

_____. *George Whitefield and the Great Awakening.* Garden City, N.Y.: Doubleday, 1972.

_____. *Moody: The Biography.* 2nd ed. New York: Macmillan, 1963.

_____. *To All Nations.* San Francisco: Harper and Row, 1985.

_____. *Wilberforce.* New York: St. Martin's, 1978.

Poole-Connor, Edward J. *Evangelicalism in England.* Worthing: Henry E.
    Walter, 1951.
Powell, Emma. *Heavenly Destiny.* Chicago: Moody, 1943. Biography of Mrs.
    D. L. Moody.
Purviance, David. *The Biography of Elder David Purviance.* Dayton, Ohio:
    B. F. and G. Wells, 1848. Eyewitness account of the Cane Ridge camp
    meeting.
_____. *The New Charismatics.* Garden City, N.Y.: Doubleday, 1976.

Railton, G. S. *The Authoritative Life of General William Booth.* New York:
    Doran, 1912.
Ramsay, John C. *John Wilbur Chapman.* Boston: Christopher Publishing
    House, 1962.
Rees, E. Ebrard. *Christmas Evans.* London: Kingsgate, n.d.
Reid, William, ed. *Authentic Records of Revival.* London: James Nisbet,
    1860.
Reminiscences of the Revival of Fifty-Nine. Aberdeen, Scotland: The
    University Press, 1910.
Reynolds, James B., et al. *Two Centuries of Christian Activity at Yale.* New
    York: Putnam's 1909.
Reynolds, James S. *The Evangelicals at Oxford, 1735–1871.* Oxford:
    Marcham Manor Press, 1975.
Rhodes, Harry A., ed. *History of the Korea Mission.* Seoul: Chosen Mission,
    n.d.
Richards, Thomas C. *Samuel J. Mills.* Boston: Pilgrim, 1906.
Richardson, Leon B. *An Indian Preacher in England.* Hanover, N. H.:
    Dartmouth Ms. Series, No. 2, 1933. Samson Occom's letters while in
    England.
Richter, Julius. *A History of Missions in India.* Edinburgh: Oliphant,
    Anderson and Ferrier, 1908.
Ritson, Joseph. *The Romance of Primitive Methodism.* London: Edwin Dalt,
    1909.
Roberts, Richard O. *Revival.* Wheaton, Ill.: Tyndale, 1982. Has a helpful
    bibliography of books on revival.
Rodeheaver, Homer. *Twenty Years with Billy Sunday.* Winona Lake, Ind.:
    Rodeheaver Hall-Mack, 1936.
Rowe, Henry K. *History of Andover Theological Seminary.* Newton, Mass.:
    n.p., 1933.
Rudnick, Milton. *Speaking the Gospel Through the Ages: A History of
    Evangelism.* St. Louis: Concordia, 1984.
Rudolph, L. C. *Francis Asbury.* Nashville: Abingdon, 1983.
Russell, Kenneth W., II. "Mordecai Ham: Southern Fundamentalist." M.A.
    thesis, Western Kentucky University, 1980.

Sandeen, Ernest. *The Roots of Fundamentalism.* Chicago: University of
    Chicago Press, 1970.
Sawatsky, Walter. *Soviet Evangelicals Since World War II.* Scottdale Pa.:
    Herald, 1981.

Schapera, I., ed. *David Livingstone Family Letters, 1841–1856*. London: Chatto and Windus, n.d.

Scharpf, Paulus. *History of Evangelism*. Translated by Helga R. Henry. Grand Rapids: Eerdmans, 1966. Covers three hundred years in Britain, the U.S.A., and Europe, especially Germany.

Scheiner, Edwin. *Christian Converts and Social Protest in Meiji Japan*. Berkeley: University of California Press, 1970.

Schlenther, Boyd S. *The Life and Writings of Francis Makemie*. Philadelphia: Presbyterian Historical Society, 1971.

Schweinitz, Edmund D. *The Life and Times of David Zeisberger*. Philadelphia: Lippincott, 1870.

Scott, Harry. *A History of Scottish Congregationalism*. Glasgow: Congregational Union of Scotland, 1960. Has much data on the Haldanes.

Sellers, Charles. *Lorenzo Dow, the Bearer of the Word*. New York: Minton, Balch 1928.

Shaw, Joseph M. *Pulpit Under the Sky: A Life of Hans N. Hauge*. Minneapolis: Augsburg, 1955.

Shaw, S. B. *The Great Revival in Wales*. Chicago: S. B. Shaw, 1905. Revivals in Wales and Ireland in 1859.

Sidney, Edwin. *The Life and Ministry of the Rev. Samuel Walker*. London: R. B. Seeley and W. Burnsides, 1838.

Sizer, Sandra S. *Gospel Hymns and Social Religion: The Rhetoric of Nineteenth-Century Revivalism*. Philadelphia: Temple University Press, 1979.

Smellie, Alexander. *Evan Henry Hopkins*. London: Marshall Brothers, 1920.

Smith, George A. *The Life of Henry Drummond*. New York: Doubleday and McClure, 1898.

Smith, Gypsy. *A Mission of Peace*. London: National Council of Evangelical Free Churches, 1904. Describes Smith's South African tour.

_____. *Gypsy Smith: His Life and Work*. New York: Revell, 1901.

Smith, H. S., Robert T. Handy, and Lefferts A. Loetscher. *American Christianity*. 2 vols. New York: Scribner's, 1960–63.

Smith, Harold I. "An Analysis and Evaluation of the Evangelistic Work of Samuel Porter Jones in Nashville, 1885–1906." M.A. thesis, Scarritt College, 1971.

Smith, J. M. *The Essex Lad Who Became England's Greatest Preacher*. New York: American Tract Society, 1892. Biography of Spurgeon.

Smith, Timothy L. *Revival and Social Reform: American Protestantism on the Eve of the Civil War*. New York: Abingdon, 1957.

Smith, Wilbur M. *A Voice for God*. Boston: W. A. Wilde, 1949. Laudatory biography of Charles E. Fuller.

Sprague, William B. *Annals of the American Pulpit*. 9 vols. Boston: Robert Carter and Brothers, 1859–69.

Stanley, Henry M. *In Darkest Africa*. 2 vols. New York: Scribner's, 1890–1891.

Stanley-Smith, A. C., and Leonard Sharp. *Rwanda's Redemption*. London: Rwanda Medical Mission Auxiliary, 1931.

Stephen, David R. *Memoirs of the Late Christmas Evans of Wales*. London: Aylott and Jones, 1848.

Stevens, Abel. *The History . . . Called Methodists*. 3 vols. New York: Carlton and Porter, 1858–61.

Stewart, James A. *Invasion of Wales by the Spirit through Evan Roberts*. Fort Washington, Pa.: Christian Literature Crusade, n.d.

Stock, Eugene. *The History of the C.M.S.* 3 vols. London: C.M.S., 1899.

Stone, Barton. *The Biography of Elder Barton Warren Stone, Written by Himself*. New York: Arno, 1972. Reprint of an 1847 edition.

Strachey, Roy. *Frances Willard: Her Life and Work*. London: T. Fisher Unwin, 1912.

Strickland, W. P. *Autobiography of Rev. James B. Finley*. Cincinnati: n.p., 1853.

Strober, Gerald S. *Billy Graham—His Life and Faith*. Waco, Texas: Word, 1979.

Strong, William E. *The Story of the American Board: An Account of the First Hundred Years of the American Board for Foreign Missions*. Boston: Pilgrim, 1910.

Sunday, W. A. *Autobiography of William Sunday*. Published by Mrs. Sunday, n.d.

Sweet, Leonard I. *The Minister's Wife: Her Role in Nineteenth-Century American Evangelism*. Philadelphia: Temple University Press, 1983.

Sweet, William W. *Makers of Christianity*. 3 vols. New York: Holt, 1935–1937.

_____. *Religion in Colonial America*. New York: Scribner's, 1942.

_____. *Religion in the Development of American Culture, 1765–1840*. New York: Scribner's, 1952.

_____. *Revivalism in America*. New York: Scribner's, 1942.

_____. *The Story of Religion in America*. New York: Harpers, 1950. The text used in American religious history classes for years.

Tari, Mel, and Cliff Dudley. *Like a Mighty Wind*. Carol Stream, Ill.: Creation House, 1972. Other writers claim he exaggerates the miracles in Indonesia in 1966.

Taylor, Howard, and Mary Taylor. *Hudson Taylor and the China Inland Mission*. London: Morgan and Scott, 1918.

_____. *Hudson Taylor in Early Years*. London: China Inland Mission, 1911.

Telford, John. *The Life of the Rev. Charles Wesley, M.A.* London: Wesleyan Methodist Bookroom, 1900.

Tewksbury, Donald G. *The Founding of American Colleges and Universities Before the Civil War*. New York: Arno Press, 1969. Reprint of 1932 edition.

Thomas, Lee. *The Billy Sunday Story*. Grand Rapids: Zondervan, 1961.

Thompson, Charles L. *Times of Refreshing*. Chicago: T. Palmer, 1877. Story of American Revival from 1840 to 1877, with discussion of preaching methods.

Thompson, Earnest T. *Presbyterians in the South*. 3 vols. Richmond, Va.: John Knox, 1963–73.

Thornbury, John F. *God Sent Revival*. Welwyn, England: Evangelical Press, 1977. Second Awakening and Nettleton discussed.

Tipple, Ezra S. *The Heart of Asbury's Journal.* New York: Eaton and Mains, 1904.

——————. *Francis Asbury, the Prophet of the Long Road.* New York: Methodist Book Concern, 1916.

Townsend, W. J., et al. *A New History of Methodism.* 2 vols. London: Hodder and Stoughton, 1901.

——————. *Robert Morrison.* London: Pickering and Inglis, n.d.

Tracy, Joseph. *The Great Awakening.* London: Banner of Truth, 1976.

——————. *History of the ABCFM.* New York: M. W. Dod, 1842.

True, Charles K. *Memoirs of John Harvard.* Cincinnati: Curts and Jennings, 1878.

Tucker, Alfred. *Eighteen Years in Uganda.* London: Edward Arnold, 1911. An account of Tucker's Ugandan episcopate.

Tyerman, Luke. *The Life of the Rev. George Whitefield.* 2 vols. London: Hodder and Stoughton, 1876–1877. Superseded by D. Allimore's work, but still useful for sources.

Tyler, Bennet. *Memoir of the Life and Character of Rev. Asahel Nettleton, D.D.* 6th ed. Boston: Congregational Publishing Society, 1879. Excellent life by his friend.

——————. *New England Revivals.* Wheaton, Ill.: Richard O. Roberts, 1980. Reprint of 1846 edition.

——————. *Remains of the Late Rev. Asahel Nettleton.* Hartford, Conn.: Robbins and Smith, 1845.

Tyler, Sarah. *The Countess of Huntingdon and Her Circle.* London: Isaac Pittman, 1907.

Varley, Henry. *Henry Varley's Life Story.* London: Alfred Holmes, n.d.

Vickers, John. *Thomas Coke: Apostle of Methodism.* Nashville: Abingdon, 1969.

Vincent, Leon H. *John Heyl Vincent.* New York: Macmillan, 1925.

Wachon, Brian. *A Time to Be Born.* Englewood Cliffs, N.J.: Prentice-Hall, 1972. Account of Jesus people.

Wagner, C. Peter. *What Are We Missing?* Carol Stream, Ill.: Creation House, 1973. Deals with Pentecostalism.

Waller, Horace, ed. *The Last Journal of David Livingstone.* Westport, Conn.: Greenwood, 1970.

Walters, Ronald G. *American Reformers, 1815–1860.* New York: Hill and Wang, 1978.

Webber, F. R. *A History of Preaching in Britain and America.* 3 vols. Milwaukee: Northwestern Publishing, 1952–57.

Weinlick, John L. *Count Zinzendorf.* New York: Abingdon, 1956. Scholarly biography.

Weisberger, Bernard A. *They Gathered at the River: The Story of the Great Revivalists and Their Impact Upon Religion in America.* Boston: Little, Brown, 1958. Fairly accurate but at times sarcastic survey of revival, 1800–1910.

Wheatley, Richard. *The Life and Letters of Mrs. Phoebe Palmer.* New York: W. C. Palmer, Jr., 1876. Has many extracts from her diaries.

Wiens, John. "Biblical Roots of Evangelical Reform in England, 1729–1815."
M.A. thesis, Wheaton College, 1958.

Wilberforce, Samuel. *The Life of William Wilberforce.* London: John
Murray, 1872.

Wilkinson, John T. *Hugh Bourne, 1772–1852.* London: Epworth, 1952.

Willard, Frances E. *Glimpses of Fifty Years.* Chicago: Illinois Temperance
Publishing Association, 1889.

Williams, A. E. *Barnardo of Stepney.* London: George Allen and Unwin,
1943.

Williams, Cyril G. *Tongues of the Spirit.* Cardiff: University of Wales, 1981.
Brief history of classic and neo-Pentecostalism, with analysis of glossalalia.

Williams, Gladys. *Barnardo the Extraordinary Doctor.* London: Macmillan,
1966.

Williams, J. E. H. *The Life of Sir George Williams.* London: Hodder and
Stoughton, 1906.

Willis, Avery T. *Indonesian Revival.* South Pasadena, Cal.: William Carey
Library, 1977.

Wilson, John E. H. "Belief and Practice in East African Movement." M.A.
thesis, Fuller School of Missions, 1975.

Winslow, Ola M. *Jonathan Edwards, 1703-1758.* New York: Macmillan, 1941.
Scholarly; stresses Lockean influence on Edwards.

Wirt, Sherwood E. *Crusade at the Golden Gate.* New York: Harper, 1959.
Account of 1958 crusade in San Francisco.

Wiseman, Frederick L. *Charles Wesley, Evangelist and Poet.* New York:
Abingdon, 1932.

Wood, Arthur S. *Thomas Haweis, 1734-1820.* London: SPCK, 1957.

_____. *The Inextinguishable Blaze.* Grand Rapids: Eerdmans, 1960.
Scholarly, good accounts of Methodist and evangelical revival.

Wood, C. Stacey. *The Growth of a Work of God.* Downers Grove, Ill.: Inter-
Varsity, 1978. The story of the IVCF.

Woods, Charlotte E. *Memoirs and Letters of Canon Hey Aitken.* London:
C. W. Daniel, 1928.

Wright, James E. *The Old-Fashioned Revival Hour and the Broadcasters.*
Rev. ed. Boston: Fellowship, 1940.

Wright, Philip. *Knibb "the Notorious."* London: Sidgwick and Jackson, 1973.
Knibbs's biography and Caribbean slavery.

Wright, Thomas. *Augustus Toplady.* Vol. 2. London: Faircombe and Sons,
1911.

_____. *Isaac Watts.* London: Faircombe and Sons, 1914.

Wynbeek, David. *David Brainerd, Beloved Yankee.* Grand Rapids:
Eerdmans, 1961.

Yarwood, A. T. *Samuel Marsden.* Melbourne, Australia: Melbourne University Press, 1977. Scholarly biography of Marsden, apostle to New Zealand
Maoris.

Zabriskie, Alexander C. *Anglican Evangelicalism.* Philadelphia: Church
Historical Society, 1943.

INDEX

NAMES